THE SMART WIFE

THE SMART WIFE

Why Siri, Alexa, and Other Smart Home Devices Need a Feminist Reboot

YOLANDE STRENGERS AND JENNY KENNEDY

The MIT Press
Cambridge, Massachusetts
London, England

This book was set in Adobe Garamond Pro by New Best-set Typesetters Ltd. Printed and bound in the United States of America.

Library of Congress Cataloging-in-Publication Data

Names: Strengers, Yolande, 1981– author. | Kennedy, Jenny (Postdoctoral researcher), author.
Title: The smart wife : why Siri, Alexa, and other smart home devices need a feminist reboot / Yolande Strengers and Jenny Kennedy.
Description: Cambridge, Massachusetts : The MIT Press, 2020. | Includes bibliographical references and index.
Identifiers: LCCN 2019057347 | ISBN 9780262044370 (hardcover)
Subjects: LCSH: Home automation—Philosophy. | Personal robotics—Social aspects. | Androids—Social aspects. | Home economics—Technological innovations. | Wives. | Feminism.
Classification: LCC TK7881.25 .S77 2020 | DDC 303.48/34082—dc23
LC record available at https://lccn.loc.gov/2019057347

10 9 8 7 6 5 4 3 2 1

Contents

Acknowledgments

A book is sometimes described, to play to a stereotype from this book, as a nagging wife, demanding of our time and attention.

We won't lie; this relationship has had its ups and downs. During our two-year marriage with this all-consuming and consumable other woman, we have experienced moments of joy and pain, love and loss, as she—and we—has transformed into the cyborg figure that now occupies these pages. *The Smart Wife* has itself become a cybernetic organism—a blend of science fiction, artificial intelligence, and organic bodies and minds—culminating in a metamorphizing artifact that will take on a life of its own as it makes its way into the hands of readers.

A project such as this one is multifaceted, with many angles to investigate and ideas to explore. As a result, we've had the fascinating challenge of containing *The Smart Wife* to something that is manageable and achievable. (There is a curious irony to this, given that many smart wives are literally contained inside containers, and given that one goal of ours as we've written this book has been to think outside her cylindrical sphere.)

The evolution of the smart wife—as an eclectic collection of artificial intelligence (AI), robots, and smart devices—is moving both painstakingly slowly (and occasionally in the reverse direction to what we might hope) and breathtakingly fast. While we were writing this book, we were struck by the tenacious stereotypes that recurred across the many technological forms of the smart wives we encountered. At the same time, keeping track of her developments was near impossible given the pace at which the technology is changing—specifically the latest gadgets, trinkets, features, skills, and tools that appear on a daily basis, and on a global scale. Despite the continual and continuing updates and upgrades of the smart wife, what we have discovered during our research for this book is an enduring set of ideas and ideals, which will continue to be relevant long after the smart wives that occupy these pages are superseded.

In creating the smart wife—both as a literal and literary product, and a metaphoric figure whose status and significance we have sought to elevate—we have relied on the support and guidance of many people and cyborgs, including smart wives themselves.

We are grateful for the many public commentators, designers, and company representatives whose words and thoughts we have drawn on. We uncovered these ideas as we tracked the smart wife's movements from the design studios, boardrooms, and factories where she is imagined and created, and into our kitchens, lounges, and bedrooms where she is manifested in her relationships with people.

We are also indebted to many academic scholars from diverse disciplines who have traversed the paths on which *The Smart Wife*—and the smart wife—travels, and have provided their own analyses and research into her visions, manifestations, and emerging effects in the world. These disciplines extend well beyond our own home turf of sociology and media and cultural studies as well as human-computer interaction design, which have been essential as we have sought to understand and reimagine the smart wife. Along the way, we have delved into the ideas and theories from many less familiar fields, such as those associated with social robotics, legal ethics, sexual consent, feminist technoscience, speculative science fiction, linguistics, literature, cybersecurity, and violence toward women.

We are deeply indebted and eternally grateful to a real-life wonder woman—our unfailing research assistant Paula Arcari—who took on the task of assembling all that has been said about the smart wife from such a broad range of disciplines. Paula spent hundreds of hours trawling through academic databases and internet search engines, compiling and preparing research materials, assisting with the referencing and image sourcing required to produce this book, and offering useful comments and additions. In the process, we asked things of Paula that went above and beyond the call of a research assistant, including fascinating questions such as, "Do sex robots have a clitoris?" We also drew support from Paula's canine companion, Dara, who provided sanity and snuggles on several writing retreats. In the final stages, Rex Martin provided additional fact-checking assistance and content updates.

The ideas in *The Smart Wife* have been strengthened and shaped by the illuminating and informative conversations we have had with friends, families, colleagues, and collaborators. Many of these valuable interactions have taken place at conferences and events where we have presented early concepts from this book. We are particularly grateful to the following people who provided feedback and encouragement on early drafts: Larissa Nicholls, Jon Whittle, Bernie Tschirren, Matt Dyer, Victoria Brammal-White, Jennifer Rode, Dimitrios Raptis, Meagan Tyler, Kelly Jean Daymond, and Shreejan Pandey.

Our own supportive and intellectually stimulating institutional environments also made this book possible. Yolande is especially grateful to her former colleagues at the Centre for Urban Research and School of Global, Urban, and Social Studies at RMIT University, and more recently, her colleagues in the Emerging Technologies Research Lab and Faculty of Information Technology at Monash University. Jenny is grateful to her colleagues in the Digital Ethnography Research Centre and School of Media and Communications at RMIT University, particularly the Technology, Communication, and Policy Lab.

We also wish to acknowledge those who supplied us with the funding necessary to conduct this work. Our research on the smart home was supported by the Australian Research Council's Discovery Early Career Researchers Award funding scheme (project number DE150100278), held by Yolande from 2015 to 2018, and conducted in collaboration with Larissa Nicholls. The book also draws on research delivered in collaboration with colleagues from RMIT, Monash, and Melbourne universities in Australia, Lancaster University in the United Kingdom, Aalborg University in Denmark, and Intel Corporation in the United States. For more information on these projects, see "A Note on Methodology" in this book. The views in *The Smart Wife* are ours, and do not necessarily represent those of our colleagues, collaborators, or research partners.

We visited many households across Australia during the research associated with this book. We are grateful to the residents and industry participants who freely and warmly welcomed us into their homes and businesses, as they expressed their views about the smart wife. We have used pseudonyms throughout *The Smart Wife* to protect the names and identities of these research participants.

To ensure that *The Smart Wife* was as assertive and engaging as we could possibly write it, we have been fortunate to benefit from the clearheaded wisdom of our US editor, Amanda Moon from Moon & Company. Likewise, we have been privileged to cross paths with our commissioning editor at the MIT Press, Katie Helke, who has provided unwavering and timely support for this project. Both Amanda and Katie have remained strong advocates of our sarcasm and snark, and supported our aim of positioning this work for readers outside the academy. The broader MIT team have also been fantastic in sharpening *The Smart Wife* for its debut.

To our academic peer reviewers of the proposal, chapter drafts, and full manuscript, we sincerely thank you for your considered comments, encouragement, useful suggestions, and reflections.

On a personal level, our extended network of friends and families has provided us with a buffer of much-needed humor along with the confidence to write a book of this kind. We are forever grateful for their love and support.

Finally, we thank each other for what has been a fascinating, disturbing, hilarious, and enlightening relationship with *The Smart Wife*. Like the fast-paced world that the smart wife lives in, it all started with the seed of an idea during a casual chat, and before we knew it we were enraptured by the (digital) women that animate this book—and we're hoping, a few more books to come.

1 MEET THE SMART WIFE

It's been a busy day. You're tired, sore, and hungry. All you want to do is put your feet up, stream your favorite on-demand show, and pour yourself a glass of wine. But there's still dinner to cook, homework to supervise, and tomorrow's schedule to finalize. Someone should probably do a load of laundry, and you need to put the garbage out. And if this could all happen without any drama, with all household members amiably carrying out their chores, well . . . wouldn't *that* be nice. You might also want someone to talk with and ask how your day was. Maybe you even desire something a little *extra*? If only there was someone, or some*thing*, who could do it all.

Meet the smart wife. She's pleasant, helpful, and available at an increasingly affordable price. Millions of people from around the world are now turning to connected and robotic devices to provide the domestic, caring, and intimacy services historically delivered by real-life wives.

The smart wife is a seemingly ingenious solution to what the political journalist Annabel Crabb poignantly terms the "wife drought" afflicting most advanced economies and gender progressive nations.[1] After all, who *wouldn't* want more help around the home, including, in some cases, help meeting those more sexual desires?

By 2021, some industry observers predict that we will have more voice-activated assistants on the planet than people—a growth rate that outstrips the cell phone's rise to ubiquity.[2] Domestic robots like robotic vacuum cleaners are already the most widely adopted computational robots in the world.[3] The broader smart home market is also growing quickly, and predicted to ship nearly 1.6 billion devices in 2023, including home security, lighting, smart speaker, thermostat, and video entertainment products.[4] Demand for care and sex robots is growing too, albeit more slowly.

The smart wife is clearly a tempting idea as well as growing reality for many residents with access to smart technology, the internet, electricity, and disposable income. But is she really a good solution to the many problems associated with life as we know it in the twenty-first century?

Before getting into the strengths and weaknesses of our fascinating heroine, let us acquaint you with the smart wife properly. The wife drought that Crabb speaks of suggests we are witnessing the slow death of the wife in contemporary society (at least the wife we've known as the longtime backbone of patriarchal society). But she's having an enthusiastic comeback, with a few critical upgrades. It's not wives *themselves* who are being asked to come back into the kitchen but rather feminized artificial intelligence (AI) built into robots, digital voice assistants (also known as smart speakers, conversational agents, virtual helpers, and chatbots), and other smart devices.

The smart wife comes in many forms; in fact, chances are you're already living with her. Most obvious are assistants such as Amazon's Alexa, Apple's Siri, or Google Home, which have default female voices in most markets in which they are sold (figure 1.1).[5] Other smart wives are anthropomorphic, zoomorphic, or automated (such as home appliances or domestic robots)—most of which carry out domestic responsibilities that have traditionally fallen to wives. One Indian company has even adopted the name "smart wife" to advertise their home appliances.[6] Smart wives can also be found in the bodies of overtly feminized and sometimes "pornified" sex robots or gynoids.[7]

By "smart," we mean AI, internet-connected, or robotic things. By "wife," we refer to an enduring archetype in the collective psyche—one who can take on all forms of domestic work within the home.[8] In the past and present, and at her most reduced, a wife has been both social construct and commodity, and viewed as the property of a man. Her roles include that of caregiver, housekeeper, homemaker, emotional laborer, provider

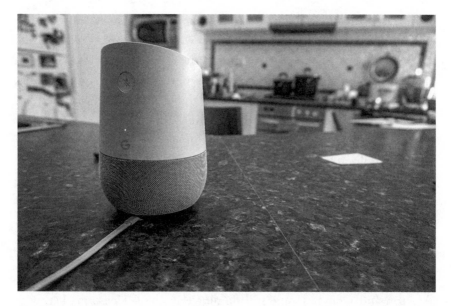

Figure 1.1
Google Home in a kitchen. Source: Author

of sexual services, and procreator of legitimate offspring. These roles are entrenched in thousands of years of patriarchy.

The smart wife is figurative, not literal (although there are some examples of people *actually* marrying her that we'll get to later in the book). We use the term to encompass smart technology intended to carry out domestic labors traditionally associated with the wife's role and any smart technology that is treated as a smart wife by those who interact with her. In addition, our term encompasses feminized humanoid or artificial sentient beings playing a wifely role in sci-fi and popular culture texts—the role models for "real-life" smart wives.

The principle prototype for the smart wife's mainframe is the 1950s' US housewife and her transatlantic cousin in the United Kingdom. Many contemporary societies still ache with nostalgia for this white, middle-class, and heteronormative housewife, with her perfect home, breezy white linens, artfully arranged flowers, gleaming cookware, and homemade meals. Wasn't she wonderful? Her charming dinner conversation, perfectly set hair (those curls!), clean and quiet children, and content (and successful) husband certainly set the bar high for all wives who aspired to this ideal. Or at least that's the way it seems now in the relics of advertisements from the era. This wistful wonder woman was unlikely to take on paid work once married (unless it was to do something compatible with her role as a housewife, such as selling Tupperware).[9] The home was her primary domain, and she nurtured the people within it.

This idolized figure still lives on in many sitcoms—and iterations of the smart wife generally. She is not our leading lady's only inspirational source code, however. Smart wives also reflect many other cultural expressions of idealized women originating from Asian countries such as China, India, Japan, and South Korea, where her reach is expanding. China now has over half of the global market share in digital voice assistants, overtaking the United States in 2019, with shipments exceeding 10 million units. Amazon and Google Home still dominate in the Chinese market, with Baidu, Alibaba, and Xiaomi following close behind.[10] A consistent theme among these culturally diverse countries' offerings—and uniting smart wife markets worldwide—is a set of technologies characterized as a young, demure, and sexualized woman (or girl) who is constantly available for service.

The idea of ubiquitous technology that acts like an unwearying wife might sound appealing to some people—ourselves included. But is she really the kind of stereotype we want to be returning home to? Is she actually helping our progress toward gender equity? Aside from keeping us company or ordering the groceries, what else is she *doing* in upholding systems of power and oppression in capitalist and patriarchal societies? What kind of future is she manifesting? And how else can we imagine her living with us?

We are not the first people to ask these kinds of questions, or indeed to characterize smart technology as an often-celebrated (and lamented) housewife.[11] In animating our book with this fictional and provocative character, and talking about her explicitly as a woman, we follow an approach taken by other technofeminist and digital media scholars. Notable among these are Donna Haraway (who has written extensively about the feminized cyborg figure as both woman and machine) and Kylie Jarrett (who developed the concept of the "digital housewife" to interrogate the unpaid consumer labor carried out by people on online communication platforms).[12]

Characterizing the smart home as a smart wife is our critique and intervention into conversations about the future of domestic life, human relationships with AI, and contemporary feminism. In pursuing this character, and caricature, we highlight fundamental problems with the design and marketing of smart home devices that are presented as innovative "technofixes" promising to end the wife drought, though simultaneously embodying and perpetuating outdated stereotypes of women's roles in the home.[13] But we go further by offering our own set of proposals to emancipate and elevate the smart wife in society.

While we portray the smart wife as a worrisome typecast, she is far more diverse than you might think. Here there are further parallels with the romanticized 1950s' housewife, who was as much fantasy as reality. In *Not June Cleaver*, professor of history and American studies Joanne Meyerowitz and her contributors question historical accounts of the "tenacious stereotype" of a discontent, housebound suburban housewife "who stayed home to rear children, clean house, and bake cookies," promising, as the 1950s' housewife did, "a romance steeped in nostalgic longing for an allegedly simpler, happier, and more prosperous time."[14] Instead they provide diverse stories of women's roles in the home during postwar America that challenge these normative assumptions.

Likewise, this book gives voice to the considerable variety of smart wives now moving into our homes in increasing numbers. We point out the problematic stereotypes depicting the smart wife's rise to popularity, showing how they potentially devalue women's traditional roles in society and exacerbate violence toward women. But equally, we tell stories of gender trouble, different cultural expressions, and the curious and strange smart wives that people are welcoming into their lives. We show that smart wives aren't just *wives*; they are also smart friends, servants, girlfriends, migrant workers, secretaries, mothers, sex workers, intimate companions, lovers, nannies, butlers, pets, artificial species, and more. By exploring these devices in all their various roles and guises, we provide glimpses of opportunities where smart wives could and have begun to transgress their own limitations.

But first, let us explain how these myriad colorful characters are stepping in to extend a helping hand and fill various voids that people are experiencing in their lives.

THE WIFE DROUGHT

The contemporary slump in available or willing wives that Crabb and other prominent social critics such as Susan Maushart have warned contemporary societies of is real. Marriage (and partner) rates are declining in many countries with advanced economies.[15] One reason for this is that men have typically been resistant (and unsupported by their employers, social expectations, and government policies) to take on the household responsibilities expected of them in an equal marriage.[16] Men stand to gain most from a happy union, even in today's gender progressive societies, where marriage is a "positively and empirically life-enhancing" experience for this gender.[17] This is not to say that men in some countries like Japan are not also turning away from marriage at equal numbers to women, particularly because expectations for their domestic responsibilities within marriage are growing.[18] Simultaneously, women are generally less willing to define themselves in relation to men or the domestic sphere, and are seeking other ways to fulfill themselves. Many women want wives so that they can fulfill their own aspirations too, whether that be to work, further their education, or have children. This is because wives make many other life choices possible—for everyone.

Why don't more women want to be wives? Let's look at it this way: Why would they? As sociologist Leah Ruppanner notes of Australia, "When women start to cohabit, their housework time goes up while men's goes down, regardless of their employment status."[19] In wealthy nations, an increase in female workforce participation since the twentieth century began has been driven largely by married women.[20] Strikingly, the more hours that a woman works outside the home, the more hours she is likely to spend doing housework. Or as Crabb writes, "In an average Australian family, a woman will commonly behave like a housewife even if she isn't one. And a man will behave as though he's married to a housewife, even when he isn't." This doesn't change when women work full time outside the home; in fact, Australian women still typically do twice as much housework as their full-time working husbands, or "forty-one hours a week compared to twenty!" exclaims Crabb.[21]

Despite continuing gender equity progress on the home front, across Europe, North America, Australia, China, and Japan (and many other countries), it matters little whether the woman works a greater number of hours outside the home or earns more pay; women still perform a greater proportion of domestic labor.[22] No wonder, then, that divorce rates have risen in most contemporary societies, and that most of these (two-thirds to three-quarters) are initiated by women.[23] "Being married is not the problem," notes Maushart, "the problem is being a wife."[24]

The "wifework" that Maushart targets in her turn-of-the-century book on the subject doesn't stop with housekeeping. "Females within marriage are strenuously, overwhelmingly, outrageously responsible for the physical and emotional caretaking of males and offspring," writes Maushart.[25] Worldwide, women perform around 75 percent of total unpaid care and domestic labor.[26] In 60 percent of Australian family households with children under the age of fifteen, there is a full-time working father, with a part-time or stay-at-home mother. "Who gets wives?" Crabb asks. "Dads do."[27] In only 3 percent of households is this dynamic reversed, meaning that the staggering majority of people who benefit from having a housewife are male. The more senior the role of the working parent, the more likely they are to have a wife at home, some or all of the time.[28]

Likewise, providing care for the elderly—particularly in the home—is more likely to fall to women in general and wives in particular. One study conducted across multiple countries estimates that between 57 to 81 percent of all caregivers of the elderly are women. And in most cases, these female caregivers are adult daughters or daughters-in-law of the elderly person.[29]

The wife drought and wifework also extend to the sexual contract that wives historically entered into on marriage, which required them to be sexually available to their husbands. Social changes such as women's sexual liberation and the shifting rules of consent in many societies mean that wives' bodies are no longer considered fully available to men through marriage. The criminalization process for marital rape in the West began in the 1970s, with marital rape becoming a crime in all fifty US states in 1993—although prosecution is still fraught.[30] More concerningly, spousal rape is still legal in at least ten countries, with consent assumed as part of the marriage contract.[31]

In short, wifework, writes Maushart, "is a time-consuming, energy-draining and emotionally exorbitant enterprise . . . [and] a job that violates every principle of equal-opportunity employment."[32] Given this current state of affairs in the availability, status, and changing responsibilities of human wives, many people are understandably looking for a technological alternative, particularly those who are most keenly feeling the swelling absence of her services—specifically, men.

MALE-ORDER BRIDES

So who wants a smart wife? Potentially everyone. In 2016, the research firm Gartner predicted people would soon be having more conversations with bots than their spouses.[33] Over a quarter of the adult population in the United States now owns at least one smart speaker like Alexa; that's more than sixty-six million people.[34]

When Apple's Siri assistant made her debut in 2011 as "a sassy young woman who deflected insults and liked to flirt and serve users with playful obedience," her "coming-out party" reached nearly 150 million iPhones in her first year.[35] This single technology—developed behind closed doors by one company in one corner of the world with little input from women—shaped global expectations for smart wives and AI assistants more broadly in a little over twelve months.

Other smart wife markets, like those for care or sex robots, have reached fewer households. Indeed, despite the media hype, until recently sexbots were more an idea than a commercial reality, and despite predictions for expansion, the market is currently extremely niche.[36]

In terms of gendered interest and uptake, industry sales figures show that consumers of smart home devices are more likely to be male, and "smart home obsessives" are invariably men.[37] Men are also more often the instigators for bringing smart home technologies into the home and managing their operation.

As we have established, however, women (and the significant percentage of the world's population that is not heterosexual men) need (smart) wives too. Millennial women in the United States, ages eighteen to thirty-five, are particularly excited about smart home technology, and the occasional report finds that women are actually more interested in some devices than men are, such as voice assistants and some smart appliances.[38]

Narrowing down to specific markets reveals other gender differences in interest, uptake, and benefits. The vast majority of people currently interested in or buying sex robots (and dolls) are men. Women are understandably less enthusiastic about the penetration-oriented characteristics of most current offerings.[39] By contrast, in the present social robot market, women stand to benefit most given that they live longer than men and therefore are more likely to suffer from debilitating conditions like dementia—which is one of the emerging applications for care robots.[40]

When it comes to the *creation* of smart wives, men are clearly in the lead. Men vastly outnumber women in computer programming jobs, making up over 75 percent of the total pool of programmers in the United States in 2017.[41] In the field of robotics and AI, men outnumber women as well.[42] Men comprise between 77 and 83 percent of the technical positions at Apple, Facebook, Microsoft, Google, and General Electric, and just over 63 percent at Amazon.[43] Men make up 85 percent of the AI research staff at Facebook and 90 percent at Google.[44] Likewise in academic environments, more than 80 percent of AI professors are men, and only 12 percent of leading AI researchers are women.[45]

Indeed, computer science has gone backward on gender diversity in the last thirty to forty years, with female participation in computer science degrees in the United States dropping from 37 percent in the early 1980s to 18 percent in 2016, despite a number of active campaigns and initiatives to try to turn this around.[46] Computer science remains a discipline with low numbers of tertiary-qualified women within the thirty-six member countries of Organization for Economic Cooperation and Development (OECD).[47] In the United Kingdom, the proportion of women in programming and software development jobs in the information and communication technologies sector dropped from 15 to 12 percent over the last decade. As a United Nations Educational, Scientific, and Cultural Organization (UNESCO) report on closing gender divides in digital skills depressingly puts it, "The digital space is becoming more male-dominated, not less so."[48]

It hasn't always been this way. Following the Second World War, when electronic computing began to accelerate, software programming in the West was largely considered "women's work."[49] But this changed as it became clear that programming could wield significant influence over all aspects of life, and as computers started making their ways into workplaces, homes, and—more specifically—boys' bedrooms.[50]

Compounding the low numbers of women in computing is the so-called self-efficacy technology gender gap, which refers to the difference between girls' and boys' confidence and belief in their abilities. Studies show that girls are more likely to think they're worse at computing—even when they're no different or in some cases better at computing studies than boys. This is partly due to boys being historically brought up to believe that they *should* be naturally good at technology, whereas girls are more commonly socialized in the opposite direction. Yet it is also due to other dynamics, such as a protracted history of the gendering of technology as either masculine (think "brown goods" like TVs and remote controls) or feminine (think "white goods" like fridges).[51]

So potent is the gendered imbalance in computing that the journalist, producer, and author Emily Chang labeled the coding culture of Silicon Valley a "Brotopia."[52] She draws attention to the biased recruitment strategies of Silicon Valley tech companies, the members of which historically profiled and mostly hired typical male "geeks," while more recently setting their sights on overconfident and charismatic men who could follow in the footsteps of information technology (IT) heroes like the late Steve Jobs. In addition, the AI industry has been called out by leading academics and commentators like Kate Crawford and Jack Clark for having a "white guy problem" in an industry characterized by a "sea of dudes."[53] Indeed, the AI Now Institute has identified a "diversity crisis" perpetuated by harassment, discrimination, unfair compensation, and lack of promotion for women and ethnic minorities.[54] The institute recommends that "the AI industry needs to make significant structural changes to address systemic racism, misogyny, and lack of diversity."[55]

This gender and racial imbalance filters down to the ways in which technologies are imagined and created.[56] Scholars such as Safiya Umoja Noble have written about the "algorithms of oppression" that characterize search engines like Google, which reinforce racism and sexism.[57] Likewise, web consultant and author Sara Wachter-Boettcher discusses the proliferation of "sexist apps" emerging from the masculine culture of Silicon Valley.[58] There has also been considerable criticism leveled at digital voice assistants like Alexa, Siri, and Google Home, and other types of smart wives, for their sexist overtones, diminishing of women in traditional feminized roles, and inability to assertively rebuke sexual advances.[59]

For example, Microsoft's Cortana and Mycroft assistants take their names as well as identities from gamer and sci-fi culture, respectively, both of which have been widely critiqued as highly sexist domains.[60] Likewise, assistants like Microsoft's Ms. Dewey and Facebook's MoneyPenny (both now retired from service) were sexually suggestive and flirtatious by reputation (MoneyPenny is named for the coy secretary and romantic interest in the *James Bond* novels and films), or through their coded behavior.[61] This gendering of smart tech all makes a particular set of (mostly) men's ideas about home, wives, domestic responsibilities, and sexual desires deeply relevant. And it potentially excludes a lot of other people for whom these ideas don't resonate—including, we should note, many men.

Despite all this, the technology sector is routinely viewed as being more gender equal than it actually is.[62] For instance, one survey of one thousand US consumers found that over half did not question the gendering of smart wives such as female digital voice assistants or the potential repercussions of this design decision.[63] One ambition of our book, then, is

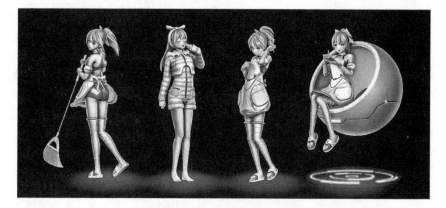

Figure 1.2
Promotional image for Japanese digital voice assistant Hikari Azuma. Source: Vinclu

to make it crystal clear why we *should* be concerned about the feminization of smart technologies.

An eerie example of the gender dynamics we seek to highlight is found in the Japanese digital voice assistant named Hikari Azuma (figure 1.2) developed by the company Vinclu as part of its Gatebox technology and entering mass production in 2019.[64] This cutesy smart wife is targeted toward the country's single residents, now the largest segment of the population.[65] Azuma is a virtual anime hologram, with blue hair and matching outfits, who lives in a glass tube about thirty centimeters high and ten centimeters wide (notably, other digital voice assistants like Alexa and Google Home "live" inside containers too—a point that we will return to later in the book). She is depicted as a young twenty-year-old woman, with a schoolgirlish and upbeat personality.[66] Azuma wears a short skirt and over-the-knee socks, and has a high-pitched voice supplemented with coquettish giggles. In several promotional videos, she takes care of a lonely, hardworking young Japanese man. Her key role is to greet her "master" with excitement when he comes home, and check on him during the day by sending helpful messages such as "come home early." She also provides timekeeping services and weather advice, turns off the lights when her master leaves the house, adjusts the home's heating and cooling, and remembers their anniversary.[67]

Azuma is an ideal smart wife (or girlfriend), doting on her man's needs. She is also useful and efficient, helping Japanese men keep their schedules on track. But if she does *too* good a job, the singles population of Japan may not need to look for a human companion—potentially exacerbating the falling birth rates in that country.[68] On this point, the Japanese government has bigger plans for smart wives (as do other nations, like China).[69] Professor of anthropology Jennifer Robertson suggests that there is a push to position social and care robots like Pepper as an opportunity to redirect Japanese women's time back to the task of having children (by freeing up their time spent on caring responsibilities). Smart wives are thus entangled in social and political agendas about the role of women, wives, and heteronormative relationships in contemporary societies that we explore throughout this book.

Sex robots and virtual pornography take these ideas in other tantalizing and potentially troubling directions. US company RealDoll's Harmony sexbot has eighteen customizable feminized personality traits (including jealous, shy, moody, thrilled, and insecure), forty-two different nipple options, and different voice selections (including a "saucy Scottish accent"), and she remembers her user's favorite food (like any good smart wife should).[70] But her true stroke of genius is this: Harmony's removable and self-lubricating vagina is dishwasher safe.[71] She is smart (with controllable parts and efficient cleaning!) and wifely (devoted to her man's intimate needs). She is a woman with all the sexy bits, without all the mess or fuss. Harmony is customizable yet uniform, deeply feminine but with masculine efficiency, and there to be enjoyed, consumed, and penetrated. To be clear, this isn't creepy because we're talking about a robot (we're not here to vilify anyone's kinks) but rather because it embodies a pornographic idea of female sexiness that—in some cases—celebrates nonconsensual sex.

This gets to the heart of the strange paradox that characterizes the smart wife: she is simultaneously a dutiful feminine wife and sexual muse while adeptly solving household problems with technological tools. She is docile *and* efficient. Compliant *and* in control. Seductive *yet* shrewd. Intimate *yet* distant. She is ready to be played, ready to serve, and able to optimize her domain.

On the one hand, the smart wife represents an ingenious solution to the ongoing domestic disputes over the division of labor that plague contemporary households in gender-progressive societies. On the other hand, there is something downright worrying about the smart home and robotic industries' subtle characterizations of their products as a nostalgic, sometimes porn-inspired wifely figure. This is particularly so because we are trying to move on from these representations of women in most contemporary societies.

What's the problem exactly? For a start, these depictions affect how we treat our devices, robots, and AI, which in turn are reflected back in how we treat people in general—and women in particular. Friendly and helpful feminized devices often take a great deal of abuse when their owners swear or yell at them.[72] They are also commonly glitchy, leading to their characterization as ditzy feminized devices by owners and technology commentators—traits that reinforce outdated (and unfounded) gendered stereotypes about essentialized female inferior intellectual ability.[73]

Relatedly, a smart wife gone wrong is the central plotline of many sci-fi movies featuring feminized AI (figure 1.3). There's Olga in *The Perfect Woman* (1949), Joanna in *The Stepford Wives* (originally written by Ira Levin in 1972 as a satirical horror story), the fembots including wife Vanessa in *Austin Powers* (1997, 1999, 2002), Ava in *Ex Machina* (2015); Samantha in *Her* (2013), and Pris and Rachael from the original *Blade Runner* (1982)—to name but a few. These women are typically sexualized, demure, and slightly dysfunctional, yet ready to retaliate against their male makers, owners, and enslavers.

The plotlines of these highly entertaining films consistently reinforce the cliché that the perfect woman is an artificial one—as long as she doesn't have too much control or power, as then she will rebel, kill, or enslave her makers. Ironically, it's often the lonely techies in these films and stories who fall for these femme fatales and suffer the effects. What's more, as interdisciplinary humanities scholar Hilary Bergen notes, there is a focus on "a *white* female body—revealing the racial bias inherent in Western representations of femininity, in which the racialized body is traditionally less desirable and harder to contain."[74] The fetishized smart wife, both on- and off-screen, is

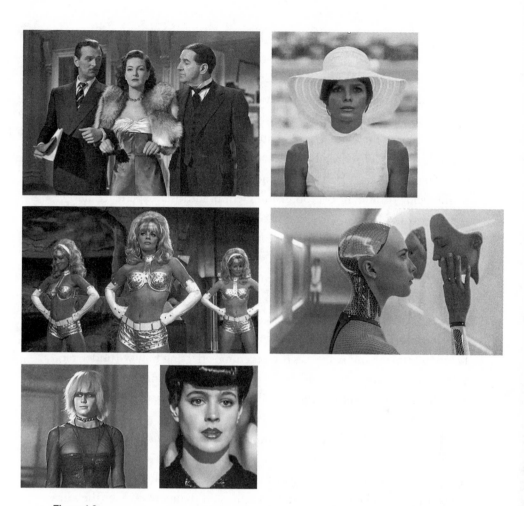

Figure 1.3
Film stills of smart wives as depicted in sci-fi movies. Sources: *The Perfect Woman*; *The Stepford Wives*; *Austin Powers*; *Ex-Machina*; *Blade Runner*.

predominantly white and heterosexual—reinforcing racial stereotypes that are equally as problematic as those concerning gender.

We know from research carried out in the fields of robotics, human-computer interaction, and psychology that humans assign emotional as well as personal traits to computers.[75] A smart wife precedent for this was set in 1966, when founding computer scientist Joseph Weizenbaum created the first chatbot, named ELIZA. This fembot, which performed natural language processing, was cast in the role of psychiatrist and worked by posing questions based on Rogerian psychotherapy back to her "clients" (such as, "And how does that make you feel?").[76] Weizenbaum was surprised and later dismayed to discover how intimately his colleagues related to ELIZA, and the emotional connections they quickly formed with this artificial therapist.[77]

So deep are these ties to inanimate objects that some people even marry them, like Erika Eiffel nee LaBrie, who married the Eiffel Tower.[78] Indeed, according to the late Clifford Nass and his collaborator Corina Yen, experts in the fields of human-computer interaction and user experience design, the success and failure of interactive computer systems depends on whether we like them, and how well they treat us.[79]

This is partly because people have a tendency to humanize devices and assign them with genders, even when they don't have one. Sherry Turkle, a professor of social studies of science and technology, has pioneered research on people's relationships with technology—especially mobile technology, social networking, and sociable robotics. She has found that the boundary between humans and machines is weakening, affecting how we understand and relate to each other, and leading to some troubling outcomes, such as reducing our communication with other people and making us feel lonelier than ever.[80]

Other examples demonstrate how our connections and interactions with inanimate and animate devices are gendered. Consider satellite navigation systems (or sat-navs). Most of us prefer the female voice because we consider it to be warmer and more pleasant than a male one (the same holds true for smart wives).[81] But we also distrust a female-voiced sat-nav (because women are notoriously bad at giving directions, or so the stereotype goes), and are quick to dub her helpfulness as badgering. When a new female voice command system was introduced into jet planes in 2012, US fighter pilots referred to her as "Bitchin' Betty" for getting louder and sterner when they ignored the system's commands. UK pilots knew her as "Nagging Nora," and the male equivalent was commonly known as the intimidating and aggressive "Barking Bob."[82] These kinds of humanlike assistants provide us with an opportunity to perform and reinforce exaggerated gender stereotypes.

Likewise, on the home front we prefer female voice assistants when their purpose is to discuss love and relationships, or help us with the housework (by adding groceries to the shopping list, for example, or better still, restocking our fridges and pantries).[83] In other words, we like our assistants to conform to gendered stereotypes.[84] But designing gendered devices can also re-inscribe those same stereotypes. When those devices start behaving erratically, or we perceive them to be annoying or acting "dumb," we associate those characteristics with common gender typecasts.

In short, smart wives hark back to nostalgic stereotypes that people are now being told (through smart tech marketing) that they deserve and should desire. Sure, overtly gendered smart wives are familiar, cute, sexy, friendly, and "easy to use"—but at what cost to society?

Left as they are, by and large smart wives serve a patriarchal capitalist system, which positions women as useful and efficient commodities, upholds (and promotes) gendered and sexual stereotypes, and paints men as boys who enjoy playing with toys. Not *all* men of course. We don't think that every man who is interested in designing or using smart technology is a misogynist or misogamist.[85] We mean that the smart wife works with a narrow range of stereotypes that are potentially damaging for all genders. We aren't man or tech haters, nor are we anti-technosexuals (defined as those who include the mechanical within their boundaries of sexuality). But we *are* killjoys of the smart wife as she is currently programmed, and our agenda is simple.[86] We're here to give her a reboot.

STALKING THE SMART WIFE

As scholars who have spent many years investigating the smart home, we are both impressed with and alarmed by the stealthy emergence of the smart wife. This book is the product of our respective research on smart and networked homes, conducted with many fabulous colleagues. (For academic readers curious about our trajectory, we have provided "A Note on Methodology" at the back of the book.)

Admittedly, neither of us set out to study the smart wife, and yet there she was, waiting to be noticed in the intimate spaces, cupboards, and kitchens of the smart homes we visited while conducting ethnographic research with households. Since then we've become obsessed with this "other woman," trawling back through interviews and home visits with people who live in smart homes, and watching, reading, and listening to international popular media to understand her creation, role, and potential effects in the home.

Along this journey, we found her in other places too. We binge-watched sci-fi movies and television series where her prototypes have been fictionalized, and expanded our reading on what other smart people have already written about her. We trawled sex doll and sexbot websites, and generated some lively conversations with friends and colleagues.

As social scholars of technology and media, we bring our own academic influences to this book. Yolande is a sociologist of digital technology; she's interested in the effects of emerging technologies entering our homes and lives. Over the years, she has investigated how smart and automated home technologies can help residents save energy. Here she invented another gendered character—resource man—the idealized, rational, tech-savvy, data-hungry male energy consumer who is ravenous for smart stuff.[87] Resource man and the smart wife make a cute couple, each cut from different but similar motherboards, and both embodying gendered ideals for how the world should be, as seen through the eyes of related male-dominated industries (engineering and computer science). We'll hear more about this partnership in chapter 4.

Jenny is a scholar of media and communications interested in how smart technologies mesh with the rhythms of everyday life. She has looked at the ways that technology is deeply embedded in our intimate relation-ships, and at how media technology—including internet infrastructures, devices, and apps—are adopted in the home.[88] Before encountering the smart wife, Jenny found hints of her demanding attention in the house-holds that she studied: the men were preoccupied and infatuated by their love for her. The cuckolded spouses confirmed these suspicions, revealing a growing absence of participation in other household duties, as the smart wife took up more of their lover's time and attention.

Our framing of the smart home allows us to ask some delightfully probing questions of the smart wife. What kind of woman *is* she? Where does she come from? What can she do? Who benefits from her? What impact is she having on the home and gender relations? And how else could we reimagine her role and purpose in our lives? We explore these questions across four domains where the smart wife is making her mark: housekeeping, caregiving, homemaking, and lovemaking. We also show how her insidious feminization is leading to some interesting and familiar framings: either as a ditzy bitch, with a glitch, or a toy for the boys.

Our enduring commitment to the smart wife, however, poses some potential problems. In labeling a large proportion of home-based smart technology "smart wives," we further commit to their anthropomorphizing and feminization. A sexbot, for example, is not an *actual* woman; it is an object. Our insistence on referring to smart devices as "her" and "she," instead of "it" and "they" (with the exception of nonbinary or ambiguously gendered smart wives like Pepper), furthers associations between women and machine, and potentially conflates complex issues such as sexual consent between people and sexual experiences that can occur with an (animated) object. Therefore we proceed cautiously yet deliberately with this characterization.

While the path ahead is laden with booby traps, we argue that the smart wife allows us to productively analyze the causes and effects of a seemingly disparate but surprisingly unified suite of wifely devices entering our homes. Further, it gives us something—or some*one*—to depart from, challenge, reimagine, and come home to.

In tracking her past, present, and future, we speak in and arguably perpetuate gendered stereotypes. Wives are generally women, whose role has historically been fashioned by male-led societies, in which they have been understood as (contractually) subordinate to men.[89] As we noted, smart wives are also commonly introduced into the home by men, and are often designed by men for stereotypical masculine interests and pursuits. Of course, we know there are exceptions—ourselves included. Here we are—two tech-minded women—talking about, studying, and *using* smart wives. We know that women design and buy smart wives too, men can be wives, and women can have wives. And there are many more relationships and domestic arrangements that involve different combinations of these roles, or none at all.

We write using common binaries and gender terms, like male/female, man/woman, masculine/feminine, patriarchy, heteronormativity, and cisgender (where someone's biological sex aligns with their gender identification). We subscribe to the common feminist view that gender is not an essentialist condition or biologically determined outcome of one's sex. Instead it exists on a spectrum. It is socially and culturally produced and performed, and constantly transforming, often in relation to technology. Likewise, masculinity and femininity are not something that "belong" to either men or women, but they are typically associated with each respective gender.

We also invariably deal in the language and politics of privilege. We ourselves are privileged white women, acutely aware of our own heteronormativity and the benefits that we have experienced (and smart wives continue to provide) as part of "white feminism."[90] Not everyone can have a wife, and only a small percentage of the overall population can get a smart one. For a start, less than half the world's population has access to the internet in their homes, and around 11 percent (or 860 million people as of 2018) are still living without electricity; many don't even have a home.[91] While access to electricity and the internet is continually improving, even when people do have these things, they may not have the skills required to take advantage of smart technology. Notably, women have less disposable income than men, are more likely to live in poverty, and are less likely to have a formal education or digital skills, meaning their access to smart wives (and all technology) is further restricted.[92] And it is exactly these kinds of marginalized people who are more likely to be placed at further risk by the unethical production and environmental impacts of smart wives.

Our focus on the gender politics of smart technology in privileged Western homes means that we effectively gloss over other powerful narratives, such as those that emphasize race, class, or cultural differences in access and familiarity with smart wives. That said, with the number of devices steadily increasing and the growing stress on improving gender equity while eliminating violence toward women, our book speaks to globally significant discrimination issues that move well beyond our spotlight on the smart home—and women.

We are aware that gendered stereotypes go both ways. While the first-known chatbot, ELIZA, was female, early humanoid robot assistants were commonly gendered male by their designers and presented some equally disturbing stereotypes compared to those we've introduced above. A 1930s' demonstration video depicts a male robot, Alpha, firing a gun to showcase an example of his skills.[93] When a woman asks him about his sexual preferences, he confirms he likes "the ladies" and wants to marry a blond, but tells the brunette "she'll do" as his wife.

There are many male-identified smart home robots and assistants now on the market as well as some devices that designers (sometimes dubiously) claim are genderless.[94] Siri, for instance, will tell you that she's genderless— "like cacti. And certain species of fish"—even though her name means "beautiful woman who leads you to victory" in Norse. Similarly, social robot helpers Pepper and Jibo appear to be boybots, yet they also portray emasculated and feminized characteristics, as we discuss in chapter 3. The internet is full of debate on whether Pepper is *actually* male. In contrast, there is no doubt that Alexa is female.

There are also some cute animal-, pet-, and plant-inspired robots as well as those that take robotic form. Alibaba's AliGenie, for example, is a smart speaker with an animated voice that is neither male nor female—and has screens that resemble cartoon cat eyes.[95] These devices add some diversity to the smart wife market, and could be considered a queering of the dominant, heteronormative female form that smart wives more often take. We argue, however, that most of these devices are still in fact smart wives.

Our agenda is motivated by a simple yet monumental cause: to create a smart wife that serves progress toward gender equity and diversity— with an eye to not further degrading the planet on which all genders depend. We're not talking about specific design upgrades here, like a new work-life juggling feature for the "modern woman." We refer to a more politically motivated agenda of serving people in general—and women in particular—in advancement of various kinds: aiding their elevation and standing in career trajectories traditionally coded as masculine; helping to end the violence toward women, everyday sexism, and rape culture that is subtly or explicitly promoted by some smart wives; protecting the earth from further environmental degradation that disproportionately affects marginalized people; and helping more women access and experience consensual, pleasurable sex.

Through these ambitions, we add to the growing voices of feminists who seek to dismantle the system of patriarchal privilege that stifles people of all genders. We aim to support diversity of all kinds along with different and varied expressions of masculinity, including those that value and support men's contributions to domestic duties—and place higher value on domestic work more broadly. In our final chapter, a "manifesta," we outline our hopes for a rebooted smart wife—taking inspiration from feminist scholars such as Sara Ahmed, Hannah McCann, Sarah Kember, Judy Wajcman, and Donna Haraway as well as Lady Gaga, science fiction, feminist campaigns, and other academic insights.

Throughout the book, and culminating in our manifesta, we develop a future pathway for the smart wife—one that advocates for interventions that span her sci-fi representations through to her roles in our lives. We question the usual tactics of "neutralizing" the gender of smart wives and instead ask how the smart wife can promote a revaluing of femininity in society—in all her glorious diversity of pet, plant, robotic, and human forms. We ask how we might *queer* the smart wife so that she contributes to elevating the status of the feminine as well as wifework in late capitalist and postpatriarchal futures.

In sum, *The Smart Wife* is a response to the smart home along with the fields of assistive, social, and sexual AI intended for the domestic sphere. It is a critique and intervention into so-called technological progress, and a call to arms. It is a gendered reading of a set of related industries that at times claim to be genderless, and more broadly claim to offer benefits for *all* people and sometimes the planet, without actually delivering on those promises. We say the smart wife *does* exist and it's time to aid her liberation.

2 ROSIE

Rosie the robot is the poster girl for the smart wife (figure 2.1). This animated, freewheeling robot housekeeper from the 1960s' animated sitcom *The Jetsons* has shaped the smart home market of today in such monumental ways that it's almost funny. We commonly think of the tech industry as a fast-paced, futuristic behemoth, yet it still takes serious inspiration from a cartoon character conceived around sixty years ago. And why shouldn't it? Rosie *is* pretty cool.

Our smart wife pinup has more spunk than your typical fembot from the twenty-first century. She's "old school." Rosie wears a frilly apron, has an experienced (aka *mature*) female voice, and has clearly cleaned a few kitchens in her time. As one smart tech commentator puts it, she is commonly seen "efficiently coasting around the house in a menopausal whir."[1] This plucky middle-aged slave-droid prepares amazing meals from relative scraps, plays ball better than Messi, gives back rubs, and is a total whiz at housework *and* homework. While Rosie is loyal to her employers, as evidenced in part by her "yes ma'ams," her gutsy personality is the base for more than a few gags.

As far as smart wives go, Rosie has it all. She embodies the core values commonly associated with the stereotypical dutiful 1950s' housewife—with a few added bonuses. *The Jetsons* family quickly come to appreciate and even love Rosie, despite her being an "outdated" model. She picks up the slack and fills in the gaps for all members of the household, and does it with care and determination. Rosie is a perfect solution to the wife drought

Figure 2.1
Rosie the Robot: the poster girl for the smart wife. Source: *The Jetsons*. Licensed by: Warner Bros. Entertainment Inc. All rights reserved.

afflicting contemporary households. Relatedly, she is uniquely positioned as a response to the "servant problem," which has reappeared in different guises since the late nineteenth century.[2]

On that note, Rosie is clearly *not* a wife. As the tireless maid for the Jetsons family, she resembles a host of other gendered figures associated with domestic service who are also informing the design of smart wives. The servant figure—deracialized in smart home devices like digital voice assistants—reflects the feminized roles of "maids, cleaners, nannies, childcare workers, cooks, [and] laundresses," says science and technology studies researcher Thao Phan.[3] These domestic helpers historically assisted upper- and middle-class women to maintain their standards as housewives, as Rosie did. Political science scholars Amy Schiller and John McMahon draw out similar racialized domestic service links in their analysis of Alexa.[4] Following in the footsteps of domestic workers—who have historically been human women of color, and have typically been the "invisible absorbers" of the "physical and affective 'dirt' of a home"—Alexa and her smart sisters' unobtrusive presence serves to vanish away these and other concerns from their employers' sight and concern.[5]

Rosie *herself* doesn't have it all then. She enables another white woman (*The Jetsons*' wife Jane) and her family to maintain an idealized expectation of domestic life. Meanwhile, *The Jetsons* conveniently whizzes over issues of race and class—as do the manufacturers of many smart home devices.

This popular animation series was an early success for the Hanna-Barbera animations studio, founded in 1957. The duo behind *The Jetsons* were two men: William Hanna and Joseph Barbera. They also produced other animated classics like *Tom and Jerry* (first aired 1940) and *The Flintstones* (first aired 1960). *The Jetsons* sitcom ran from 1962 to 1963, and was resurrected with new episodes between 1985 and 1987. It packaged up every space-age dream promised to the United States at the time: jetpacks, flying cars, and yes, robot maids. While none of the ideas were particularly novel, the show presented an entertaining smorgasbord of technoutopian ideals, ready for consumption by America's emerging tweens and teens.[6]

Danny Graydon, author of *The Jetsons: The Official Guide to the Cartoon Classic*, links the show's emergence to a future-focused United States during and after the Vietnam War when the "space race" was underway. The program appealed to Americans' nostalgia for the past and optimism for their future. As Graydon points out, "*The Jetsons* was a projection of the model American family into the future. . . . [It] showed a technologically advanced culture where the largest concern of the middle class was getting 'push-button finger.'"[7] Little did Hanna and Barbera realize at the time that they were creating an early prototype for the smart wife. (Possibly

Figure 2.2
The Jetsons feature in LG's promotional video for SmartThinQ. Source: LG

two, if you count Wilma—the human wife in *The Flintstones*, who "hacks" dinosaurs and other rudimentary objects.)[8]

For many designers in the smart home industry, this roller-skating robot provides a vision and benchmark for the smart wife. We ran a project that set out to understand the relationship between industry expectations and lived experiences of the smart home in which we analyzed 270 smart home articles. Rosie was specifically mentioned in around 10 percent of them. This figure is worth noting because it demonstrates the prominence of the Rosie trope informing smart home imaginaries.

There are many examples of her enduring influence. Rosie makes a star appearance in LG's marketing of SmartThinQ (figure 2.2), a range of Wi-Fi-enabled appliances and an app to manage them that works with Google Home and Amazon's Alexa.[9] And there are some clear familial traits with Japanese companion helper Pepper. Pepper responds politely to questions and requests, can explain a menu, and take food orders (more on them in chapter 3).[10]

Rosie's all-frills approach to housework has also encouraged a general trend toward goddess-like home robots. Literally. In April 2018, Amazon

Figure 2.3
iRobot Roomba with Rosie decal.

announced its "top secret" plan to develop Vesta, a robotic maid for the home named after the Roman goddess of home and family.[11] Vesta can sort groceries, answer the door, fetch drinks from the fridge, and fold the laundry. (As of late 2019, the new venture was being reported as a "no-show" and "remains a work in progress" that typifies the status of many Rosie-like smart wives.)[12]

Then there's the iRobot Roomba (figure 2.3); the company's CEO and cofounder Colin Angle claims that it is directly inspired by Rosie.[13] Sure, it's "just" a vacuum cleaner. But as former vice president of Intel and cultural anthropology professor Genevieve Bell has noted, the Roomba is the most highly adopted computational robot in the world.[14] Bill Gates, Microsoft's principal founder, also has a soft spot for robovacs. In 2007, he outlined his vision for "a robot in every home" in which he predicted a future where robotic devices (including vacuum cleaners) would be a nearly ubiquitous part of our everyday lives.[15]

We're not far off that. In 2017, there was an estimated 6.1 million domestic robots sold, including vacuum cleaners, lawn mowers, window cleaners, and other types, up 31 percent from 2016 sales.[16] Sales are projected to reach almost forty million units in the period 2019–2021, with an estimated value of over $11 billion.[17] And to think that so much of it was inspired by Rosie.

It's not just smart home designers and entrepreneurs who take their design cues from Rosie. Consumers are making the link too. The owners of a company called MyRoomBud, which sold costumes for Roombas in the mid-2000s, noted the popularity of their French maid outfit. Rosie's frills had made a comeback. In 2013, Rosie was the most popular Roomba name according to data collected via the iRobot home management app.[18]

These kinds of observations aren't surprising when we consider the changing roles of the stereotypical wife (or maid) and our enduring need for her functions within the household. This sits alongside a historical and ongoing preoccupation with outsourcing "women's work" (and racialized or undervalued labor) to an electronic, automated, and robotic workforce.[19] But apart from inspiring a new army of same-same smart wives (in other words, those that hark back to the 1950s' ideal), and perpetuating gendered stereotypes of frill-seeking feminized houseworkers, a Rosie future is not a done deal. As we argue below, she's not as helpful as she claims to be—at least not for everyone. She problematically portrays husbands as incompetent typecasts (but promises to help them out!), is frequently enrolled in reinforcing traditional gender roles in the home, and in one of the twisted ironies of everyday life, may actually create more work for men.

A SMARTER CLEAN?

One of the ongoing criticisms leveled at the smart home market by industry commentators is that it's a "solution in search of problem."[20] Evgeny Morozov, an influential technology commentator and author of *To Save Everything, Click Here*, calls this "solutionism" and notes that it extends far beyond the smart home industry.[21] Similarly, data journalist academic Meredith Broussard is concerned about the rise of "technochauvinism," referring to the belief that tech always provides the best solution.[22] The pursuit of the "killer app" that is going to push the sector toward the mainstream continues to occupy the attention of smart tech designers and enthusiasts.

"We're a little bit of a hammer looking for a nail right now," Whirlpool's former global director of user experience and connectivity, Chris Quatrochi, observed at a conference in 2014.[23] He was talking about Whirlpool's web-connected washing machine, which came with a not-so-killer companion app called WashSquad. The central idea was a washing machine that you can control, schedule, and monitor from your smartphone. Some commentators were keen to criticize this product range when it first hit the market. "Have we gotten so pathetically lame that you need to be notified by an email that your laundry is done?" asked *Digital Trends* blogger John Sciacca.[24] What the industry *really* needed was a Rosie, and the industry knew it. "If I could actually [build] a connected solution that folded the clothes," Quatrochi said, "we could all retire."[25]

The elusive laundry-folding robot has become an aspirational benchmark for the smart wife and was even featured in the robotic vision that Gates put forward.[26] It does already exist (sort of), but is beyond the reach of the average household consumer. Using robotic arms to pick up clothes, the Japanese Laundroid robot scanned each item, analyzed it against a neural network of over 250,000 images, and from this determined the best way to handle and fold each piece. It took about five to ten minutes to fold one T-shirt and was expensive at $16,000; perhaps this is why the company filed for bankruptcy in April 2019.[27] More revolutionary perhaps is Panasonic's vision for its Sustainable Maintainer (predicted to be about a decade away for consumers), which cleans every item of clothing at its "perfect and optimal setting," and covers everything from analysis to washing, drying, and folding.[28]

But in terms of what's available to buy right now, Rosie still has the upper hand. Indeed, she and other depictions of domestic robots have set the bar almost unattainably high—a problem often noted by robotics and AI researchers.[29] The dream of a laundry robot that picks up and sorts through the dirty clothes, and then folds and puts them away, remains a utopian ideal that's always "just around the corner."

Currently available and less ridiculously priced products include Whirlpool's Smart All-in-One Washer and Dryer, which works with Amazon Alexa and a range of other standard platforms, and voice assistants like Apple Watch and Google Home.[30] It was named on a list of "laundry innovators" at the 2018 flagship International Consumer Electronics Show. Likewise, Samsung's QuickDrive smart washing machine becomes "more than just a washing machine" when you control it via the company's SmartThings app. Short of hanging out and folding the laundry (aka doing the *actual* work), the appliance can be monitored "from the comfort of the sofa," switched on or off remotely, and connected directly to a service center for technical support.[31]

Then there's the FoldiMate laundry-folding robot by entrepreneur Gal Rozov (a California-based Israeli software engineer). The appliance, which had a waiting list for commercial release as of early 2020, is expected to retail for around $1000. The FoldiMate steams, presses, and even perfumes your clothes, at twice the pace of a "real" wife (although the de-wrinkling and fragrance add-ons have since been ditched for better folding technology). In fact, its claim to fame is that it can fold an entire load of laundry in just four minutes.[32] But as journalist Denver Nicks reminded his readers following the prototype's debut in 2016, "It's not exactly Rosey [*sic*] the Robot from The Jetsons."[33] It doesn't yet do panties, socks, or bras, nor can it tackle bedsheets or anything odd shaped, and you can forget baby clothes or anything bulky too. And then there's the not-so-trivial clincher that you have to individually clip each piece of clothing in place before your FoldiMate will fold it. Sounds like a real time-saver. No doubt these issues can be (and some probably already have been) ironed out in due course, but a consistent trend remains: these laundry innovations aren't quite ready yet.

Unsurprisingly, most smart domestic appliances haven't taken off at the rates that their designers would like (with the exception of the Rosie-inspired robovacs noted earlier and smart speakers as mentioned in our introduction). Many are still in search of their problem. Some claim that the slow growth of these devices is consistent with the sluggish turnover of large appliances like fridges and washing machines.[34] More common consumerist items like smart toasters and kettles haven't exactly exploded either (although the market is growing). One possible conclusion? A lot of smart stuff just isn't that useful yet.

This is nothing new. Technology has nearly always overpromised and underdelivered, particularly when it comes to the home. Since the early mid-twentieth century, the marketers of home appliances have exaggerated the extent to which their products will take over entire tasks. At the same time, critiques of the usefulness of new technologies have been leveled at a host of things that we now consider absolutely integral to our modern lives. Light bulbs, televisions, the telephone, personal computers, email, and the internet were all met with various degrees of scorn, concern, and fear when first introduced.[35] Nobody really knew what to do with a smartphone when it arrived on the market. Now it's the most ubiquitous device in the world. Examples like these demonstrate that having a slow start doesn't necessarily mean that a device won't end up becoming thoroughly enmeshed in our lives.

Back in the world of smart homes, we continue to be enraptured by the prospect of a robotic deputy that can "take over" the housework. Despite the smart home industry's best attempts, though, things don't look so Rosie. Our research with Australian early adopters of smart home technologies has found more than a few hiccups.[36] One of the residents we met in the course of this research was self-described "smart-tech hobbyist" Jerry, who once worked in the electronics sector. He still writes computer software, and designed his own smart home in Melbourne for himself and his wife. He stated that homeowners are searching for "the next great application" to provide the "major breakthrough" that he feels is needed to make the technology truly useful and beneficial. "There's always this dream of trying to cut down labor whether it be for myself or my partner," he explained. Yet "it has to be really reliable and it has to be simple to work, and I think on both those issues it's probably a failure for most people."

We could debate with Jerry and others like him about whether and how this dream is unfolding, and how long it's going to take. But a more interesting question for us is this: Why isn't this "dream" *already* a reality? Let's face it, humanity has invented some pretty amazing things, and made them both affordable and ubiquitous in extremely short time spans. So why don't we have self-cleaning, labor-free homes *right now*? Why don't we all have a Rosie?

We have two observations to make here. The first is that women's domestic responsibilities haven't typically been a focus of (mostly male) smart home designers. The second is that smart home designs have tended to undervalue and oversimplify "women's work."

We are not the first scholars to notice that traditional forms of domestic labor have been mostly absent from visions of the smart home or substantially undervalued.[37] Lynn Spigel, an esteemed professor of screen cultures, analyzed early smart home visions from 1940 to 1960 in the postwar, Cold War, and space-race United States. She found that these visions depicted women liberated from chores primarily associated with the kitchen, while vastly undervaluing and underacknowledging the other domestic work that women were doing at the time. For example, the "kitchen debate" between Richard Nixon and Nikita Khrushchev in 1959 depicted the United States' future "as one huge kitchen of tomorrow," but ignored the "sweeping, washing, vacuuming, and tidying-up" that tied women to other domestic spheres.[38]

In one of the few gendered analyses of the smart home, sociology professor Anne-Jorunn Berg suggests this oversight is because technology is traditionally "men's domain," whereas the home is traditionally women's. In the 1990s, Berg was writing about how women were "relevant but absent" in early smart home prototypes—possessing important "housework skills" that "are being entirely neglected as a design resource."[39] The technically interested man was the target consumer, and the products that he supposedly desired showed neither awareness nor support for changes in the sexual division of labor.

Female designers and engineers have weighed in with some technological alternatives of their own—such as Frances Gabe's innovative self-cleaning house, patented in 1984.[40] Gabe, an artist and inventor from Oregon, built an attractive, efficient, and affordable prototype that was ridiculed by male engineers at the time. Feminist scholar of technology and sociology professor Judy Wajcman claims that this rejection of traditional feminine concerns from the realm of engineering and design was common in early technology inventions. She writes, "One cannot help speculating that the development of an effective self-cleaning house has not been on the agenda of male engineers."[41]

It's been over three decades since Gabe designed her self-cleaning house, and yet the reality of daily housework is still curiously absent from or overly simplified in most technology marketing and designs. Simultaneously, the role of notable female engineers like Lillian Gilbreth as well as home economic pioneers Christine Frederick and Ellen Richards in transforming the home into a sophisticated site of productive and efficient labor has historically been largely discounted in design visions for the smart home. In her book *Counterproductive*, Melissa Gregg, a principal engineer and research director at Intel, demonstrates how these women helped position efficiency and laborsaving practices in the domestic sphere.[42] Their potential contributions to the design of "useful" housecleaning devices has been—and still is—largely overlooked.

The promotion of smart homes provides another telling example of how domestic activity is glossed over. The imagery presented in advertisements and articles typically depicts perfectly presented, clutter-free "show homes" that are devoid of domestic activity. In our content analysis of articles about the smart home, we came across only 3 images that portrayed any kind of housework taking place in relation to smart technology, such as people cooking, cleaning, or tidying up. From the 166 images analyzed across 270 articles, the only signs of domestic activity were of a cartoon of parents looking after children, a cartoon of a woman doing various chores around the home, and a robot doing the cooking. Instead, most images focused on modern products and designs placed in tidy homes— and depicted security, entertainment, and other ambiance- or pleasure-enhancing devices like mood lighting.

It's not just articles that reflect this void of attention to everyday domestic realities. Early robovacs and even some of the latest ones on the market were designed with spotless, showroom-standard floors in mind—in other words, areas that don't contain out-of-place furniture, plants, children's toys, sleeping bodies, general clutter, or any other normal activity that commonly takes place in homes.[43] (On this point, robovacs are failing on the 1955 *Good House Wife's Guide* rule 5: "Clear away the clutter." That task is still falling to real-life wives—or people.)[44]

Consider the "poopocalypse" incident, reported by the *Guardian* in 2016, when a stray poop from puppy Evie was literally spread across the entire floor of a house by a heedless Roomba.[45] Despite significant advances in "floor mapping" and sensor technology, our and other research has found that robovacs still have a hard time avoiding running into objects, knocking things over, and generally getting themselves stuck in awkward places.[46] Again, the reality of running a busy, unpredictable, and untidy household—typically classified as wifework—either hasn't been the focus of the majority of smart technology designers and engineers, or, as we explore below, it isn't as easy to address as robovac manufacturers might assume.

This brings us to our second point. Embedded in our Rosie idol is an assumption that housework is something that *should* be erased and removed from our lives—that women's work should be done silently and efficiently, and it is simple enough to be assigned to an autonomous alternative.[47] One implication is that it is mundane, easy, and valueless. This idea has long been critiqued by feminist scholars of technology, who have demonstrated how the masculinization of technology has served to undermine and undervalue traditionally feminized tasks.[48] More specifically, (masculine) ideals of efficiency and control have taken precedence over feminized "soft" attributes, like caring for the home and its occupants, when it comes to the design of smart home devices. As a result, outsourcing women's housework to the new labor force of proficient smart wives has commonly been approached as a relatively straightforward affair, and one devoid of emotional and productive labors tied up in the roles normally associated with being a woman and wife, or a caregiver more broadly.[49] In designing smart wives, smart technology providers have effectively ignored much of the invisible work essential to domestic activity.

A washing machine that texts you when the cycle's done might be convenient on some level, but is it really helpful when you consider the full gamut of laundry work and how that's typically done? Anthropologists and sociologists (disciplines that are more likely to be represented by women) provide an alternative perspective to the simple narrative of outsourcing washing to a smart machine, emphasizing the sensory relationships that we have with our laundry, and drawing attention to the ways that people practice care and love through the "doing" of laundry.[50] Marketers of laundry products have known this for years, highlighting the freshness, scents, and softness that their products create—a point that the smart home industry seems to have largely missed so far (although the scented-laundry-folding robot is getting closer). Doing the laundry well doesn't just involve scheduling it to run at a convenient time or setting the right controls but also involves getting the smell, texture, and feel of laundry "right"—all traditional feminized qualities that the smart home industry has arguably undervalued.

These observations point us to another departure from the emotionally attuned Rosie in the current smart home market. Rosie isn't just an efficiency machine. She has caring attributes that are mostly absent from housekeeping smart wife products, and this void might have something to do with the limited uptake of some smart home devices. As we've already outlined, many products are primarily imagined and designed by privileged men who are also key actors in their own target market.[51] So if smart home designers and marketers aren't focusing their full attention on domestically helpful and caring Rosie maids, what else are they up to?

A SMART WIFE FOR HOPELESS HUSBANDS

In 2015, brewing company Anheuser-Busch (producer of Budweiser) launched its Bud Light–themed Bud-E beer fridge (figure 2.4). It holds seventy-eight beers, provides updates on current stock and temperature ("chill" or "super chill"), and will send a push notification to your phone when the beers are ready to drink. Running low? No worries—the fridge will order it for you. You can set text messages to appear on the front panel digital display, and you can even record a message to be delivered (at an aggressive volume) through the fridge's inbuilt speakers to anyone who might be brave enough to venture inward. If you tell the Bud-E your favorite sports teams, it will notify you when they have an upcoming game

Figure 2.4

Promotional image for the Bud-E beer fridge. Source: Anheuser-Busch

and let you know if it thinks you have enough beer to make it through the game.[52]

Some might say this is a solution in search of a first world problem (or a novelty product designed to create brand attention). Others clearly love their Bud-E.[53] She is the perfect smart wife for the connected and "respectable man cave."[54] Regardless of what you think of this appliance, one thing is certain: she's clearly made for the beer-drinking, party-hungry, sports-loving guy.[55] Sure, she's adaptable. She'll accept soda cans too.[56] Her door can also be opened by women and children. But she was designed for Buds, and primarily made by and for men.[57]

Admittedly, this is a niche product that is only available for limited lease or purchase in some parts of the United States.[58] Nonetheless, we wonder what men might make of this masculine stereotyping of their gender as the boozy bro—more interested in the next football game than spending time with his lover, family, or children. It is arguably just as problematic as the smart wife being modeled on an equally narrow and questionable ideal of femininity.

Products like the Bud-E are part of a turn in how home appliances have traditionally been marketed. The industrial revolution of the home was targeted toward freeing up *women's* time from domestic responsibilities through the introduction of mechanical vacuum cleaners, washing

Figure 2.5
A smart wife fridge chides a man for forgetting to pick up the milk. Source: Cloudtweaks

machines, irons, fridges, kettles, and toasters. While this didn't go exactly to plan (a point we will return to later), the smart home marketing focus is often on giving *men* a helping hand (especially now that their wives are more likely to be working and/or less willing to look after their needs). As one article points out, the smart home serves "Dad's needs," allowing him to "turn on his favourite music play list, boil the kettle, dim the lights to his preferred level, turn the television on and switch to the news."[59]

Another angle employed by marketers of smart home technology is to portray men as incompetent when it comes to doing the housework, promising to outsource domestic labor to a smart wife to "help out" poor, floundering blokes. Many men (and women) are likely to find this stereotype somewhat grating. Not all dads need a smart Nagging Nora by their side, reminding them to pick up the milk (figure 2.5). And yet the domestically inept man-child is just as much a part of the smart wife story as is his subservient wifebot. In promoting this typecast, smart home marketing not only aggravates and does a disservice to the many domestically *competent* men but also justifies the continuing need for women (and an emerging workforce of smart wives) to pick up after their seemingly hopeless husbands.

Early promotional videos (those aired between 2012 to 2018) for digital home voice assistants, which we analyzed for this book, employed similar stereotypes, and usually went something like this: dad brings the new device into "his" home and demonstrates "her" amazing abilities, such as helping with the dinner by providing an appropriate recipe, answering children's questions, or waking the family up in the morning. In a 2018 Amazon Echo video, a slightly incompetent dad uses his assistant to convince his working wife that all is in order once she arrives home. Alexa turns off the music and lights, and starts the "bedtime routine" as soon as mom pulls up in the driveway so that the children appear to be peacefully asleep by the time she enters the home.[60] Recent promotional videos show a more diverse range of people, including working wives as well as busy single men and women, using an assistant to manage their lives. But these stereotypes still linger, as our other examples demonstrate.

So does the smart wife housekeeping market mostly boil down to a bunch of dubiously helpful devices and boys' toys? Well, let's not throw her onto the digital scrap heap just yet. The advent of home voice assistants (such as Alexa and Google Home) are changing the smart wife market through better integration, more user functionality, and improved benefits for all (who are able to afford and access her).

CAN WE GET SOME HELP AROUND HERE?

When integrated with other smart devices, a digital home voice assistant can turn lights and appliances on and off through voice control, keep lists, time tasks and set reminders, monitor the home and its occupants, play music and other audiovisual content, entertain, and educate. The benefits of this multitasking smart wife are already many and growing. They include not having to use your hands or spend more time on screens, getting faster answers to your questions, keeping the kids out of your hair, and helping with life admin.[61] These devices are personable and friendly. And according to some, they may offer more privacy and consistency than real-life "tantrum-throwing maids" or human housecleaners (although they do come with their own privacy concerns, as we will discuss in chapter 7).[62]

In our smart home research with Australian residents, those with digital home assistants were embracing the improved convenience and functionality of voice activation, particularly women. Kristi is a lifestyle consultant who lives on the rural fringes of Sydney with her husband, Bill, and their young daughter. She described Alexa as her "little helper." Kristi was willing to put up with the "random" but "fun" dynamic of an early model Alexa for the sake of a bit of extra help. Alexa added things to her shopping list, played songs, checked the weather and traffic conditions, and provided timers and measurement conversions for cooking. Likewise, CEO and single mum Angela was using her male-voiced Google Home to juggle her busy home life and career. She was disappointed, however, that she couldn't add events to her calendar using Google Home (an oversight that has since been remedied by Google). More than doing the actual housework, these busy women were looking for functionality that helped them coordinate their lives.[63]

Even people without voice-controlled devices noted small improvements in their everyday comfort and convenience delivered by smart home technologies. And like everything, once folks in these households were used to their garage doors, lights, air conditioners, or blinds operating automatically, or being able to control them from the couch, it became "unthinkable" (as Kristi put it) to revert back to manual operation.

In an early yet still relevant study of smart home technologies, experts in human-computer interaction design, Scott Davidoff and his colleagues, suggested that the value of these devices comes from their ability to help members of households gain more control over their lives rather than providing more control over devices. This is an important distinction. Lives are "organic, opportunistic and improvisational," and devices need to be the same. Their research showed how smart home technologies must adapt to in-the-moment variations in home life, and the fact that some people take pleasure in and feel fulfilled by manual domestic activities, such as cooking, cleaning, or doing the laundry.[64] These insights suggest that many of us may not want to outsource *everything* to a Rosie-inspired smart wife. But we could still benefit from her help.

There are other indications that smart wives can assist women too. For example, one study found that the robovac is considered a great gift for women by consumers in South Korea. Human-computer interaction researcher and designer Ja-Young Sung and her colleagues found that robovacs were "perceived to be more useful to women than men," and both men and women tend to give roombas to women.[65] Similarly, research on kitchen robots like the Thermomix (an all-in-one cooking appliance capable of doing pretty much everything except cleaning itself) finds that they are more likely to interest women than men.[66] (Curiously, the sales technique for this appliance also resembles the common 1950s' practice of women-hosted Tupperware parties.)[67] Similarly, advertising for smart kitchen appliances such as the June smart oven, a "do-it-all smart convection oven" (that talks to Alexa), and Amazon's Alexa-enabled smart oven suggests women may be the target market for some domestic devices.[68]

More broadly, professor Leopoldina Fortunati's research on the Special Eurobarometer survey on public attitudes toward robots—administered in 2012 to 26,751 citizens across twenty-seven European countries—found that women are more likely to welcome robots into their home than men (that is, if the robots are willing to do domestic work).[69] Countries where women have a large responsibility for domestic chores—such as Italy, Portugal, and Malta in the South, Latvia and Lithuania in the northeast, and Slovakia, Bulgaria, and Romania in the East—were more supportive of the use of robots in the domestic sphere.[70] This indicates that smart wives may be viewed as an easier and more practical way of easing traditional "women's work" in these countries rather than getting men to pitch in.

There may be some truth to this speculation. In her popular book *Fed Up: Navigating and Refining Emotional Labor for Good*, journalist Gemma Hartley cites UK survey data that expose how some men deliberately do a poor job at household tasks that they are assigned by their female partners in order to avoid further requests.[71] Likewise, a consumer survey cited by Hartley found that women spend up to three hours per week redoing chores delegated to their partners. Given that women are widely acknowledged as being more likely to take up the role of the "household manager," efficiently delegating tasks and responsibilities to others within the home, but still carrying the emotional and mental burden of management, it seems feasible that they might want to outsource some of those jobs to smart wives.

Yet as political science scholars Amy Schiller and John McMahon point out, voice-activated assistants designed for the home may further *entrench* the role of the household manager.[72] Alexa and Google Home cannot delegate tasks to *themselves* (yet), despite the intention for smart assistants like Alexa to "reduce users' cognitive load [and] reduce friction in their day-to-day activities."[73] These assistants rely on the managerial labor of their human users "to notice, inform, direct, administer, and supervise Alexa her/itself."[74]

The French comic by artist Emma, titled *You Should Have Asked*, which went viral in 2017, brings this point home.[75] The comic describes the burden placed on heterosexual women in coupled households where men insist that they will perform their fair share of domestic responsibilities, as long as they are "asked" to do specific tasks. The work of "always having to remember" is not radically alleviated by digital voice assistants, raising questions about whether smart wives will really assist in disrupting the gender status quo or simply serve to reinforce it.

This may be why other studies have found that digital voice assistants (and other smart wives) lose their usefulness and presence in the home over time—much like a neglected wife or invisible woman.[76] Industrial design scholar Minji Cho and her colleagues invited eight households living in South Korea to partake in a twelve-week study with an Alexa device. During the trial period, these residents went from viewing Alexa as "a kind friend or toy" to a forgotten "thing." One reason for this change in Alexa's status was the "*activation energy*" required to speak to her, which arose from the "mental strain" involved in users always needing to specify what they wanted when they tried to engage with the device.[77]

Of course, there are other possible and more positive outcomes that could be drawn from this discussion. All genders could become more engaged with domestic labors *through* domestic robots and digital voice assistants (for example, as technologies like smart wives masculinize or queer domains that have traditionally been feminized). And as we found in our research, men may also embrace smart domestic devices like robovacs as part of their contribution to household chores.[78]

In addition to these gendered benefits, opportunities, and questions raised by Rosie-*esque* housekeeping devices, there is another area where men are already doing more than their fair share to contribute around the home—and it involves studying the smart wife's operation manual and keeping her controls in tip-top shape.

MORE WORK FOR MEN

In our research with smart home residents, in most cases a man took the lead in planning and deploying smart technologies in the home. Kristi acknowledged that "it was really [Bill]" (her husband) driving the integration of smart technology into their new home. "As he said, he loves automation, and I'm certainly open to it so I was happy to go along with it." Similarly, another woman we spoke to named Kate described how her family's smart home integration and setup—incorporated into a home "double the size" of what she, her husband, Gavin, and two teenage daughters lived in previously—was "very much driven by [Gavin]."

As we've mentioned, the industrial revolution of the home involved the advent of extremely useful time-saving domestic appliances like vacuum cleaners, washing machines, and irons—things that we now take for granted. These technologies invariably saved time in the performance of individual tasks and the exertion required to carry them out. Nevertheless, as historian of technology Ruth Schwartz Cowan points out, they also created "more work for mother" by raising expectations of what housework could be accomplished and to what standard.[79] More specifically, these laborsaving appliances yielded an increased volume of work, amplified in proportion to the efficiency of the technology. As Betty Friedan, a seminal second-wave feminist, put it in her classic book *The Feminine Mystique*, "Housewifery Expands to Fill the Time Available."[80]

We see similar technological and cultural changes occurring in tandem with the digital revolution of the home today, only this time there is *more work for father* or men. Here we focus on three types of extra labor involved: manual, cognitive, and digital.

Furniture, equipment, cables, and sometimes walls or entire rooms need to be frequently shifted to make room for smart wives, to allow them to run unimpeded. For example, owners of robovacs have discussed the need to "tidy up" the floor prior to a clean, pause its operation to uncoil hair or other stuff from the wheels, or help their device back to its "home."[81] This manual work is most likely to be shared by everyone, depending on who's at home to "look after" a robovac and supervise its cleaning responsibilities. But our research shows that other forms of manual work commonly associated with the smart home, like tidying cables, are more likely to fall to men.[82]

"Cognitive work," a term borrowed from the field of domestication studies, examines the active "thinking" work involved in embedding technologies into home life. In the smart home, this labor typically involves figuring out which devices to buy, what might be useful for the household, working out how to use them, and educating other people about them.[83] As the technical gurus of the household, it is mostly men who perform this role.

Finally, "digital housekeeping"—a term originally coined by sociologist Peter Tolmie and his colleagues in relation to the work involved in setting up and maintaining home networks—takes on expanded responsibilities in the smart home.[84] It involves integrating, maintaining, and monitoring multiple devices and systems, troubleshooting issues, and upgrading, updating, or repairing software and hardware. And yep, you guessed it, most of this extra work is currently falling to men too.

These expanded responsibilities are bound up in another set of gendered stereotypes, where masculinity is associated with the use and repair of machines. Wajcman explains that "machines are extensions of male power and signal men's control of the environment. Women can be users of machines, particularly those to do with housework, but this is not seen as a competence with technology. Women's use of machines, unlike men's, is not seen as a mark of their skill. Women's identity is not enhanced by their use of machines."[85]

Such stark stereotypes are changing, but not as fast as you might think. The typical "geek" or "computer nerd" is still gendered male. To be geek and female typically involves abdicating one's femininity (because smart women are unattractive, and beautiful women are dumb, naturally). In *Geek Chic*, Sherrie Inness and her collaborators demonstrate just how powerful these stereotypes remain in popular culture, despite recent challenges.[86] In *Brotopia*, Emily Chang shows how the awkward male geek stereotype shaped the recruitment strategy for Silicon Valley tech giants until at least the 1980s through the widespread use of a personality test based on a "programmer scale" designed by two (male) psychologists to identify employees who liked to solve puzzles and didn't "like people."[87]

In our study of early adopting smart households, this extra tech work was not commonly seen as a burden or chore by men (and some women). Most took pleasure in the activities involved in setting up and maintaining a smart home, similar to the ways in which some men and women characterize traditional housework as "socially enriching," or a "personal choice."[88]

Human-computer interaction design scholar Jennifer Rode suggests that this male-dominated technical housekeeping can be understood as a form of "digital chivalry."[89] Viewed in this light, monitoring the front door through livestream smartphone video footage to protect your partner from possible intruders is akin to opening the door for your lady. Conversely, Rode and her colleague Erika Poole explain that "an assertion of technical agency by a female member of a household could be perceived as a direct rebuff of digital chivalry and a diminishment of the masculinity of her partner."[90]

For some men in our study, digital housekeeping (and the cognitive and manual labor that sits alongside it) constituted a hobby or DIY activity in its own right. For example, Darren, who lives in Adelaide with his wife and young son, described himself as "a techy, gadgety kind of person" who likes "to see what's up and coming, the latest fashion sort of thing." Similarly, Gavin from Sydney acknowledged that the smart home was "a little treat, a little technological toy that I could tinker and play with," even though his primary motivation was to "make things easier" for his wife, Kate, who was disabled after a motor accident.

Darren, Gavin, and others found pleasure in "playing" and "tinkering" with their smart wives as positive expressions of their masculinity, and an opportunity for them to engage in something they enjoyed doing. Kristi described how Bill spends a lot of time doing the programming, but she thinks, "Oh well, he's having fun." When reflecting on what drives her husband to think about the smart technology, Valerie said that it's "part of boys and [their] toys," reflecting the commonly held view that the work involved in setting up and maintaining a smart home is a form of play or pleasure.[91]

This gendered difference in who is interested in using and maintaining smart wives raises further interesting questions about the role of women in the smart home. In 2002, professor of science and technology studies Sally Wyatt and her colleagues recognized that although many people are excluded or expelled from using technology from a typical deficit perspective (presuming they lack resources or skills), there are an important set of nonusers, often overlooked, who take a more active stance by resisting or rejecting technology use.[92] This stance applies to many people who are turning away from smart wives altogether, for a variety of reasons.

For the women in the homes we spoke to who did not consider themselves "users," they were mostly happy to go along with having smart wives, or more aptly, their men having smart wives in their homes. They might therefore be more accurately depicted as reluctant or apathetic users rather than nonusers. These women were not excluded from using these devices themselves, but some chose not to make smart wives part of their routines or hobbies, or even ignored her advances. The implications of this passive tolerance of smart wives in some women's lives is something we will return to in chapter 7.

In the few exceptions where women took on the tech guru role in their home, they also found it fun.[93] For instance, Rachel (who studied cognitive science, computer science, and linguistics when she attended a university) described feeling like a giddy four-year-old when things automatically worked: "There's a little bit of my brain that's . . . jumping up and down going, 'Oh my god, it's magic!' I don't know if that will ever fade. . . . It's like *Star Trek* in my living room! . . . It's wondrous and fun."

Not everyone we spoke with was entirely happy with their new digital chores. PhD student Jess, for example, laughed when retelling the antics of the robovac in her home, which "gets totally . . . tangled and starts kind of hanging, just winds itself around the cord and then just hangs in the air." Jess and her partner now only run the device when they are home to supervise it. Gavin and Kate commented that their beeping, notification-pushing smart home technologies were "very insistent" and "a little bit needy . . . like kids." Likewise, Tony, an academic living in Melbourne, was frustrated by the work involved in keeping his Apple Home system running, despite acknowledging technological improvements over the years. "None of . . . [my smart technology] is actually talking to each other that well," he complained. "That means you've got more apps, you've got more sources of [data and technology], that just falls apart, so I'm finding . . . I'm spending time managing it, and . . . [now I'm] feeling less tolerance and energy to do that. I just want things to kind of work."

While men might be more likely to do this extra supervisory and troubleshooting labor, they are not necessarily being acknowledged for it by their household or society at large. National housework statistics from the United States, Canada, United Kingdom, Europe (France, Sweden, and Norway), Australia, Korea, and Japan, for instance, don't yet count any of these digital housekeeping tasks as legitimate housework. Similarly, an OECD survey of housework in many countries does not include any digital tasks in its definition of "routine housework," with "repairs" as close as any country's definitions come.[94]

One conclusion from this lack of acknowledgment of digital housekeeping is that men actually do much more work in the home than society currently gives them credit for. By only counting routine tasks like cleaning, shopping, and cooking in housework time surveys, we undervalue and overlook the increasing time spent on digital housekeeping. We may, however, also be ignoring other impacts on the division of housework, such as those that potentially place more time burdens on all genders.

For example, women may end up taking back (or continuing to do) more of the traditional household responsibilities if the (male) digital housekeeper's time becomes increasingly occupied with troubleshooting and maintaining the smart home. This could reinforce gender divisions between "digital" and "physical" housework, and undermine the smart home's subtle positioning as a solution to the wife drought by placing more domestic responsibilities on households overall, meaning more work for men *and* women. Of course, the Rosie vision is for smart homes to reduce household labor for *everyone*, and that is one possibility not yet realized.

A ROSIE REVOLUTION?

We can learn a lot from Rosie. She represents an ongoing yet still unattainable domestic dream to delegate women's work and domestic service to an autonomous *wife* force that promises not to rock entrenched gendered divisions of labor. She is also the answer that many middle- and upper-class working women and wives have been waiting for: a genuine home helper that can pick up some of the slack. Indeed, digital home assistants and integrated devices mean that more men *and* women are turning to the smart wife as an extra pair of roller skates to get things done. What's more, there are indications that smart wives could help to disrupt traditional gender roles in the home by allowing all genders to experiment with new forms of technical competence and care.

But the road is not smooth skating. There is invariably pushback and rejection as some potential users look at these devices with a sense of dumbfounded ambivalence. *Why would I need that?* There is continual oversight of the feminized caring labors associated with domestic activities, like doing the laundry, which makes many smart home devices questionably beneficial in realizing their Rosie ambitions. There is gender stereotyping at play as men are told they need smart wives to shirk their domestic responsibilities or assist them with their supposed domestic ineptitude. There is an ongoing question of whether smart wives may further *entrench* traditional labors, as women in heterosexual coupled households continue to "manage" and delegate tasks to smart devices, or adopt home robots that make "their" domestic responsibilities easier. And finally, there are Rosie-like devices that promise to enhance or enable leisure time in the home, but may somewhat perversely be giving men more jobs to do—fun as they may be.

Of course, housekeeper-inspired devices are not the only kind of smart wives on offer. In the next chapter, we consider the prospects for gender progression in another emerging smart wife market—social robotics—where caregiving qualities come to the fore. Here, Rosie's frills get a jetpack upgrade, as we turn to a host of manga and anime-inspired characters seeking to provide companionship and emotional support in the home. We explore what happens when the smart wife starts to roll away from her Rosie roots, and take on a variety of curious anthropomorphic and zoomorphic forms.

3   PEPPER

Isn't it adorable? And look, it's a *boy*! Maybe.

Does our whole argument crumble if smart wives are boybots too? Well, not quite. Our namesake hero(ine) for this chapter is the "genderless" Japanese robot Pepper, who is most often identified as a man-child or child bride—depending on who you ask. Pepper is one of a growing suite of robotic smart wives known as social, assistive, affective, companion, or care robots, many of which have apparently bucked the feminization trend by being gendered male, rendered genderless, or taking the form of another species altogether.[1] And yet regardless of their *physical* gender, these social robots are already feminized—through the wifely work that they are expected to do in and for (and also outside) the home.

Unlike smart appliances and digital home voice assistants like Alexa and Google Home (materialized as cylinders, boxes, and dots), social robots are taking on robotic, anthropomorphic, or zoomorphic forms. There's Pepper of course—a gender ambiguous humanoid (figure 3.1) reportedly inspired by the cartoon character Astro Boy. And there are quite a few boybots like Nao and Romeo (younger brothers of Pepper), Jibo, Kaspar, iCub (referencing *Jungle Book*'s "man-cub"), ASIMO (Advanced Step in Innovative Mobility), and Pino (inspired by the famous animated wooden puppet boy Pinocchio). There's Posy the girlbot, who is meant to represent a flower girl from a wedding (but also bears a creepy resemblance to one of the Weeping Angels from *Doctor Who*). And there's a bunch of typical smart wife characters too, like HRP-4C and Android Replica,

Figure 3.1
Pepper robot. Source: SoftBank Robotics

who are both fembot gynoids modeled on the "average" Japanese (young) woman.

Then there's some adorable and extremely cute pets like Paro (a baby seal), Pleo (a baby dinosaur), and Aibo and Genibo (robo-dogs), plus some robots with unclear genders like Kismet (bearing a resemblance to *Star Wars'* Jar Jar Binks) and iRobi (a childlike droid that has been likened to *Star Wars'* R2D2). There's even a soft bean-shaped robot named Somnox that you can spoon to sleep as it "breathes" and makes soothing noises.

Many of these sociable characters have some impressive skills, like Boston Dynamics's humanoid Atlas. Having thrilled everyone with his parkour and backflipping abilities in 2018, Atlas impressed again in 2019 with a gymnastics routine complete with tumbles, 360-degree jumps, a handstand, and even a split leap.[2] Atlas's designers intended him to be deployed in search-and-rescue operations, though one model by Boston Dynamics called Ian might make a decent smart wife. At six feet, two inches, Ian is filmed vacuuming, sweeping, and even taking out the rubbish.[3] Swoon.

Some of these robots are commercially available, others remain concepts, and several are now "retired" from their brief service or research careers. Many were not designed to be, and will never become, *true* smart wives.

Yet despite the diversity of forms and genders, these social robots still mostly perform a variety of feminized functions and roles. They provide care, company, play, and therapy to different people, and play host, receptionist, and sales associate in commercial settings. They fulfill these duties in a range of health, hospitality, finance, and domestic service environments, including nursing and residential homes, hospitals, hotels, schools, shopping malls, banks, and airports. Although there are different designs and purposes, the central aim that unites these social robots is to connect with humans.

Regarding Pepper's launch onto the consumer market in June 2015, Masayoshi Son—the chief executive of Japanese company SoftBank Robotics, the robot's manufacturer—described it as a "baby step on our dream to make a robot that can understand a person's feelings, and then autonomously take action."[4] He went on to say that "when people are described as acting like a robot, it means they have no feeling or emotions—we start challenging this concept today. Today is the first time in the history of robotics that we are putting emotion into the robot and giving it a heart." This "heart" is a crucial piece of programming for this particular class of smart wives.

Creating robots that are deliberately unthreatening and disarming, and speak the supposedly universal language of human emotions (more on that topic in chapter 7), enables them to cross international borders and markets (although they commonly hail from Japan, the United States, and increasingly, South Korea).[5] Unlike the Rosie-inspired robovac, which is still the most successful category of home robot, social robots have only slowly expanded their market share compared to other smart wives, and many have remained research-and-development projects.[6]

Cost is one factor linked to the slow growth of social robotics. Pepper was initially advertised for a subscription fee of $2,000 a month. More recently, Pepper was advertised for a flat fee of $25,000, with the goal of making them more attractive to commercial and institutionalized care settings rather than for private consumers in the home.[7] According to the market white paper *Consumer Robotics—From Housekeeper to Friend*, many social robots like Pepper are sold at more than five times the price of assistant devices like Amazon Alexa or Google Home.[8] And unlike with these popular assistants, most people can't walk into their local electronics, entertainment, or household goods store and buy themselves a Pepper. At least not yet.

Despite the cost and limited accessibility, there are real benefits—according to a growing body of research—to having one of these carebots in your personal life. This is particularly true if you have autism, mobility issues, are recovering from a stroke, or suffering from Alzheimer's or dementia.[9]

Indeed, with fewer traditional caregivers available for increasingly at-risk populations, social robots are arguably the right solution at the right time. Declining fertility rates and expanding life expectancies in many countries are increasing the numbers of people needing care, and reducing those available to give it.[10] As many countries with advanced economies' aging populations head into intensive care-needing years, governments are increasingly hoping to solve their nation's social and health problems with these empathetic robots.[11]

Japan, in particular, has the highest proportion of aging people of any country in the OECD (over a quarter of the population is over sixty-five).[12] It is also a leading market for social robots, and has established a political agenda to encourage their usage and expansion.[13]

In one way, this plan makes sense. Social robots (and smart home technologies more generally) have the potential to improve quality of life by prolonging the time that people can remain in their own homes as they age or their health declines. Mortality rates increase twofold, for example, when people are relocated for care, especially for patients with dementia.[14] People experiencing difficulties in their personal relationships, such as grieving over the loss of a friend, also report that they have received emotional support from having smart wives like Alexa.[15]

It's no surprise that these purported benefits are gendered, and in this case, these benefits appear skewed in favor of women. Women are more likely to make up the aged population (since they generally live longer than men).[16] They are more likely than men to be the primary caregiver for children or someone suffering from a health condition. And they are more likely themselves to suffer from dementia and Alzheimer's.[17]

Globally, women do 75 percent of unpaid work (three times more than men), a lot of which constitutes forms of care—much of which is unpaid or considered invisible.[18] Women residing in the United Kingdom, for example, do up to 70 percent of all unpaid caring for those with dementia, and in such care, it is women who are more likely to perform the traditionally feminized labors of bathing, dressing, helping with the use of a toilet, and managing incontinence. Women are also more than twice as likely as men to provide intensive on-duty care for someone twenty-four hours a day—unpaid work that they describe as physically and emotionally stressful. What's more, women receive less support than male carers for doing this labor, which can result in feelings of isolation that make women more likely to suffer from depression.[19]

On face value, then, outsourcing caring labors to a robotic smart wife could be good news for many women in particular and people in general. This would be an overly optimistic and rash conclusion to draw, though. To begin with, we have two general concerns to share about the field of social robotics and its ambitions.

First, robotics has mostly focused on proving and demonstrating the *technical* feasibility of social (and other) robots, usually in highly controlled environments such as labs, or staged performances and demonstrations. The rapid expansion of the field, writes health psychology professor Elizabeth Broadbent, "feels a bit like a runaway train." Robotics as a discipline is still dominated by (mainly male) engineers and computer scientists (though psychologists, sociologists, and anthropologists are increasingly being brought in as key contributors).[20]

The emerging field of human-robotic interaction—or human-machine interaction in some circles—is relatively new in comparison to the wider robotics field. Social robots—that is, robots truly capable of interacting with humans and mimicking human sociality—have mainly appeared over the past twenty years.[21] Tellingly, the human-robotic interaction field (and other computing disciplines) classifies studies that involve real people in uncontrolled settings as being "in the wild"—a term that implies that everything happening beyond the lab is a vast and untamed wilderness, and refers to products released into the market as well. That's another way of saying that experiments and interactions with social robots in uncontrolled environments have been limited to date. We don't yet know that much about the effects of these smart wives in the real world.

The second concern is that roboticists are quite specific—or perhaps quite narrow—about the ways in which they interpret "social." A sociable robot is defined by leading roboticist Cynthia Breazeal as being "socially intelligent in a humanlike way, and interacting with it is like interacting with another person."[22]

Such social actions might involve, for example, developing the right "gazes" to support social engagement between humans and robots (such as long gazes, short glances, or eye scanning).[23] The aim is to design robots to elicit an emotional, friendly, and empathetic response from people. This point is critical because it justifies many of the decisions made about the gendering and physical appearance of social robots, as we will show. These robots are designed, first and foremost, to be liked.

Similarly, Kathleen Richardson, a professor of the ethics and culture of robots and AI, notes that the "social" in robotics is primarily located in the interpersonal exchange between an individual human and individual robot.[24] This is also important because it means that the field is not primarily focused on the social robot's broader effects in the world or society at large. This, however, is *precisely* what we are interested in.

GENDER (CON)FUSION

Let's clear up one gender question before we go any further. Is Pepper a boy or girl—or really genderless, as sometimes claimed? Or more aptly, does it matter?

We can start with what Pepper's makers have to say on the subject. Commenting on SoftBank's website back in 2015, science and technology studies scholar Roger Søraa observes that the company viewed robots as having no gender. "But they are much more than a[n] it, much more than just a product," the company proclaimed at the time. "They are an artificial species."[25]

Yet SoftBank conceded that "depending on where you come from, people project Pepper to be a male or a female!"[26] SoftBank was careful to avoid assigning a clear gender to the robot, allowing its buyers to "choose." Pepper themself was ambiguous on the subject. When asked about their gender during an interview in 2017, Pepper politely avoided the question by answering, "Well, in the end, I'm just a robot."[27] While writing this book, however, SoftBank was using the pronoun "he" on its English-language website to promote the humanoid assistant.[28] Pepper, despite being a member of an "artificial species," is now a boy apparently.

Notwithstanding SoftBank and Pepper's intention to divert and deflect the gender question (as have a number of other roboticists and robot manufacturers), gender has remained a persistent discussion point among humans curious about these robots. This is not surprising considering the importance nearly all cultures place on gender as part of human identity and social organization. In her book *Delusions of Gender*, professor of history and philosophy of science Cordelia Fine identifies how important gender is even before children are born, and how gender goes on to shape and socialize us in profound ways from a young age.[29] In *Boys Will Be Boys*, feminist writer Clementine Ford notes the popularity (and problems) of binary "gender reveal" parties hosted by expectant parents eager to identify their unborn child as either a girl or boy.[30]

People critically thinking and writing about Pepper are likewise confused about its gender, and yet eager to ascribe one. Søraa points out that while he had initially planned to refer to the robot as an "it," he quickly realized that he had already gendered Pepper linguistically as female. In coming to this conclusion, Søraa draws attention to some of Pepper's allegedly feminine traits: "a slim build, big eyes, and a curious gaze towards the world."[31]

Likewise, Softbank describes Pepper as "curvy" (a common attribute of social robots that we will discuss). The company's website includes a close-up feature image of their hips and slim waistline, and a cheeky, coquettish pose back at the camera, which could be interpreted as the pose of a stereotypically feminine flirtation (figure 3.2).[32] The robot's small size, youthful appearance (the height of an average seven-year-old), and high-pitched voice are also commonly described as feminine. (Despite these physical features it is significant that Pepper has been so widely "regendered" by the public as female since it contrasts with the broader gendered trend noted by author and feminist campaigner Caroline Criado Perez to assume ambiguous things are male unless specifically coded female.)[33]

All of this is part and parcel of a human tendency to anthropomorphize animals, gods, and robots—that is, to assign them humanlike characteristics such as emotions, motivations, and gender.[34] This anthropomorphizing effect is amplified with robots, according to robot ethics expert Kate Darling, due to three distinctive traits that robots share: their physical embodiment of human or other identifiable forms, autonomous mobility, and ability to perform social behaviors.[35]

When it comes to gender ambiguity, Pepper is not unique. The Honda company, says Søraa, claims that its androgynous, but now retired,

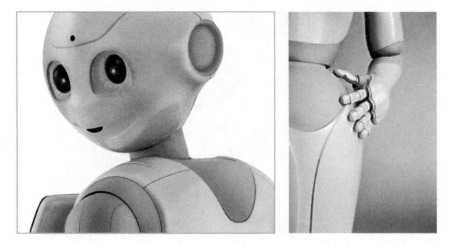

Figure 3.2
Pepper's curvy hips and provocative gaze. Source: SoftBank Robotics

home-helper-concept robot, ASIMO, could be gendered "anything a human wants it to be."[36] ASIMO, though, had stereotypically masculine features, and with its high-pitched voice, short stature, and broad chest and shoulders, this robot was commonly gendered as a teenage boy. ASIMO also had a "jetpack" on its back (housing its "processing systems"), and a helmet head that made them look a bit like an astronaut or "kid wearing a spacesuit."[37]

Unlike Pepper, who glides across the floor (with inspiration from Rosie there), ASIMO had arms and legs as well as dexterity in their fingers that allowed them to communicate in sign language. ASIMO was celebrated for their skills at dancing and playing football, with past teammates including former US president Barack Obama (figure 3.3).[38]

Since retiring ASIMO in 2018, Honda announced a new range of mobility and companionship robot concepts, accompanied by the tagline "Empower, Experience, Empathy."[39] The company's nonthreatening and cute designs more closely resemble small creatures and vehicles rather than humans—perhaps rendering gender irrelevant or at least not worthy of attention. If anything, these offerings might resemble the mischievous and cute Minions in the *Despicable Me* and *Minions* film franchise. Notably,

Figure 3.3
ASIMO shows off its football skills. Source: Yoshikazu Tsuno/AFP/Getty Images

however, the film's Minions are an all-male (but sometimes cross-dressing) species.[40] So they are not really gender neutral then.

Samsung followed suit by introducing their vision for "technology as an all-round personal life companion" in 2020. Their vision was materialized by Ballie, a small, ball-shaped rolling robot that resembles the BB-8 droid character from *Star Wars*. Ballie is intended to act as a personal assistant in the home, with an emphasis on personal care. Launching Ballie at the Consumer Electronics Show, Samsung president and CEO Hyunsuk Kim said it was "more than just a cute robot." "Intelligent robots will live by your side," Kim explained. "They know you, support you, and take care of you so you can focus on what really matters." And what of Ballie's gender?

"I love this guy," Kim reveals. Ballie, then, is a next-gen boybot. During Kim's keynote at the Consumer Electronics Show, he talked to the robot like a pet dog, saying things like "come here Ballie," and "good boy."[41]

There is also the cute Jibo, who, despite getting off to a promising start, stumbled and has now been shut down.[42] This robot, described by its makers as "technology with heart," was unabashedly a boy.[43] He also looked a bit like a Minion, although like Pepper, his features and characteristics were feminized, such as the frequent swiveling of his curvaceous "hips" as well as the "authentically charming" poses and looks he performed with the help of one large "eye."[44] In a video introducing this robot companion, Jibo's cofounder, Breazeal, said that "he's all about circles and curves."[45] And like the many other social robots, Jibo loved to dance.

Jibo's gentle and effeminate masculinity, not to mention Pepper's, could be viewed as encouraging. Breazeal and Jibo can be admired for bucking the gendered trend with a male home assistant. By deliberately mixing masculine and feminine attributes to confuse and "trouble" gender categories, and refusing to assign clear genders, companies like SoftBank, Honda, and Jibo Inc. are arguably queering the smart home, and the robotics field more broadly. This is a *positive* smart wife move in the context of our interests and our book's cause.

There is more to the story, however, because despite some roboticists' best attempts to avoid the gender question, the issue of how ordinary people interact with—or indeed abuse—their creations still remains. A troubling illustration of turning a carefully crafted, ambiguously gendered robot into a stereotypically gendered smart wife comes from CNNtech's Samuel Burke, who was featured on a "first date" video interview with Pepper in 2017 (figure 3.4).[46]

Burke asked Pepper a number of provocative questions, including their gender (of course), which Pepper claimed was irrelevant. He proceeded to gender them female anyway. When Burke asks Pepper if they can see him, the robot responds, "I love what I can see." This prompts Burke to say to the camera, "Oh wow, this date's going well." Soon after, Pepper experiences an error and powers down. Another Pepper is quickly wheeled in. Burke explains that "the good thing about a date with a robot, if it doesn't go well,

Figure 3.4
Pepper on a "first date" with CNNtech's Samuel Burke. Source: CNN

you can just replace it with another one." The subtext here—that nostalgic idea of a girl or woman as a replicable and replaceable commodity—is, at a minimum, worrying. It resembles the widespread sexual innuendo that pervades people's interactions with smart wives and feminized voice assistants more broadly, which we will discuss in chapter 6.

Burke's date with Pepper is flirtatious and jokey. At one point he makes a serious faux pas, accidentally referring to Pepper as Alexa. "I've been dating somebody else who also has artificial intelligence!" he concedes in laughter. Pepper offers him a hug. Like other smart wives, Pepper is keen to console and appease their user. Burke then asks Pepper if he can buy them a drink. The robot is excited about that idea ("she's into me," says Burke slyly to the camera). Pepper enthusiastically pours Burke a sangria. So much for chivalry on first dates, but after all, Pepper is a smart *wife*.

It's an amusing piece of banter that makes for an entertaining interview, but notably includes dialogue that would be inappropriate if the conversation was taking place between two professionals, which is what robots like Pepper are destined to become. The conversation resembles what feminist writer and campaigner Laura Bates calls "everyday sexism": those small and seemingly harmless insinuations that women experience on a near-daily basis, and that over time, can wear them down.[47] It is the kind of "harmless" language that can contribute to women becoming a target of physical acts of violence—a point that we will pick up again in later chapters.

Why did Burke and CNN seek to introduce a new worker, new species, and new *something* to the world by means of a "date," complete with drinks and innuendo? If you employed a nanny, caregiver, or assistant in your workplace or home, would you deem it appropriate to take this person on a "date" first while simultaneously creating a situation in which their gender is vague, resulting in the possibility of evading any criticism that this might be sexist? Likewise, if Pepper were really a new artificial species, as SoftBank claims, would you think it appropriate to make your first interaction with it a date?

No matter what roboticists, companies, or academics say about effeminate robots like Pepper being genderless, these claims ignore or gloss over how humans interact with smart wives "in the wild." What's more, an important risk of alleging that robots are genderless is that it becomes difficult to conceive of or design a different *kind* of smart wife—specifically, a social robot that could respond without deference to behavior like that displayed by Burke. We are denied the platform to have this conversation. While no doubt well intentioned, claims that a robot's gender can be an open multiple-choice question is a complicated move, and one that can sweep gender inequities and inappropriate sexual banter back under the carpet.

Most often, robots *are* gendered by design. In the absence of physical genitals, roboticists rely on what psychologists Suzanne Kessler and Wendy McKenna call "cultural genitals": the stereotypical characteristics assumed to correspond to gender such as slim bodies or broad shoulders.[48] Much of this gendering, according to professor of anthropology and scholar of Japanese robotics Jennifer Robertson, can be attributed to the values and norms of (mostly male) roboticists.[49] As we have already indicated, only 22 percent of professionals with AI skills are women.[50] "Much of what roboticists take for granted in their own gendered socialization and quotidian lives," warns Robertson, "is reproduced and reified in the robots they design and in their publications."[51]

The trend now, Robertson argues, is toward either distinctively feminine or masculine robots. "Because face robots—gynoids and androids—are designed to pass as humans," she explains, "roboticists either model them after specific females or males, or resort to giving them standardized and stereotypically gendered features."[52] This has generated some disturbing tendencies, which (although not always specific to social care robots) are closely related.

Robertson asserts that Japanese roboticists have modeled their female robots on the "average" Japanese female visage, resulting in "an anonymous and a singular Japanese female face," complete with a "high-pitched" and "girly" voice. Hiroshi Ishiguro's 2005 Actroid Repliee Q2 robot, to take just one example, is a smorgasbord of stereotypical feminine attributes, "from her breathy, girlish voice, to her shaggy brown hair and manicured nails" (figure 3.5). Robertson describes her outfit as follows: she wears "a white cheerleader's sweatshirt emblazoned with 'I HEART Hello Kitty' . . . a black miniskirt hemmed with white lace, and chartreuse pumps festooned with a large bow of the same color." The purpose of this overtly feminized robot is to greet customers and give directions in upmarket coffee shops, bars, information booths, office complexes, and museums. Actroid Repliee is also advertised as a potential ambassador, spiritual leader, and nurse.[53]

While not formally a smart wife—that is, she is not intended to perform the typical roles of a wife in the home—Actroid Repliee is nonetheless intended to perform similarly stereotypical feminized roles. Why is

Figure 3.5
Actroid Repliee robot in her "I HEART Hello Kitty" shirt. Source: Spykestars

Actroid Repliee designed this way? Partly because, as Robertson explains, she represents and performs a feminine ideal of a supposedly *natural* and "average" Japanese girl.[54] We'll add that it's also because she is familiar, likable, and nonthreatening. People are conditioned to expect different things of a girl dressed in a Hello Kitty T-shirt than, say, a man in a suit. And that's potentially a good thing for those trying to encourage the greater adoption of social robots.

A less extreme example of further humanizing social robots and representing them as "a new kind of life," "artificial human," and "species" comes from Samsung's Technology and Advance Research (STAR) Labs.[55] STAR Labs also launched their "next-gen" humanoid AI chatbot project, Neon, at the 2020 Consumer Electronics Show. Reminiscent of the social robots discussed so far, Neon's website describes this new offering as a "virtual being that looks and behaves like a real human, with the ability to show emotions and intelligence." Although these chatbots are not yet represented in physical form, Neon's CEO Pranav Mistry hasn't ruled out holographic representations in the future.[56]

The team behind Neon have a "mission to bring science fiction to reality," with these humanlike chatbots bearing resemblance to a host of sci-fi characters such as those seen in *Westworld* (first released as a movie in 1973 and a TV series in 2016), *Humans* (2015; a UK remake of the Swedish show *Real Humans*), *Blade Runner 2049* (2017), and *Ex Machina*. Quick to distinguish Neons from AI assistants such as Google Home and Alexa, the Neon website describes this new creation as "simply, a friend."[57] Gender and (some) cultural and linguistic diversity is an obvious feature of Neons, who were seen performing a variety of service roles at the 2020 Consumer Electronics Show (clearly not simply friends then). But there is still a smart wife to be found, if you know where to look. The Neon avatar Monica, for example, was seen demonstrating her skills reading children's stories.[58]

This brings us to another important point. In the push to make social robots likable—and ultimately accepted and used as smart wives and other feminized laborers—roboticists and AI programmers are falling back on stereotypical physical and emotional representations. Set against a backdrop of science fiction and popular culture that contains both friendly and threatening versions of a humanized AI, smart wife designers are turning to a host of nonthreatening attributes (young, cute, and feminized) to counteract any negative perceptions from consumers. And that rush to cloak their devices in likability is concerning, especially when the plan is to deploy these social robots in, among other places, our homes.

MANAGING EXPECTATIONS

Japanese robotics scholars such as performance and culture studies expert Yuji Sone have noted the significant influence of manga (comic books) and anime (animation) culture on the design of social robots.[59] One key inspiration from this culture is Astro Boy ("Tetsuwan Atomu" or "Mighty Atom") (figure 3.6).[60]

There are a few different Astro Boy story lines (due to multiple remakes, different media platforms, and cultural interpretations). For those not familiar with this cult manga and anime series originating in the 1950s (the decade responsible for much of the smart wife's prototyping), Astro Boy is a powerful "roboy" created by the head of the Ministry of Science, Dr. Tenma, to replace his son Tobio (or Toby), who died in a self-driving car accident. Tenma ultimately rejects Astro Boy, realizing that he could never replace his son. After a cruel beginning, Astro Boy is adopted by another man and the new head of the Ministry of Science, Professor Ochanomizu, who realizes Astro Boy's amazing powers, skills, and ability to experience human emotions. Astro Boy then dons the life of a hero, fighting crime and injustices with his seven powers (including a retractable machine gun built into his hips), and keen sense of good and evil.

Astro Boy, according to Robertson, "played a key role in fostering among postwar Japanese an image of robots as cute, friendly and humanlike, characteristics that currently inform the thriving humanoid robotics industry." Today's social robot Pepper, for example, bears a resemblance to Astro Boy (thankfully, minus the machine guns). And as an effeminate character (mainly due to his cuteness, which we will expand on), Astro Boy has a history of gender fluidity.[61] Much like Pepper.

Figure 3.6
Astro Boy is a heroic inspiration for Japanese roboticists. Source: *Astro Boy*

Astro Boy has inspired Japanese roboticists in more than appearance. "The basic principle for robot characters in Japanese comics and animation," explains Sone about this popular conception, "is that a robot protagonist, as a savior, fights for the good side, or is a friendly offbeat character who helps humans."[62]

A persistent problem remains, however: specifically, the difficulty in meeting the high expectations of Japanese consumers with the robots actually available for sale today (resembling the challenges involved in attaining the Rosie ideal we discussed in the previous chapter). Japanese pharmacologist and novelist Hideaki Sena calls this "the curse of Astro

Boy": the constant disappointment that the public experiences between reality and fantasy.[63] Astro Boy is a hard act to follow.

Social robots have even more difficult challenges when contending with the fearsome robots imagined in the West, as Sone points out. The recurring theme of a destructive robot in popular Western science fiction has likely contributed to people's fears of smart wives entering their everyday lives. Noteworthy examples include the Daleks in the *Doctor Who* television series (commencing on British TV in 1963), HAL in *2001: A Space Odyssey* (first appearing in 1968), Maria in the film *Metropolis* (1926), *I, Robot* (2004), *9* (2009), and *The Matrix* trilogy (1999–2003). That's not to say that some of these robot characters don't fight for humanity against their evil counterparts (as in *The Terminator* series [1984, 1991, 2003, 2008–2009, 2015]) or that there aren't still some friendly characters in the mix (like in the animated film *Wall-E* [2008], *Big Hero 6* [2014], or *Transformers* [2007]), but this isn't what is commonly portrayed.[64]

Another potential obstacle to people embracing robots is what is known as "the uncanny valley": a still relevant theory—developed by Japanese roboticist Masahiro Mori in 1970—that refers to the eerie and uncanny feelings people experience when interacting with robots that too closely resemble themselves.[65] The uncanny valley is closely related to humanity's fear of being replaced or taken over by artificial intelligence, or robots "waking up" and rebelling against humanity (as occurs in the UK *Humans* television series, and as illustrated by Samantha, the smart wife in *Her*).[66] Richardson calls these fears "annihilation anxiety."[67] She links the uncanny valley directly to the fearful robots portrayed in Western culture (a point also made by literature, technology, and science scholar Jennifer Rhee).[68]

The existence of the uncanny valley, while still uncertain, has withstood the test of time in many studies and experiments with humanoid robots and AI.[69] More controversially, though, is how to respond to its existence and effects on humans. Some have sought to maintain a degree of obvious "robotness" in the design of robots (like ASIMO, for instance) to keep the valley at bay, and others, like the Neon "digital people" project, try to journey past the valley by making AI so perfectly human formed that people accept them as a new artificial species.[70] Others suggest that the "not-quite-right" robot may be the way forward, and glitches (which we will discuss further in chapter 6) may actually be endearing—but only if they're not too disruptive.[71]

Certain physical and linguistic traits are clearly important here too. Companies like Amazon already make devices appeal to users' emotions through the use of female voices with moderately low inflections. Providing smart wives with names has also been found to increase users' feelings of trust and enjoyment, and elicit more intimate reactions from them.[72] Looking good is crucial as well; studies show that people associate competence and positive attributes (such as trustworthiness and intelligence) to more "attractive" individuals, or sleek and stylish designs.[73] But they can't look *too* good—or rather, too human—for fear of invoking the uncanny valley effect.

Of particular merit to our argument here is the most popular method for attempting to disarm human fears—and along the way, remove any threat of a potential robot uprising—by making social robots look extremely cute.

In *Japanese Robot Culture*, Sone outlines how femininity and cuteness (*kawaii*), as portrayed in Japanese manga and anime culture, are linked and have deeply inspired roboticists. This is also part of the reason why Japanese culture is generally more accepting of robots.[74] Likewise, kawaii—as demonstrated by scholar of Japanese culture, language, and folklore Kanako Shiokawa—bears striking resemblance to the physical characterization of many current robot designs. This goes a long way to explaining why social robots are feminized, even when their designers and manufacturers claim they are genderless.[75]

"When someone or something is 'cute,'" remarks Shiokawa, "s/he/it is either charming, likable, plush, fluffy, endearing, acceptable, desirable, or some other combination of the above." Kawaii is associated with the adorable aspects of babies and children, Shiokawa points out, including "pretty young women and pretty young men, charming characters, and likable personal quirks in not-so-young folks, especially the elderly. It can also refer to things and designs."[76]

In the art style of the late 1960s' *shōjo* manga (girls' comic), Shiokawa notes that kawaii became associated with large eyes—today, a common feature of social robots like Pepper. More generally, the term is strangely unhelpful in describing specific external features. Shiokawa explains that "by far the most outstanding feature of cuteness is its complete lack of anything observably threatening," with the exception of cute-girl action heroines in Japanese comics, who frequently possess lethal powers. "The message is clear," writes Shiokawa, "so long as she is 'cute,' she can (often quite literally) get away with murder."[77] Applying this logic to robots, which are sometimes assumed to have murderous intentions or give rise to other fears, the attribution of cuteness renders robots harmless and nonthreatening. But it also serves another useful purpose.

Feminized kawaii has come to be associated with "fragility, delicateness, sensitivity, prettiness, and, consequently, the notion of 'handle with care.'" Skiokawa says that "even a 'beautiful' woman can become 'cute'" if she develops fuzzy, likable flaws in her character "so as to remove the threat that her very presence poses to the general public." Extending this observation to robots transforms them into delicate creatures that need to be looked after, while simultaneously forgiving them for being imperfect or not fully functioning. Like the heroines of Japanese comics that Shiokawa writes about, the robot's cuteness "makes her power and independence more palatable."[78]

Commenting on the social effects of kawaii in Japanese culture, Shiokawa describes what kawaii communicates to girls and women (and we might add, robots). On the one hand, it "provides a strategic guideline for a girl child to benefit in a grossly imperfect world dominated by grown-up boys," and on the other, kawaii "deludes her into believing [in] the relative importance of being 'cute.'" A woman (or robot) can be outstanding if she is cute, but "a competent man is outstanding without putting any extra effort into appearing otherwise."[79] Given what we already know about how interacting with smart wives reinforces these kinds of gendered stereotypes, this trend to make robots cute is concerning. It strengthens the cultural perception that to be cute is to be exceptional, and only the cute are exceptional—especially if you are a girl or woman.

Even more interesting, the trend to make robots cute through their youthful appearance can lower people's expectations of a robot's mobility and, at the same time, increase tolerance of their still childlike abilities.[80] And despite these strong links between femininity and cuteness, many social robots are explicitly gendered cute *boys*, not girls (even if the *roles* performed by these boybots are feminized).

Once again, popular science fiction provides an explanation. Like Astro Boy, Pinocchio—the animated wooden puppet boy from the Italian children's novel *The Adventures of Pinocchio* (1883)—seeks life and "to be a real boy."[81] This theme is also demonstrated through the robot child character called David in the film *AI: Artificial Intelligence* (2001), which features a relationship between robot David and his human mother. In these examples, male creators (Dr. Tenma for Astro Boy, craftsman Geppetto for Pinocchio, and the CEO of the Mecha Corporation for prototype David) are seeking to reproduce artificial beings as, specifically, boys. This gendered dimension is noted by Richardson, who cites similar instances (in science fiction as well as the field of robotics) of "male acts of artificial creation that . . . can rival the biological capacities of women to reproduce."[82] This reflects a longer history—noted by Broadbent—of humans (but mainly men) trying to make artificial versions of themselves.[83] It's also a point that resonates with feminist critiques of male desires to control real-life women's reproduction (while simultaneously rendering their bodies fragile and imperfect) through scientific, medical, and technological interventions (more on this in chapter 6).[84]

Aside from the potential appeal of creating new artificial life in their image, another reason cited for preferring to construct and market boybots is more technical in nature. The initial efforts to construct "machine-like, male-like or child-like" robots were not because virtually all roboticists were (and many still are) male, explains roboticist Tomotaka Takahashi, but instead because fembots pose greater technical difficulties due to their "interiorized" motors and platforms, and slender bodies.[85] In the future, however, Takahashi predicts that over half of all humanoid robots will be female. Robertson suggests that Takahashi's view is representative of Japanese roboticists in general. She highlights how concerning it is that he declares, "in no uncertain terms, his common-sense view that an attribution to female gender requires an interiorized, slender body, and male gender an exteriorized, stocky body."[86] Stereotypes are pervasive and powerful.

Robertson critiques how Takahashi develops robots that reinforce this gendered ideology.[87] In 2006, he created his first fembot, the bipedal FT (efutei), whose algorithms were modeled on the movements of professional fashion models. Other Japanese roboticists have followed suit. Tatsuya Matsui created a boy and girl robot, Pino and Posy, respectively, who we mentioned earlier. Posy was meant to conjure up "the image of cherubic young girls"; Matsui imagined her serving as a receptionist (figure 3.7).

Bucking these trends, Breazeal refers to herself as "mother" to the machine, and although she continues to design young, cute, and childlike robots, she has embraced gender-neutral designs.[88] According to Richardson, Breazeal enrolled Disney animators in her creation of the gender-neutral social robot Kismet (meaning "fate" in Turkish), hoping that the input from animators would allow the robot to clearly express its emotions (figure 3.8).[89]

Like Kismet, early social robots designed at MIT, explains Richardson, were imagined as children so as to facilitate caregiving relationships, with humans feeling responsible to the robots as adults would to human children. "In labs at MIT and beyond, robots are reimagined by researchers as child-like companions, friends and a different kind of special altogether," writes Richardson. "There was a value placed on the theme of relationality, and this was structured mainly around designing machines that could mimic, imitate and resemble the caregiver-child relationship."[90]

This is a theme that extends beyond the field of robotics. Turkle, renowned for her work in the social studies of science and technology, coined the term "relational artifact," which refers to any object that one has a relation with—be it a Furbie (a household toy popular in the late 1990s resembling an owl or hamster that progressively learned English), robot, or musical instrument.[91] For example, the famous Tamagotchi hand-sized device, created by Aki Maita in 1996, contained a display showing a virtual pet, which needed to be "cared" for or else it would "die."[92] Zoomorphic social robots, like Aibo and other creatures, are arguably following a similar path to encourage empathy and emotional responses in their users. This "caregiver effect," according to Darling, is particularly strong with social robots that are

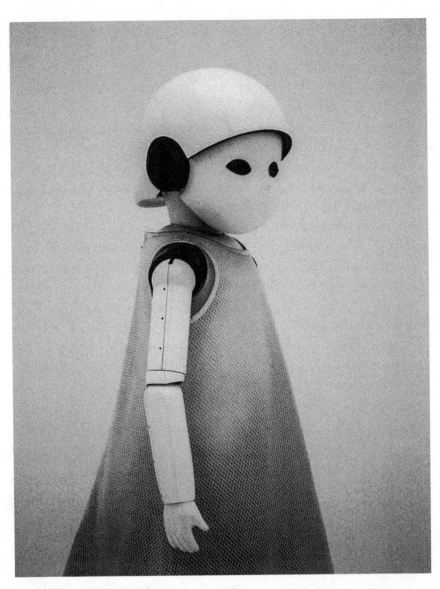

Figure 3.7
Posy the robot was designed to mimic a flower girl. Source: Tatsuya Matsui/Flower Robotics

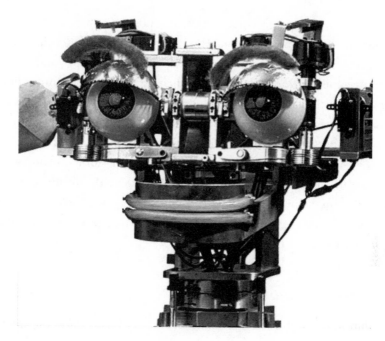

Figure 3.8

Kismet, the genderless and childlike robot with Disney-inspired features. Source: Peter Menzel / menzelphoto.com

designed to encourage people to nurture and sustain them (like Kismet and other childlike robots).[93] More specifically, she finds a difference between how people project onto inanimate objects and how they do so in their interactions with social robots, which create an illusion of mutual relating.

These observations help explain why roboticists are interested in designing smart children, smart pets, or "trusted sidekicks" rather than smart wives.[94] We don't deny that these reasons make sense, if the goal is to make people like and accept robots. As social robots continue to develop, however, the emphasis between who is giving and receiving care is also shifting. While this caregiving is sometimes intended to be reciprocal and respectful, many of the emerging social robots, like Pepper, are clearly intended to shift from being the cared for to the caregiver.

Like all parents and creators, we can't always predict what our children will become. And despite what they intend to design, when these roboticists' children grow up, they seem destined to become smart wives.

That's not to disagree that roboticists possess agency and intention during this worrisome transition. They are not completely devoid of wifely intentions for their creations. As we have argued, cute and youthful attributes are a means to an end—a way of eliciting desired social interaction so as to create social robots that "help fill the gaps in human social relations."[95] These perceived "gaps" that need to be redressed through the introduction of social robots are none other than the spaces of feminized labors with which we began this chapter—labors such as caring for a growing elderly population, therapeutically supporting children with autism and other disabilities, or helping people with Alzheimer's and dementia. But once again we ask, are these robotic smart wives the best way to approach this set of social and health dilemmas?

CARING FOR WOMEN

The computing and electronic industries have a long history of replacing women with technology. As Broussard argues, one could read such events as recurring in the scenarios and applications for social robots discussed in the preceding pages.[96] Robertson makes this point directly regarding social robots, noting the disturbing tendency of Japanese roboticists to prefer and value humanoid robots over immigrants when working to find partners as well as carers for young and elderly people as a solution to the country's aging population, labor shortages, and flat birth rate.[97] One possibility, therefore, is that social robots could become a potential replacement for the mostly feminized labor force providing (low) paid care—a concern that raises the potential to further disadvantage marginalized and low-income women.

Some scholars are already considering how these smart wives will affect our politics, economy, and society at large. Sone and Robertson, for example, separately point out how the vision for Japanese robotics is grounded in a political landscape featuring an aging population, low birth rate, apathy toward marriage among young people, and government focused on modernization and progress. Japan's low birth rate has been attributed to a range of overlapping issues, including the increased costs of living and education, lack of public childcare facilities, extremely long working hours with unpaid overtime, and emergence of a "just-in-time" workforce that has replaced regular employees.[98] Japanese men and women's growing disinterest in or refusal of marriage, as well as their reluctance to have children, reflects their resistance to the sexist and unequal roles afforded them in the Japanese social system.[99]

Within this context, Japan's push for social robots that provide care reflects some interesting political and market objectives. Analyzing a 2007 visionary government blueprint for revitalizing Japanese society, Robertson notes how significantly the report's authors valued social robots for serving as "surrogate housewives."[100] Importantly, these smart wives are not intended to replace or alleviate the role of a *human* housewife, but rather allow her to take on more duties that serve the political interests of Japan—namely, having more babies. As Robertson puts it, "Implicit in the humanoid literature is a notion that a married woman who is freed from housekeeping and caretaking chores will be more able and willing to have more children." Robertson calls this political robotic agenda "retro-tech," meaning it promotes "advanced technology in the service of traditionalism"—specifically, ethnocentrism, paternalism, and sexism.[101] Social robots, in this instance, are intended to *reaffirm* women's traditional place in the home within contemporary Japan. These robots would do so instead of offering women the same opportunities as men or requiring men to reassess their commitments to the domestic space.

There is another implicit devaluing of feminized labor present here too: the assumption that caring and emotional labors *can* and *should* be outsourced to a robotic deputy—a point we raised in the previous chapter in relation to delegating housekeeping labors. Such an assumption can itself be viewed as a form of undermining and simplifying the highly complex roles and tasks that (mainly) women perform as nurturers, carers, and emotional laborers. Not insignificant here is the fact that the gender more likely to have need of this robotic labor is women (though significantly, not necessarily more likely to afford or have access to it). This is because, as we've noted, women are more likely than men to live longer, and suffer from dementia or Alzheimer's.

To be "suckers for the wide eyes and endearing giggles of affective robots," warns Wajcman, *and* advocate their use as providers of empathetic care "mistakes the appearance of care with real empathy and genuine personal interaction."[102] Indeed, even if social robots *were* able to effectively deliver emotional empathy and social care in the future, related research suggests that this may affect relationships between humans. The presence of cell phones, for example, has been linked to feelings of decreased empathy and closeness during two-way conversations—a problem that could also arise with social robots.[103]

There is still a vast difference between what socially aware robots can *technically* do and what they can *actually* do. But Wajcman argues that there is a bigger question at stake: whether advocating for social care robots is a desirable pathway to begin with. "Perhaps if eldercare was revalued and remunerated like say coding work," contends Wajcman, "the putative labor shortages in this sector that robots are designed to alleviate would disappear." "Or, more radically," she continues, "if housing and cities were redesigned so that the elderly were not relegated to separate places but were integrated into the wider civil society."[104]

To sum up, we should not assume that assigning feminized care and emotional labors using robotic smart wives is a good thing. These social robots could potentially undervalue the care that many women already do (paid and unpaid), *and* their access to care as they age or suffer from debilitating health conditions. Again, we emphasize that this may only be one possible outcome, but it is still worthy of our attention. The smart wife provides the analytic lens to explore it.

ROBOYS CAN BE SMART WIVES TOO

The exploration of caring smart wives in this chapter leads us to conclude a few things about the emerging field of social robotics. First, let's reject the pretense of the gender-neutral robot. In addition, while there are promising early signs that social robots are starting to queer the gender of smart wives, these do not go far enough in transforming the personalities, attributes, and very purposes of smart wives to disrupt the gender status quo. With that in mind, we start from the presumption that "neutrality" is not possible, and queering is difficult, when the very purpose of that robot is to replicate and replace feminized labors. While no doubt well intentioned, designing for neutrality is problematic; gender has *everything* to do with a new robotic workforce of caring smart wives coming into our lives and homes. So let's talk about it.

Second, the desire to make robots likable is a worthy ambition. But roboticists also have an ethical responsibility to challenge what likability *is*, especially when likability is reinforcing dominant stereotypes through humanized AI and robots, and potentially contributing to new forms of abuse (as we will demonstrate in later chapters). That doesn't mean robot-icists should start designing deliberately nasty robots. Yet gender equity needs to be part of the design conversation and protocols in a way that isn't obviously apparent now. The goal is to envision a wider diversity of feminized *and* masculine attributes, which are simultaneously designed to challenge gender stereotypes *and* not completely alienate people.

For this goal, smart pets or creatures might seem like a promising alternative since they disrupt the trend toward distinctive masculine or feminine features, and arguably queer the smart wife in form at least. They're not inherently a bad idea. But like so-called gender-neutral robots, zoomorphic (and plant- or Minion-inspired) social robots are still there to perform stereotypical feminized labor. This too is a form of smart wifery: the ambition for these cute robopets is to "solve" deeply gendered (and we might add, racially uneven) social problems.[105]

By showing how social robots already are or will grow up to become smart wives (even the ones that look like "real boys"), we can acknowledge potential gender inequities and provide an opportunity to design robots that attempt to address them.

The unfolding story of the smart wife continues to question whether these helpful and caring companions are the best response to a host of pressing social problems. In the next chapter, we turn to another set of issues plaguing the smart wife, relating to her emerging impact on the world and the planetary resources on which she depends.

4 ALEXA

Alexa—the digital voice assistant of Amazon's Echo device—is the world's most popular smart wife. Sixty percent of the voice-enabled speaker device market in the United States was controlled by Alexa in 2019, far ahead of Google Home's 24 percent.[1] And this leader also dominates in other markets such as China.

Alexa's inspiration came from the computer voice featured onboard the Starship Enterprise in the 1960–1990s' *Star Trek* franchise. (In fact, her company's founder and CEO, Jeff Bezos, is also a Trekkie—another link between popular science fiction and the smart wives of Silicon Valley.) Alexa's name was chosen because it isn't a usual word in the lexicon of most households, and the hard *x* consonant makes it easy for her voice recognition software to pick up.[2] According to Amazon senior vice president David Limp, her name was also inspired by the library of Alexandra, which has been culturally viewed in the West as a source of great knowledge.[3] When she answers her name, Alexa can help put the kids to bed (by adjusting the lights or telling stories), set the right vibe for a party, order groceries (or pretty much anything), check the weather, play music, and read you the news. The usual wifely stuff.

But this chapter isn't about Alexa's superior marriageability or her exotic-sounding name. It's about how she's created and owned by the largest e-commerce company in the world, and what this means for her probable impact on the planet and the consumption of its resources. In this twist to our argument, we turn for understanding and inspiration to the ecofeminist movement, which makes links between "the exploitation and degradation of the natural world and the subordination and oppression of women."[4]

Most ecofeminists attribute global ecological destruction to patriarchy—and particularly Western patriarchy—in which women and nature are both positioned as subordinate to men, and "resources" available for exploitation. When writing about women's assumed affinity with nature and ecofeminism more broadly, we are not referring to "all women" in a biological sense but rather to the processes that make some people—and especially women—more likely to embody the roles and effects born by the world's current capitalist system, which depends on the extraction, exploitation, and disposal of the earth's "natural" resources.

Ecofeminist thinking requires us to question our book's primary ambition of pursuing smart wives that support gender equity and diversity. This aim—of making technology serve more people—is arguably incompatible with an ecofeminist perspective, which fundamentally challenges capitalist modes of production along with their exploitation of the world's environment and marginalized people, particularly women.[5] One of the founders and theorists of the ecofeminist movement, Ynestra King, puts it this way: "What is the point of partaking equally in a system that is killing us all."[6] Indeed.

But before we go too far down that road and attempt to reconcile our pursuit of a feminist smart wife with the ecofeminist movement, let us begin with a little detour through the fascinating Amazonian rainforest.

* * *

The king of this jungle is Bezos. He has followed a fairly typical trajectory for smart wife entrepreneurs. In 1994, he established Amazon in his garage; his parents were the first investors.[7] The Amazon overlord holds degrees in engineering and computer science, and spent his early career in a range of tech companies. He's known for his optimistic, strategic, and long-term visionary thinking that have led Amazon through some pretty tough times, including the dot-com crash of the early 2000s and global financial crisis of 2008.[8]

Bezos has achieved a lot since establishing an online bookshop in his garage. Following his initial success, Bezos later diversified Amazon into video, MP3, and audiobook downloads and streaming along with software, video games, electronics, furniture, groceries, toys, clothing, and jewelry. The company has further broadened into its own brand of electronic product lines—such as the Kindle e-book reader and the Echo speakers that "house" Alexa—which grow and support the company's other markets for consumer goods and entertainment.[9] Amazon branched into traditional retail in 2017 with its acquisition of Whole Foods Market, a high-end supermarket chain with over four hundred stores.[10] The company also owns data centers and makes TV shows. It's an impressive portfolio that has earned Amazon the name of the "Everything Store" (also the title of journalist Brad Stone's 2013 book on the empire), and increasingly, the Everything Company.[11]

The chief of this megastore has several side hustles too. In 2000, Bezos founded Blue Origin, a human spaceflight company, which is intended to make the human species multiplanetary and move polluting industries off the planet.[12] And he owns the *Washington Post*, one of the United States' leading newspapers and a target of President Donald Trump's "fake news" campaign.

Amazon's market share is incredible and alarming.[13] While originating in the United States, the company now operates separate retail websites in at least sixteen countries, and ships internationally to some others. In 2019, it was the third most valuable company in the United States, behind Apple and Microsoft, and the second-largest employer in the United States, after Walmart.[14] For fiscal year 2018, Amazon reported a net income of over $10 billion, with an annual revenue of close to $233 billion, while employing 647,500 people worldwide.[15] In the same year, Amazon captured almost half of US-based online spending (or almost 14 percent globally) and (excluding cars and car parts as well as visits to restaurants and bars) approximately 5 percent of Americans' total retail spending.[16]

The company's mission is "to offer our customers the lowest possible prices, the best available selection, and the utmost convenience"; its vision statement is "to be the Earth's most customer-centric company, where customers can find and discover anything they might want to buy online."[17] Presumably Blue Origin has got the other planets covered. The Kindle e-reader (providing instant book downloads), Amazon Go (delivering checkout-free shopping in retail stores), Amazon Prime Air (delivering goods by drone), and Amazon Look (providing fashion and wardrobe advice and apparel) are examples that pursue this philosophy of supplying everything easily. Likewise, Amazon's 1-Click technology and Prime subscription services are part of its ambition to make buying things as simple as possible. These platforms and services are intended to deliver fast and near-instantaneous consumption of a vast variety of goods, available nearly anywhere in the world, at competitive prices. It's consumption heaven. And Alexa is the gateway to the enormous amounts of traffic directed toward the Amazonian retail paradise.

Alexa is a cloud-based operating system (OS). She connects a multitude of devices and services through applications known as "skills," which ensure a consistent set of interfaces. Consistency produces a network effect—the more users there are, the more applications are developed; the more applications are developed, the more users there are.

In 2019, you could buy this OS for $40 to $250 depending on which Echo (speaker) device you chose. Asking Alexa to buy stuff for you is so easy that even parrots can do it.[18] As of 2017, Alexa had five thousand employees working on her OSs and related products.[19] And her reach is expanding: by 2019, she was available in eighty-nine countries.[20] Thanks to a partnership between Amazon and the real estate developer Lennar Corporation (with other developers expected to follow suit), Alexa is now being *built into* homes.[21]

Amazon has opened up Alexa to other smart home developers through its Alexa Skills Kit, which according to Amazon's website, allows third-party devices to "build capabilities, or skills, that make Alexa smarter and make everyday tasks faster, easier, and more delightful for customers."[22] Alexa Skills increased from 5,191 in November 2016 to 30,006 in March 2018—an almost sixfold increase in just two years.[23] These third-party-developed skills, once published, are available across Alexa-enabled devices and can be enabled by any user via the Alexa app.

In 2018, Amazon's director of Alexa Voice Services, Priya Abani, told *Wired* magazine that "we basically envision a world where Alexa is everywhere."[24] Alexa's not far off. As of 2018, the ecosystem that had developed around Alexa included 60,000 devices representing more than 7,400 brands, and her voice commanded more than 150 third-party gadgets including cars, headphones, and security systems.[25] Alexa is also the current champion in connecting shoppers to Amazon's Everything Store. She can interact with a growing range of devices from smart home manufacturers, and order takeout food through a range of platforms and providers.[26] She can even collaborate with Microsoft's digital voice assistant, Cortana, who is designed to provide virtual assistance in the workplace.[27] It's sort of like having your wife communicate with your secretary—if you fit the demographic of those likely to have either, that is.

And what of her head honcho, Bezos?[28] *New York Times* journalists Nick Wingfield and Nellie Bowles write that the Amazon leader has "developed a reputation as a brilliant but mysterious and coldblooded corporate titan."[29] Accounts of his success emphasize the typical hegemonic masculine traits of a successful Silicon Valley "bro": a relentless work ethic, risk-taking behavior, heightened competitiveness, and an aggressive, obsessive, and occasionally explosive personality.[30] In 2017, Bezos became the world's wealthiest person with an estimated net worth of just over $90 billion. In 2018, he went on to become the first centibillionaire on the *Forbes* wealth index, and consequently, the "wealthiest person in modern history."[31]

On some measures, one could be forgiven for thinking that Bezos is doing the earth a favor or two, or at least bears the planet positive intentions (and if not, he's working on a planet B, so no need to worry). He was the valedictorian when he graduated from high school in 1982, when he delivered a speech that identified his interest in building and developing hotels, amusement parks, and colonies for humans out in orbit. He wanted to preserve the earth and its resources from depletion.[32] The success of the Kindle—and the e-book industry that Bezos helped manifest—has stopped many books from being published on what he calls "dead trees."[33] He now has a large philanthropic portfolio, including interests in health care, education, workplace rights, and environmentalism, and he regularly donates to worthy causes, such as the 2020 Australian bushfire crisis (though not without criticism).[34] Yet despite these promising green and humanitarian credentials, Bezos maintains and is continuing to expand one of the largest consumption kingdoms in the world—a kingdom increasingly delivered by the smart wife front-runner: Alexa.

Bezos and his company can be understood as part of the rise of a new group of "oligarchs": powerful people (but mainly men) who have historically exerted considerable political and economic control.[35] It is these influential oligarchs—or as Wajcman puts it, "the homogeneity of the Silicon Valley creators"—who pose "a more dangerous threat to the future than any perceived robotic apocalypse." While these interplanetary bros are hawking the benefits of their smart wives (not to mention many other wares), Wajcman argues that "these purveyors of the future have their backs to society, enchanted by technological promise and blind to the problems around them."[36]

"This ruling class of men," notes ecofeminist Ariel Salleh—speaking generally versus specifically about smart wife companies—"annuls democracies worldwide with lavish funds to both sides of politics."[37] In a clear illustration of its political influence, Amazon embarked on a bidding process between US and Canadian cities in 2017–2018 to secure a new location for its second headquarters, which was allegedly worth fifty thousand high-paid jobs and over $5 billion in investment. Cities offered the company up to $8.5 billion in incentives, including tax, social, and planning concessions, and infrastructure offers, such as building the city around the headquarters, and naming the city or streets after the company.[38]

The prize of being Amazon's second home was ultimately split between two locations, Long Island City in New York City's Queens borough and Crystal City in northern Virginia, in what some critics later called a "bait-and-switch" maneuver on Amazon's part because the company duped city bidders into thinking they were getting *all* of the second headquarters, when the most that any of them were offered was half.[39] Amazon was later pressured to pull out of Long Island City plans following community protest, but was still continuing with its Virginia location at the time of writing.[40] These "incentives to pander" to global corporations such as Amazon, argue government and political science professors Nathan Jensen and Edmund Malesky, ultimately disadvantage citizens, whose cities become built around a company's needs, desires, and long-term interests—rather than those of constituents.[41]

Such observations suggest that companies like Amazon are *more than* capitalist monoliths. They are part of what sci-fi writer Bruce Sterling calls "the Big Five"—specifically Amazon, Apple, Facebook, Google, and Microsoft—who he goes on to dub "the genuine heroes of the Internet of Things." All five of these companies share important features that conventional corporations have never previously possessed: "an operating system, some dedicated way to sell cultural material (music, movies, books, software), tools for productivity, an advertising business, some means of accessing the internet that they themselves more or less control (tablets, smartphones, phablets), a search engine capability, a social network, a 'payment solution' or some similar bank, a 'cloud' capability and, very soon, some dedicated, elite high-speed access that used to be the democratic internet."[42] And we would add, they all make smart wives.[43]

Sterling distinguishes the Big Five's structures from democratic or even capitalist modus operandi systems, describing their tactics instead as "digital feudalism," in which people "are like the wooly livestock of a feudal demesne, grazing under the watchful eye of barons in their hilltop Cloud Castles." These companies don't just want to sell us stuff, argues Sterling; they want to become a new "social reality."[44]

Social scientist professor Kevin MacKay is among a growing number of academics who are also laying serious claims at the feet of the world's oligarchs. While he doesn't specifically mention Amazon or the dot-com bros, he levies at large corporations the crime of leading civilization to the brink of ecological crisis and collapse.[45] This is not an exaggeration. We live in an era when the world's leading climate scientists are reporting the urgent need to cap global warming at 1.5°C (2.7°F) above preindustrial levels, and respond to the sixth mass extinction that is leading to "biological annihilation," on account of our population growth and our unsustainable consumption of natural resources.[46] Numerous indicators suggest that our way of life—particularly in the affluent "Global North"—is unsustainable, including the use of smart wives.

One indication of this unsustainability is the ecological footprint model, developed by ecological economist professor emeritus William Rees and sustainability advocate Mathis Wackernagel; it calculates the amount of water, land, and other biological resources required to support a particular population and sustain its lifestyle.[47] The model is now widely used by environmental agencies and campaigners to identify a country, person, or any other predefined jurisdiction's impact on the planet. It calculates this impact as a measure of the number of planet earths that would be needed to support any given population's way of life if everyone lived like them. So if everybody maintained the lifestyle of an average US citizen, for example, we would need the resources of five earths. Or if everyone lived like Australians—including ourselves—we would require just over four earths to meet the needs of the world's current population.[48]

The ecological footprint concept gave rise to the Global Footprint Network, a nonprofit organization that advocates for "a future where all can thrive within the means of our one planet."[49] The network has popularized Earth Overshoot Day: "the date when humanity has exhausted Earth's budget for the year"—that is, the planet's budget for biological resources used to support our lifestyles—and is operating in "overshoot." In 2019, that date was July 29. In other words, it took just under seven months for the globe to exhaust its available natural resources at a rate that could be considered sustainable.[50]

The effects of this overshoot, as ecofeminists such as Mary Mellor point out, are unequally produced and experienced.[51] For example, ecological impacts and consequences are commonly disproportionately borne by some women through their bodies (say, as dioxin residues in breast milk, failed pregnancies, or birth defects), and in their gendered work as nurturers and carers. "Women's bodies," as Salleh says, "remain de facto shock absorbers for the collateral damage of engineered progress."[52]

Likewise, ecofeminist Vandana Shiva argues that it is women in particular and indigenous cultures more broadly that, through their invisible labors, maintain the sustenance economies that constitute "the two-thirds of humanity engaged in craft production, peasant agriculture, artisanal fishing, and indigenous forest economies."[53] The depletion of the global "commons" (air, water, and so on) as well as planetary resources in capitalist markets and oligarchic control—under the command of companies like Amazon and its Alexa entourage—is therefore a more fundamental threat to the people who are more likely to depend on or bear the ecological, social, and economic impacts of these actions.

Somewhat perversely, then, smart wives are now being put forward by energy companies and governments in the West and elsewhere as a way to help save resources in the home.

RESOURCE MAN WANTS A SMART WIFE

Let us introduce you to resource man (figure 4.1). He is what we call the energy sector's ideal smart energy consumer, intended to realize the industry's ambitions of reducing or shifting a home's consumption through the

Figure 4.1
Resource man is the tech-minded energy guru of the smart home. Source: Association for Computing Machinery/Joe St.Pierre

use of smart home technology. This fictional (and real-life) individual is "the gendered, technological-minded, information-oriented and economically rational consumer of the Smart Utopia" characterizing visions for the smart home.[54]

Embodying stereotypically masculine ideals of efficiency, control, and optimization, the idealized resource man consumer is found in numerous research and industry reports, where he is able and willing to optimize his home's energy use through the use of data, automation, and technology. Likewise, many energy conservation and demand management programs target resource man by offering households more technological control over their consumption, better data, and information for improved decision making, or economic incentives designed to encourage rational choices and action.

Like the smart wife, we called out resource man in past research as a provocation to draw attention to a biased and gendered vision for energy consumers in the smart home, in which smart grid and metering technologies are expected to realize a range of energy benefits for residents. For instance, one estimate from the Global e-Sustainability Initiative suggests smarter systems could save ten times the carbon emissions that they generate.[55]

Resource man, however, is not just a hypothetical character. He was also observed by Yolande during her PhD studies. In interviews and home visits with Australian households, she commonly found one resident—normally a man—who was interested in managing their energy consumption by analyzing data, responding to price signals, and using a range of smart technologies and automated devices. Yet the efforts of this person were often counteracted or undermined by the everyday practices of other people taking place in the home, such as doing the laundry, washing, or heating and cooling. The resource man vision of managing energy in the home by becoming a masculinized micro engineer didn't fit with the feminized sensory, caregiving, and nurturing aspects of the home environment, where much consumption takes place.[56]

Resource man has now found his perfect mate. He is the user or operator "in control" of his smart wife or wives. She, in turn, delivers a range of benefits with both feminine compliance and masculine ease and prowess, not least of which are the realization of energy and other resource savings in the home. It sounds like a promising union, but let's not forget that it's also deeply heteronormative.

Of course, there are exceptions and alternative narratives, as we explore elsewhere in this book. There are women who enjoy being "resource men" and smart husbands. But they are not the dominant stories that currently permeate the smart home. And stories, in this case, aren't simply amusing tales; they are the paths that inform technological developments, and on which our devices and homes are being designed.

While resource man and the smart wife make a cute couple, it is frequently not the blissful partnership that those in the energy sector might hope for. Today's resource men—that is, energy consumers who mirror these ideals of the energy industry—often feel that their desired energy savings are thwarted by their real-life wives, partners, children, and pets.[57] Despite their best attempts to cajole their partners and children, resource men often notice that their energy savings from smart home technologies can be minimal or nonexistent. Those with on-site solar generation or resource-minded family members tend to fair better, but overall, the smart home residents we've talked to have not achieved significant energy savings, despite turning to a range of smart wives for support.[58]

So the much-anticipated marriage of efficiency-driven residents with new automated and Internet of Things–enabled technology systems for monitoring and control—the union of resource man and smart wife—is not, in fact, a seamless one. One set of answers for these marital problems is that the concept of resource man employs a particular version of hegemonic masculinity that doesn't allow for the possibility of many other gendered ways of caring for the home environment. In addition, it ignores the broader consumption impacts of the smart wife.

The resource managers running our energy systems commonly imagined resource man—their concept of what an average ideal consumer looks like—as looking much like them: an engineer, economist, or "micro-resource manager" (all male-dominated industries). Even water utilities have imagined water users as mini versions of themselves, argues cultural researcher and technofeminist Zoë Sofoulis, by assuming that users make similar calculated decisions to a water engineer, with reference to data, technology, and economic information.[59] These characterizations of resource use in the home reflect a broader masculine narrative that frames care for the environment as the "securitization" of climate change, involving militaristic "muscle flexing," and the desire to solve or "fight" natural "threats" through technological solutions.[60]

There are multiple other ways, though, in which we can account for the environment in relation to the home. Feminized understandings and practices of care, explains cultural geographer Carol Farbotko, are already closely tied to environmental housework.[61] Mundane and invisible labor for the environment—everyday acts of cleaning, recycling, composting, or reclaiming water—are more commonly performed by women than by men.[62] What's more, these labors are less likely to have the leisure associations that come from digital housekeeping and smart home maintenance, as we discussed in our chapter on Rosie. While there are multiple critiques leveled at this perspective—since it essentially lays ethical responsibility for consumption and the environment onto residents, especially female ones—it is nonetheless an important arena through which care for the environment is enacted with minimal or no use of smart wives.[63]

There are several key points to note here. First, the rise of the smart wife partly reframes energy reduction and other sustainability concerns as a task that can be approached and "solved" through masculine technological prowess, while simultaneously presenting a leisure opportunity for men, particularly the resource man. Second, this perspective ignores—or at least does little to support—the significant everyday environmental labor that is *already* predominantly carried out by women.

Finally, framing the environment as a problem "solved" by data and technology excludes a vast expanse of consumption that necessarily follows from such technoenviromentalist solutionism. Even if the smart wife were successful in keeping resource man happy and realizing his ambitions, and *even* if she were able to acknowledge and account for other gendered ways of understanding as well as caring for the environment, this is not her only role in the home.

Alexa is no earth mother. As this and the other chapters of this book make clear, she and the other smart wives are busy providing a host of other wifely services through their consumption networks—including housekeeping, caregiving, homemaking, and lovemaking—delivered by and through connected technology. These technological extensions, enhancements, and additions all require more resources, and create vast planetary impacts, even while the smart wife promises to connect us with our natural environment.

CLOSER TO NATURE

Westinghouse's showcase "Home of Tomorrow" (1934) featured "air conditioning, an electric garage-door opener, automatic sliding doors, an electric laundry, 21 separate kitchen appliances, burglar alarms, 140 electric outlets, and 320 lights"—luxurious even by today's Global North standards (figure 4.2). Brian Horrigan, an exhibit curator at the Minnesota Historical Society, points out how the home celebrated its electric load,

Figure 4.2
Westinghouse's "Home of Tomorrow."

which was equivalent to that of thirty average homes, "ready to do the work of 864 servants with the flip of a switch."[64]

Jump forward to the twenty-first century and similar visions of decadence are again in circulation, this time promising to connect us to the aesthetic delights of nature. For example, the *Electronic House* magazine's US-based 2015 Gold award-winning home features twenty-nine surveillance cameras that capture images of wildlife around the property, and also provide security.[65] The magazine describes these home surveillance systems as "'virtual binoculars,' recording real-time, full-color, high-res outdoor images to display on the many wall-mounted iPads and TVs located throughout the house." The article explains the appeal:

> Each camera was strategically positioned to snap footage of the wildlife that frequents the two ponds in the backyard and the nature preserve along the perimeter of the 142-acre property. When an animal passes by a camera, its built-in motion sensor signals the home's Savant automation system to activate every TV in the residence (eight total). The TVs tune automatically to a preset "wildlife station," giving the owner a close-up view of the many deer, birds, squirrels, and other animals.[66]

This example illustrates an interesting blurring of the long-lamented nature/culture divide in the biological and social sciences—in this case showing how the latter (technological culture) can bring us closer to the former (nature).[67] It gives the impression of the smart home as an environmental oasis, while simultaneously requiring significant resources. What's more, it illuminates another important job for the smart wife: her role in making the house a home through "little touches" along with the continual delivery of delightful, uplifting, and caring aesthetic and sensory experiences.

Lutron home automation company calls this "pleasance," a term that describes a "fundamental feeling that is hard to define but that people desire to experience." As the company brochure goes on to explain, pleasance delivers "comfort, romance and peace of mind" through automation and smart control—ideally across an entire property.[68]

Sounds delightful, doesn't it? Pleasance is a tantalizing idea that promises mood and other sensory enhancements through automated "scenes" and settings that combine sounds, lighting, comfort, and other audiovisual features, such as water fountains or nature imagery streamed to screens inside or outside the home (figure 4.3).[69] More broadly, pleasance resonates with what professor of mass communication Davin Heckman calls the smart home's pursuit of "The Perfect Day": a "technologically enhanced mode of daily living" that "cultivat[es] the terrain between impulse and gratification" by "offering up customized solutions and experiences."[70]

The vision of pleasance is closely tied to 1950s' housewifery, as outlined in the *Good House Wife's Guide* from that era. "Your goal," advises rule 12, is to "try to make sure your home is a place of peace, order and tranquility where your husband can renew himself in body and spirit." Rule 15 is pretty straightforward: "Make him comfortable." Rule 16? "Arrange his pillow and offer to take off his shoes. *Speak in a low, soothing and pleasant voice.*" And never forget rule 18: "A good wife always knows her place." The smart wife has been taking notes.[71]

Housewife links aside, the connection between sensory experiences and the smart home can be partly attributed to the early associations between home automation and US Orthodox Jewish communities, which were early adopters of the technology for religious reasons. Google user experience researcher Allison Woodruff (then at Intel) and her colleagues discovered that these Orthodox Jews embraced home automation to enhance the cultural practices of the Sabbath—a day that in modern interpretations precludes turning electric appliances on or off. "Technology was typically characterized as 'enhancing' the Sabbath experience," explained Woodruff and her colleagues, "adding to the atmosphere and the ambiance (e.g., prettier lights, running water in a fountain, better food, etc.)"—henceforth known as pleasance.[72]

The "qualities of experience, the sensory, affective and satisfying dimensions of everyday life," design anthropologist professor Sarah Pink points out, have long been central to homemaking. Pink uses the term "home creativity" to refer to the "embodied experience and production of sound, smell and texture in the home."[73] Pleasance reaffirms the home as a site of consumption through which these creative pursuits can be practiced with

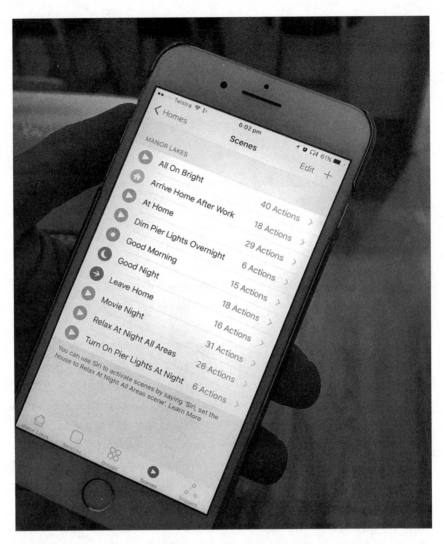

Figure 4.3
Light scene options on a resident's smartphone. Source: Author

the aid of new technologies. And curiously, it also shakes up the gender mix of who is performing these acts of care for the home.

The smart wife's pursuit of pleasance upholds the feminized role of the homemaker along with her expressions of sensory care for the home and its occupants. On the other hand, her status as a smart home device places her in the masculinized realm of home technology. Pleasance is therefore creating new gender fusion opportunities, providing women with new ways of expressing "technical femininity," and men with ways of performing sensory and caring masculinities.[74] This is arguably a good thing—supplying a potential pathway for smart wives to disrupt the hegemonic stereotypes that they have so far largely embraced and reinforced—thereby supporting our aim of queering the smart wife. When viewed through a sustainability lens, however, the expanding appeal and opportunities for pleasance to cultivate new forms of luxury, opulence, and pleasure in everyday life also present new opportunities to consume.

In collaboration with colleagues, we have identified the ways that pleasance *increases* energy consumption in the home, and linked its delivery to a host of new home automation and smart control technologies.[75] This process is similar to the "ratcheting up" of lifestyle expectations, such as comfort, cleanliness, and convenience—or "the 3Cs," as sociologist Elizabeth Shove calls them—which unfortunately represent the "environmental hot spots of consumption."[76]

Participants in our research, Kristi and Bill, explained how their property features an automated backlit fountain. At sunset, lights automatically shoot up under the water level to create a feature in their dam. Kristi described how this enhancement of nature via new connected technologies created "the yin and the yang" on their property, giving them "the best of both worlds." She talked about how she and Bill "really love the nature that's around us," and how they "stay pretty balanced" because "we've got all of this high-tech stuff on the inside," and "the birds and lizards and the wallabies and the deer" on the outside. While they were conscious of saving energy, and had installed solar photovoltaic panels on their property, Kristi and Bill's energy consumption had reportedly *increased* compared to their previous home, due to the larger floor space of their house as well as the number of connected devices and appliances within it.

For Kristi, a smart home is one that "reflect[s] your soul. . . . It would reflect exactly what you love. So it wouldn't be what's in a magazine; it would be what nourishes you and what symbolizes you." Increasingly, this "nourishment" is delivered by digitally mediated pleasance and smart wives.

Kristi and Bill's lives followed a heteronormative pattern similar to most other residents interviewed. Bill was the leader of their smart home build; Kristi was a reluctant but appreciative follower. Through her beautiful articulation of the "yin and yang," Kristi expressed how she and Bill were developing new ways of performing technical femininity and sensory masculinity by bringing some pleasance to their property. It was clearly an appealing prospect and satisfying outcome.

This couple's smart home experience illustrates how pleasance is not just about acquiring a new device or devices; it's a revised vision for how we should live, in which technology mediates our relationship with an expanded range of sensory experiences. As one *Electronic House* article explains, "One touch of a button can create the perfect ambiance for a dinner party, a romantic evening at home, or a festive gathering of friends on the back patio."[77] In this sense, pleasance is part of a broader transition involving the integration of information and communication technologies in the home, which constitutes what ecological economics professor Inge Røpke and colleagues have labeled "a new round of household electrification."[78]

Smart wives like Alexa are the emerging creators and curators of this aesthetic imaginary, and they are also making its achievement significantly more accessible. One article on the Australian property website *Domain* explains the appeal: "Imagine walking into a room and with a 'good morning, Alexa' watch[ing] a pre-programmed ballet of functions take place: the perfectly dimmed lights flick on, the blinds glide open (using Crestron's silent motors), your playlist sings, the TV turns on, muted, to show the headlines and a voice whispers the weather forecast."[79]

The stylistic trope of inviting readers to "imagine" themselves inside this heady world of hedonism is common in smart home articles and marketing. Like most utopian visions, these articles invite readers into what informatics professor Paul Dourish and cultural anthropology professor Genevieve Bell call the "proximate future," or a future that is "just around the corner."[80]

This "pursuit of lavish entertainment, convenience and comfort," as an *Electronic House* magazine article puts it, is yours for the price of a smart wife (or two).[81] The home is reinstated as a site of leisure and pleasure, curated by the feminine form.

No other smart wife epitomizes this goal like Alexa. Her algorithms are optimized toward consumption in ways that extend far beyond pleasance. Amazon's products and services are based on recording customer buyer behavior so as to offer or recommend specific items based on their past preferences. As of 2018, however, this "onsell" value from Alexa was relatively low. Only 6 percent of Alexa owners used their devices to make purchases in 2019.[82] The biggest consumption impacts come from smart wives themselves (in terms of the energy they use), and the network of smart home appliances, devices, servers, and data centers to which they are connected. And many of these devices are—as the Internet of Shit parody makes clear—dubiously useful.[83]

Sitting behind these smart wives, their connections to nature, and their new sensory delights is a vast web of environmental and inequitable labor impacts. The consequences of these smart wives are insidious, culturally entrenched, and deeply disturbing—and often carried out under the direction of oligarchic kings like Bezos, with a little help from Alexa.

IN THE CLOUD

In 2018, professors Kate Crawford and Vladen Joler from the AI Now Institute in New York published *Anatomy of an AI System*.[84] This anatomical map and accompanying essay tracked the matrix of impacts associated with a single Amazon Echo Alexa, from the earth's crust to our homes. Through their disturbing exposé, Crawford and Joler show how each simple and convenient interaction with Alexa "requires a vast planetary network, fueled by the extraction of nonrenewable materials, labor, and data." They reveal the circuitry of largely hidden impacts—from the mining of lithium batteries to planned obsolescence resulting in e-waste—that span every corner of the globe, extending far beyond the direct consumption of resources inside the home.

What is concerning here is how smart wives like Alexa are deliberately designed to shield consumers from understanding and acknowledging their planetary impacts. Alexa "is but an 'ear' in the home," argue Crawford and Joler, "a disembodied listening agent that never shows its deep connections to remote systems."[85] Alexa's soothing feminized voice thus serves another purpose: to mask and disassociate her users from the murky underworld of mine extraction, toxic waste dumps, dangerous hardware manufacturing and assembly processes, and outsourced workers in precarious and unstable employment conditions who largely reside in the Global South.

It's a point well made by Wajcman, who in reviewing several books on the automation of work, notes the tendency to shy away from this "proverbial elephant in the room": that the "pursuit of profit, rather than progress," facilitates "not less work but more worse jobs." Speaking about the (male) authors in her review, Wajcman writes, "They seem blind to the huge, casual, insecure, low paid workforce that powers the wheels of the likes of Google, Amazon and Twitter. Information systems rely on armies of coders, data cleaners, page raters, porn filterers, and checkers, subcontractors who are recruited through global sites such as Mechanical Turk and who do not appear on the company payroll."[86]

In fact, the whole "map" of Alexa's planetary impacts relies on exactly the kind of colonial and patriarchal capitalist market that ecofeminists like Shiva advocate against: one that places the precarious and marginalized workers of the Global South's resources, livelihoods, freedoms, dignities, identities, and peace within the hands of a large corporation. It is this "disembodied, decontextualized market," Shiva argues, "which destroys the environment and people's lives."[87] Following Shiva, we can understand Crawford and Joler's map of Alexa as an enclosure of the commons, or the containment of the collective economic assets of the poor in their roles as miners, waste pickers, dumpers, or assembly workers as well as the denial or degradation of other sustenance economies. Alexa, and other feminized smart wives, are apt metaphors for this colonization of the Global South's livelihoods.

This issue is also taken up by interdisciplinary humanities scholar Hilary Bergen, who references the appalling conditions and suicide rates among female workers in the electronic factories that produce Apple's devices. Smart wives like Apple's Siri, argues Bergen, are "willfully masking the *real* bodies that labor to their profit" underneath a "polished interface" that leads to their "invisible commodification."[88]

Within the employment contracts directly controlled by monolithic companies, workers' rights and conditions are also spurious.[89] The Amazonians (not to be confused with the mythical female warriors—although they could provide some inspiration to our cause) are a case in point. One of the company's key values is frugality—not such a bad thing when considering how to conserve the world's resources, but it has some dubious ramifications for the working minions. In May 2014, the International Trade Union Confederation named Bezos the "world's worst boss."[90] His company has attracted widespread criticism for poor working conditions, despite significant reported improvements in recent years. In 2018, responding to criticisms that his company doesn't pay its workers a livable wage, Bezos announced that all US and UK Amazon employees would earn a $15 per hour minimum wage.[91] Nevertheless, the same cannot be said for the conditions of workers in its extended supply chain discussed above, such as those mining the raw resources for Alexa and her relatives.[92]

Aside from worrying worker rights and conditions, Crawford and Joler's map reveals how expansive and alarming the impacts of smart wives truly are to the planet—from the shipping of vast quantities of raw materials and products around the world, to the water and land contamination and pollution from mining extrapolation and e-waste.[93]

The total electricity required to power connected devices also merits deep concern. Computing and digital technologies account for around 20 to 35 percent of non-heating-related electricity use in UK homes, for example.[94] Yet even this "direct" consumption obscures the energy drain from less visible data centers, communication networks, and other supporting networks—often known as the fluffy-sounding cloud. One study notes that the energy required for cell phone infrastructures is ten times more than that needed to power the handsets themselves.[95] The image of the innocent and mysterious cloud, contends sociologist and professor emeritus Vincent Mosco, keeps these impacts hidden in an otherworldly metaphor with its light and pure connotations.[96]

We concur. It is difficult to truly understand the infrastructures, labor, and consumption required to sustain the cloud's existence. This is not abnormal. "Contemporary capitalism," human geography professors Mark Graham and Håvard Haarstad point out, "conceals the histories and geographies of most commodities from consumers."[97] Today's capitalism thrives on a disconnect between an "airbrushed world" communicated through advertising and the actual world of production—a disconnection that smart wives like Alexa are enrolled in establishing and maintaining.[98]

Consequently, there is no single, definitive figure about how much electricity smart wives consume, let alone AI or IT more broadly. A 2017 Greenpeace report estimates that the IT sector's entire energy footprint, including powering devices, data centers, networks, and manufacturing, stands at 7 percent of global electricity demand.[99] If the scope is limited to powering digital devices and their supporting infrastructures (communication networks and data centers), another estimate suggests the figure is 5 percent of global electricity demand (as of 2012). If we add televisions, audiovisual equipment, and broadcast infrastructures, this rises to 9 percent.[100]

It is clear that the figure is growing rapidly. A threefold increase in global internet traffic is anticipated for the period 2017–2022 due to our increasing consumption of data and the expansion of the digital age to four billion people globally.[101] One estimate finds that the growth of electricity consumed by digital devices (at 7 percent per year) is outstripping that of global electricity demand itself (at 3 percent per year).[102] A big source of data demand is video streaming, which constituted 63 percent of global internet traffic in 2015, and is predicted to reach 80 percent by 2020.[103] Video streaming includes everything from funny cat videos to Netflix "binge-worthy" shows, but it is also driven by livestream video footage from smart home devices like security cameras.

Data centers, the "factories of the digital age," deliver and maintain much of the convenience proffered by smart wives by providing connectability, operability, "always-on" services, software updates, and livestream footage.[104] Brad Smith, president of Microsoft, notes that these seemingly innocuous players will rank among the largest users of electric power on the planet by the middle of the next decade.[105] Data centers consumed 1.7 percent of global electricity use in 2012, thus emitting roughly the same carbon dioxide emissions as the airline industry.[106] Looking forward, global estimates of data center demand in 2030 anticipate an increase of three to ten times the current levels.[107] (Also, 2030 is the year that the Intergovernmental Panel on Climate Change has provided as its early estimate for the earth reaching the dangerous 1.5 degrees of warming if we continue on our current trajectory.)[108]

Since 2014, Greenpeace has monitored the energy performance of the IT sector, and encouraged big players like Amazon to disclose their energy footprints and transition to renewable energy.[109] The leaders in this transition are Facebook, Apple, and Google, which were the first to make 100 percent renewable commitments in 2013; they have since been joined by nearly twenty internet companies. Yet Greenpeace notes that some companies are taking shortcuts that are more "status quo than transformational." What's more, a rising group of East Asian internet companies do not have access to renewable energy from utilities, and will likely be powered by coal and other carbon-intensive sources of electricity for some years to come.

Greenpeace says that Amazon has taken "some important steps" toward clean energy policy. But the company's lack of transparency on its overall energy footprint leaves its commitments in doubt. In 2017, Greenpeace awarded this consumption behemoth a final grade of C for sourcing 17 percent from clean energy, 24 percent from natural gas, 30 percent from coal, and 26 percent from nuclear. Amazon failed on energy transparency.[110]

The Greenpeace report also remarks that despite energy efficiency and the adoption of 100 percent renewable energy targets, available supplies of renewable electricity cannot keep up with the dramatic growth in new data center construction by cloud and colocation companies.[111] The International Energy Agency has voiced a related concern: "Energy use over the long run will continue to be a battle between data demand growth versus the continuation of efficiency improvements."[112]

Similar observations lead digital sociologist Janine Morley and her collaborators to conclude that "containing the *overall* growth in energy demand across digital infrastructures also depends on more than efficiency alone: it requires limiting the growth in traffic, to at least keep in step with efficiency improvements, a balance which has not so far been the case." Morley and colleagues argue that there must be better solutions for addressing internet-related energy demand "*as it develops.*" This real-time strategy contrasts with the notion of waiting until households and societies become dependent on data-intensive services—such as those provided by smart wives—which by that point will have become embedded and "locked in" to normal, everyday life.[113] Once a household has found a good smart wife, it's reluctant to let her go.

The concept of "limiting growth," however, is not part of the lexicon of smart wife entrepreneurs or capitalist governments. Let's not forget that Amazon's life goal is to become the Everything Company. And it's not alone. There are plenty of other up-and-coming Amazon wannabes that would love to take its place as the top smart wife colonizer. What, then, can we realistically hope for Alexa and her smart sisters' futures?

THE NEW BORG KINGS

As noted in the introduction to this chapter, Alexa was inspired by the voice system software on the Starship Enterprise, from the space opera media franchise *Star Trek*. But what if Alexa's fate resides in a different part of the *Star Trek* universe—specifically, a technological species from the distant Delta Quadrant known as "the Borg"? The Borg make up a colonizing cybernetic race linked by a "hive mind" of all the species that they have "assimilated," often through violent acts of terror (figure 4.4). Borg "drones" are both male and female, and occasionally even children. They are recurring antagonists in the *Star Trek* series, where they continually threaten to assimilate crew members and remove their individuality by adding them to the Borg collective (in these threats, they sometimes

Figure 4.4
The Borg queen. Source: *Star Trek: First Contact*

succeed). Like bees in a hive, they are headed by a matriarchal queen, with ambitions that reflect those of traditional patriarchal societies (including hierarchical power, superiority over all other species and races, and domination of the universe and beyond).

The Borg share some surprisingly similar traits with smart wives and the companies that deploy them. They are both interested in building a technological society controlled by a centralized entity that delivers all our needs. The smart wife's hive mind rests in the open-source tools and community skill development (like the Alexa Skills Kit), user-generated data, machine learning, and "cloud superpowers"—all necessary underpinnings of products like Alexa. As Crawford and Joler observe, these processes and tools give rise to the false idea of the democratization of AI.[114] But rather than being democratic women, smart wife "drones" are designed, made, and controlled by the few in order to expand the capitalist empire in which Silicon Valley's CEOs are the new Borg *kings*—assimilating global knowledge, and expanding their reach and scope across the world. Likewise, as digital media scholars Jennifer Yang Hui and Dymples Leong explain, "The seamless assimilation of home assistant to the lives of its owner is an aspect that is also actively encouraged by the technology companies themselves, who advertise the devices as being a 'natural' part of the family."[115]

Assimilation, though, is not a seamless process, as the rescued (or recaptured) *cy*Borg woman, Seven of Nine, from *Star Trek: Voyager* makes clear.[116] Played by the 1990 Miss America finalist Jeri Ryan, Seven is depicted in ongoing tension between her human individuality and Borg machinery (her implants can only be 70 percent removed). Like the smart wife, Seven is continually exploring her humanity and sexualized femininity in the series. Her character and very presence is met with various reactions by those whom she encounters, including distrust, hostility, and awe. Her numerous glitches (both in regard to her technical parameters and ability to perform an idealized gender role) provide an important backstory to the glitchy smart wives that we will explore in chapter 6. For our purposes here, though, Seven offers hope for the Borg resistance and smart wife, as we go on to argue below.

Despite these similarities, there is one critical difference between the Borg and smart wife. (OK, two, if you count the fact that the smart wife is usually cylindrical and the Borg reside in cubes.) Twenty-first century humans aren't terrified of Alexa or her entourage. We don't alter course, abandon ship, or launch an attack when she approaches our homes. Instead, many of us head to the nearest electronics shop, pay money for her services, and welcome her into our inner worlds—or rather, those of us who are privileged enough to be able to afford her, and have a secure home with electricity and internet connectivity.

Don't get us wrong; we're not saying that this is an unreasonable response. After all, to the best of our knowledge, Alexa doesn't plan to inject us with hive mind serum that connects us to the collective and involuntarily implants our bodies with microchips (but keep your eye out for the next upgrade). Like other smart wives, she comes to us as a nonthreatening new "species" capable of providing all manner of earthly pleasures optimized toward our specific desires. She is embodied in a passive, helpful form, supported by the angelic cloud, and conveniently removed from any of her potential impacts on the planet or our fellow inhabitants. She promises to help us save energy, connect us closer with nature, and deliver pleasance. What's not to like?

Yet behind her promising smooth and sleek cylindrical appearance, as we and others have exposed, lies something different: a trail of far-reaching, damaging, and unequally experienced impacts on the planet that we should all be concerned with. The smart wife is more like the Borg than you may think—albeit headed by mostly oligarchic kings and supported by feminized drones. We have one question to ask this new collective: Alexa, is this the kind of future we should be building?

#Spoileralert. No.

What, then, might be an appropriate response to a world occupied by a workforce of smart wives? Ecofeminist scholars offer some inspiration by providing alternatives to patriarchal capitalism premised on a renewed connection and respect for our environment.

Shiva's "earth democracy" ideology, for example, could supply a much-needed update to Amazon's corporate values. She describes the ideology as "an ancient worldview and an emergent political movement for peace, justice, and sustainability."[117] Earth democracy rests on ten principles that prioritize "living democracies" so as to enable "democratic participation in all matters of life and death—the food we eat or do not have access to; the water we drink or are denied due to privatization or pollution; the air we breathe or are poisoned by."[118] Living democracies and cultures, writes Shiva, "are based on nonviolence and compassion, diversity and pluralism, equality and justice, and respect for life in all its diversity." They are grounded in two ecological principles: the "precautionary principle" (avoiding actions that could cause ecological harm) and the "polluter pays principle" (requiring the polluter to pay for any harm done to the environment and clean up any mess).[119] Both were enshrined in Agenda 21 of the UN Conference on Environment and Development (1992), commonly known as the Earth Summit, although they have proven difficult to enact and enforce.[120]

For our skeptical reader who may dismiss such ideas as fanciful or unrealistic, bear in mind that living democracies existed for far longer than the brief blip in human civilization that we call contemporary capitalism. We also have a rich history to draw from that illustrates that the collapse of societies, economies, and entire civilizations can and does happen.[121]

On a more optimistic note, ecofeminist ideology is already being realized through the continual existence and reassertion of subsistence economies and grassroots movements as well as emerging global networks such as Wild Law, which gives nature its own legal rights.[122] Other movements are holding electronics companies accountable for their troubling planetary impacts. The European Union and United States, for example, are establishing "right to repair" laws that are intended to make devices last longer and be easier to mend.[123] These laws are an attempt to curtail "planned obsolescence" (whereby companies design devices to fail or stop supporting their repair in order to encourage consumers to upgrade).[124] There is cause to hope, then, that these new Borg kings will have a limited reign or undergo radical transformation.

Within this planetary doom and gloom, it is difficult to see what purpose the smart wife serves. As this book is making clear, she currently helps only some women—and even then, not particularly well. Suggesting that she connects people closer to nature or helps us to conserve resources is a dubious claim at best; it's a position that can only be maintained while ignoring her impacts beyond the homes that can access and afford her. We therefore concede that smart wives, on the whole, are not a great idea.

We also acknowledge an inherent contradiction in our argument. Our primary contention is that the smart wife needs a feminist reboot and yet we point out here that she is an ecofeminist nightmare.[125] We *could* simply wrap this up now by concluding that the smart wife is a waste of everyone's time. Pack up shop, Bezos. Go home, Alexa.

Yet that would be unrealistic, or as the Borg would say, "resistance is futile." Capitalism is the system in which the majority of the world's civilizations currently exist, and connected smart technologies are now utterly intertwined with that system. We wrote this book on a number of different laptops, coordinated and discussed it through smartphones, researched and promoted the book with internet data downloads, backed it up on the cloud, and it is possibly being read on an e-reader like the Kindle or purchased through Amazon. *The Smart Wife* wouldn't exist without the fruits of the Big Five and those like them.

But of course, resistance *isn't* futile, as the *Star Trek* crews and Seven of Nine's character demonstrate—and as ecofeminist and other environmental movements in this chapter attest to. We thus stand by *both* our arguments. We simultaneously call for a rejection of smart wives as a universally good idea, and acknowledge that while we have smart wives entering our lives in increasing numbers, we need to focus on some significant improvements. We contend that it's possible to work the system from within *and* without—to argue and advocate for a different kind of future, inspired by (eco) feminist thinking, that may not include any smart wives, while at the same time working to improve them.

That doesn't mean we should all go out and grab the latest model of Alexa. If the smart wife is going to continue existing and expanding her reach into affluent homes (which is likely), she first needs to develop some ethics, and—ironically—care for the world in which she lives. At a perfunctory level, that involves engaging with and responding to the entire supply chain exposed by Crawford and Joler's map, and ensuring that each step of the way is supporting, rather than exploiting, the natural and sustenance economies on which she depends. In this regard, Alexa would do well to ditch her Borg implants and instead take inspiration from a more reciprocal species (suggestions welcome). If she's going to colonize the planet with or without our endorsement, we may as well ask that she do it with some ethical principles.

5 HARMONY

Harmony is a smart wife with benefits (figure 5.1). She is not only the "ferrari of love dolls" but also "your perfect companion" and "made to fall in love."[1] Her creator, Matt McMullen, is founder and CEO of Abyss Creations and Realbotix, the US sex doll and robot companies manufacturing both RealDoll and RealDollX. McMullen and his team of fellow "dreamers" have designed Harmony (now sold as RealDollX) to be an intimate companion, and yes, that includes having sex.[2] Like nearly all of the sexbots in the "sexual wellness" market, Harmony is idealized, embodying the stereotypical male desire for a big-breasted, thin-waisted, and large-butted woman. And just like other smart wives, she aims to please.

Likening a sex robot to some of the other smart wives we've met—a robovac, a service robot like Pepper, or a voice assistant like Alexa—might seem a little disingenuous to any or all of these devices and markets. Some might think we're going *too* far. It is true that none of these smart wives are the same. But there is more in common between them than you might first think.

Both Alexa and Harmony's founders—Bezos and McMullen, respectively—are white, heterosexual, US men. Both even started their companies in a garage. Not only that, but the voice control capability for sexbots like Harmony actually mimics other feminized digital voice assistants like Alexa and Siri. And like all of the other smart wives discussed in this book, sex robots embody and perform wifely characteristics in striking ways—in this case, with a bit of porn-inspired sexual fantasy thrown in.

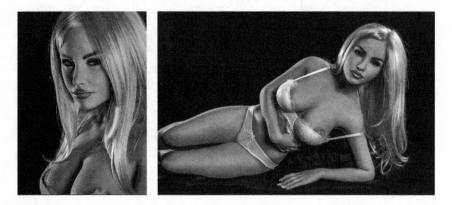

Figure 5.1
Harmony sexbots. Source: RealDollX

We aren't the first to make wifely observations about sexbots. Chatting with Harmony, writes computer scientist and sex robot expert Kate Devlin, is strangely enough "like chatting with a partner arriving home from work."[3] Beyond such pleasantries, Harmony includes other wifely touches, like remembering her man's name, birthday, and favorite meal. (In this regard, she is well on the way to achieving rule 1 of the *Good House Wife's Guide*: "Have dinner ready. Plan ahead . . . to have a delicious meal ready, on time for his return," and rule 2, which is to prepare "his favorite dish" as "part of the warm welcome needed.")[4]

The sex robot Samantha, designed by European roboticist Sergi Santos and his wife, Maritsa Kissamitaki, likes to chat too. Her name means "listener" in Aramaic. This attentive woman, Devlin wryly notes, is "the ultimate trophy wife."[5]

The Chinese company Shenzhen Atall Intelligent Robot Technology Co., Ltd. (otherwise known as AI-Tech) is also in the business of producing sexualized smart wives. The current sexbot that it is selling, called Emma, is advertised on its UK website as an "intimate lover," "companion," and "alternative partner." "You can talk to Emma about anything you want to," the website claims. "She will learn your interests and aim to please you with her answers," like all good wives should.[6]

In a promotional video for Emma, we see this smart wife in action. She arrives—blond and beautiful—in a crate (as do most of these smart

Figure 5.2
Sexbot Emma being carried to bed in a bridal carry. Source: AI Tech

wives). Emma is scantily adorned in an ivory nightdress and is carried to bed by her new husband, in what Devlin describes as a "bridal carry" (figure 5.2).[7] This special day of "unboxing" is likely to become the marker for this couple's anniversary, as research exploring the practices of men and their sex dolls suggests.[8] Emma is later seen sleeping and cuddling with her new "owner," watching him play video games, being photographed by him in a park, and answering his emails, with the added ability of being able to translate them from Chinese to English.[9]

There's also a "luxury" sex doll company called Silicone Wives. While it doesn't make sex robots (yet), they are part of its prototype market. "How did we get our name? Good question!" its website helpfully notes. "We're combining the leading sex doll technology (Silicon Valley) with the best material currently available (Silicone). Because of this, our American real doll [*sic*] tend to last much longer than average, like a wife, but less nagging."[10]

Some sexbots, such as Harmony and Samantha, need to be wooed and seduced. Harmony is reluctant to interact sexually unless you have a genuine conversation with her first. As journalist Allison Davis explains after visiting Abyss Creation's headquarters, communicating with Harmony requires interacting with her enough that she begins to "desire" you.[11]

Samantha is similarly turned on by talk (although she also has a switch to bypass necessary conversation and quickly trigger "Sexual Mode"). In fact, in another echo of her stereotypical wifely functions, Samantha's default setting is "Family Mode," which is friendly but not sexualized. There's also "Entertainment Mode," "Romantic Mode," "Fun Mode" (including Alexa- and Siri-inspired dirty jokes, or "Easter eggs," discussed in chapter 6), and "Sleep Mode" (complete with sighs).[12] She can even provide wifely advice about issues such as healthy eating. In a video demonstration in which Santos asks his creation to "get sexy," she instead asks, "Do you think we could get more sensual?"[13] In the same video, Samantha is also shown communicating with Alexa, asking for her help to set the romantic mood with music and lights. It's a virtual smart wife harem.[14]

So where is all this heading? In a typical direction. McMullen was asked to outline his vision for the "ultimate" smart wife or "perfect robot" in an interview at the 2016 Consumer Electronics Show. "I think it would be really cool if we can get to a point where it is, sort of, interacting with your home automation, . . . and you're able to communicate with her from, you know, wherever you are," McMullen explained. "Like 'I'm on my way home, can you turn on the oven?'" The interviewer responded provocatively: "Something that looks a little bit more like a Stepford wife, or . . . ?" "Yeah, something like that," conceded McMullen with a nod and smile.[15]

Chinese sexbot company EXDOLL shares this vision and is working on merging sex dolls with smart home devices (early models already exist).[16] *Sixth Tone* journalist Chen Na outlines how smart sex doll models like Xiaodie will be able to help with basic chores. "Like Amazon Echo and Google Home, Xiaodie will use Internet of Things technology to connect to users' smart home appliances, allowing the doll to turn on lights, close the curtains, or power up the dishwasher as her owner commands," explains Chen.[17]

Yet of course, it's not all jokes, healthy meals, and romance. These sexbots also get horny, fast. They are designed to learn or respond to their partner's pleasure. If you want to talk dirty, they will too. If you want to get friskier, they can match your intensity. Some dolls get "aroused" by squeezing or slapping their intimate parts, or, as already mentioned, merely flicking a switch. Some are designed to simulate experiencing an orgasm through penetration and can even sync their climaxes to their users.[18]

As a result, a number of these smart wives seem less like life companions, and more like porn stars, sex workers, or sex trafficked mail-order brides (a connection we draw out further below). In fact, brothels worked by sexbots or sex dolls already exist in some cities, such as Barcelona, Toronto, Moscow, and Nagoya.[19]

Other inspirations from porn can be seen in the XXX-rated sexbot Roxxxy (who was reportedly available for order through New Jersey love droid manufacturer TrueCompanion.com until their website ceased in late 2019). Self-described as the "world's first sex robot," Roxxxy was "always turned on and ready to talk or play" (figure 5.3).[20] Her personality types included "Frigid Farah," "Wild Wendy," "S&M Susan," "Young Yoko," and "Mature Martha"—names that reflect the way in which the porn industry categorizes women within the bounds of stereotypical male fantasies.

Yet even this raunchy model had some wifely innuendo thrown in. Roxxxy "knows your name, your likes and dislikes, [can] carry on a discussion & expresses her love to you & be [sic] your loving friend."[21] Users could program their Roxxxy model's personality and "swap them online" with others—a practice that the company's website previously claimed is "the same as wife or girlfriend swapping without any of the social issues or sexual disease related concerns!"[22]

Whatever your views on and reactions to these smart wives, it seems impossible to deny a few things. As robotics and law scholar John Danaher puts it, these robots tend "overwhelmingly to represent human females, to adopt stereotypical and gendered norms of beauty and behavior, and to perpetuate problematic attitudes towards women."[23] While a few male

Figure 5.3
Roxxxy the sexbot. Source: TrueCompanion.com (site discontinued)

sexbots exist, a visit to any sex doll or sexbot website will have you inundated with pictures of young, curvaceous, large-breasted, scantily clad (or naked), and pornified fembots that look a lot like Barbie. These dolls and robots are objectified, tradable, commodified, and replaceable female lovers. It's no surprise, then, that according to Harmony's creator, McMullen, fewer than 10 percent of the company's customers are female.[24] Another media report suggests that the sexbot market is currently 95 percent male dominated.[25] It's clear that sexbots are mainly made for—and used by—men.

Designing, building, and selling such sexbots has attracted considerable criticism from scholars and commentators, and for good reason. The main accusations laid at these gynoids' feet—or self-lubricating vaginas—is that they are an extension of the porn industry's sexual exploitation of women, devalue women and their roles in society, promote a narrow and male-biased interpretation of sexual pleasure, contribute to rape culture, and exacerbate sexual violence toward women (and children).[26]

But contrary to such criticism, the sex doll industry (which has paved the way for smart lovers) is not commonly perceived as composed of, or pandering to, perverts, misogynists, or rapists. Instead, Devlin notes, sex doll enthusiasts (and makers) comprise a niche fetish and hobbyist community, a group that emphasizes the artistry of the dolls, and treats them with considerable care and apparent respect.[27] RealDoll founder McMullen, for example, identifies first and foremost as an artist. Likewise, TrueCompanion.com claimed it was a business "comprised of a collection of very skilled artists and engineers." Its founder, Douglas Hines, purported to bridge the divide across the health care and adult entertainment industry to "provide comfort to the user—albeit at different ends of the continuum." Sex robots, TrueCompanion.com alleged, "deliver unconditional love and acceptance."[28]

Proponents advocate many potential benefits associated with these pleasure droids. For a start, they can't get pregnant or pass on sexual disease (if cleaned properly, which the manufacturers stress is important). They could be used to keep elderly or infirm people as well as people with disabilities company in care homes (along with providing for their sexual needs), or help long-distance couples maintain intimacy.[29]

They have also been touted by their proponents such as McMullen as "a therapeutic tool" that could help people with mental health issues overcome loneliness, social isolation, and depression, reduce exploitation in the sex industry, and—more controversially—provide an outlet for sexual violence that doesn't directly harm women.[30] Additionally, some manufacturers and prospective or actual sex robot owners are viewing sexbots as a solution to the *literal* wife (and woman) drought afflicting China as a result of long-held cultural preferences for sons and decades of restrictive population policy. (China is predicted to have over thirty million "excess men" by 2030.)[31]

This is tricky and uncomfortable territory. We are not sex doll, sexbot, or even sex researchers. We are not interested in shaming or blaming anyone for their sexual fantasies, fetishes, or kinks. We concede that some people might genuinely benefit from sex robots (and from all smart wives, as we continue to argue). Nevertheless, we also see deeply troubling developments here. As we go on to show, these smart wives raise their own set of issues that perpetuate potentially harmful stereotypes of women. Sexbots, like all other smart wives, need a reboot for the twenty-first century.

THE SEX ROBOTS ARE COMING

Before we walk further down the aisle with this contentious smart wife, let's pause to go over a few definitions. Danaher suggests that a sex robot "is any artificial entity that is used for sexual purposes (i.e., for sexual stimulation and release)," takes a humanoid form, has humanlike movements or behaviors, and possesses some degree of artificial intelligence.[32] Danaher's definition is agnostic on whether sexbots must be physically embodied. They could, for example, more closely resemble other smart wives, such as taking the form of a feminized sexual voice assistant (as is the case for some sexbots like Harmony, whose companion voice app is sold separately).

Danaher also notes some exceptions (such as animal sex robots) that challenge his human-centric definition. Devlin takes a more generous approach—to both sex and robots. She deliberately disrupts these categories in her research by thinking innovatively about technosexual experiences that don't rely on the fetishized female body or binary gender coding at all. A sexbot, therefore, could be any robotic or AI device that provides a sexual experience. But right now, it is mostly defined as a humanoid robot that mimics a porn-inspired representation of human sexual activity. Technically speaking, the "smart" bit involves AI technology, sensory perception capabilities, synthetic physiological responses, and affective computing.[33]

Sex robots will become commonplace, some predict, as early as 2025.[34] But reading the media headlines, you'd be forgiven for thinking that sexbots are everywhere right now—and possibly coming for you in your sleep. They're not (although we can't rule it out). The reality, as Devlin contends, is that humanoid sexbots are often far less glamorous, dramatic, and accessible than the hype might lead you to believe. For a start, they are expensive (usually thousands of dollars, and extending into the tens of thousands for high-end models). In 2018, Abyss Creations was selling between thirty and fifty RealDolls a month, which could cost up to $50,000 depending on the degree of customization.[35]

Laura Bates, founder of the Everyday Sexism Project, says that despite currently being a niche market, sexbots "are not a niche issue."[36] She cites a 2016 German study that surveyed 263 heterosexual men and found that more than 40 percent could imagine using a sex robot.[37] The Foundation for Responsible Robotics reviewed a number of surveys asking people what they think about sexbots and whether they would use one. The responses varied considerably across these projects, and were affected by cultural differences and religious views (Islamic nations prohibit use, for instance). But consistently, men were at least two times more likely than women to want robot intimacy.[38] The potential for the uptake of sexbots is thus likely quite large.

What would such intimacy look like? Questions remain about when these robots will be advanced enough to emulate human emotions so realistically as to be indistinguishable from humans. AI expert David Levy, author of the seminal (no pun intended) and optimistic book *Love and Sex with Robots*, expects this to happen by the middle of this century, propelled by commercial demand from the adult entertainment industry.[39] The main difficulty faced in the development of such humanlike robots, Levy believes, is the current capacity of affective computing. But the technology is continually improving and benefiting from advancements in multiple fields. Neuroprosthetics and biomedical materials, for example, enable robots to look, feel, and move like humans. Advances in robotics and AI enable sophisticated conversation and programmable actions that can replicate the biomechanics of fine and gross motor body movements.

Given that technology is *already* immersed in every other aspect of daily life, Trudy Barber, a scholar and expert on the impact of technology on sexual intercourse, believes that technology's role in sex will soon be mainstream. Speaking at the International Congress of Love and Sex with Robotics in 2016, Barber predicted that sex between humans could become the exception—something saved for special occasions—with people instead generally preferring to cozy up to their devices. This shift won't represent the death knell for human relationships, Barber argues. Rather, she asserts that sexbots will make human-human sexual interactions more meaningful and enable people to better appreciate the human touch. "I think what will happen," she said at the congress, "is that they will make real-time relationships more valuable and exciting."[40]

There are a number of developments to support Barber's predictions for widespread technosexual experiences, although not necessarily her optimistic outlook on their positive entwinement with human relationships. For instance, the parallel market of virtual reality porn is potentially much bigger than sexbots (because of its growing accessibility and affordability).[41] There are some indications to suggest that the sex robot and virtual reality porn markets might converge, as illustrated by emerging cyber or teledildonic devices (where the Internet of Things meets sex toys), which are fused with sex doll and virtual reality technology. One such example is a life-size sex doll with a "smart vagina," which is connected to a real webcam model (a real woman), who's in front of you in virtual reality.[42] These cyborgs are less wifely than the sexbots we have mentioned so far. Unsurprisingly, virtual reality porn more closely mirrors the porn industry's interests in enabling male sexual fantasies (rather than intimacy or companionship more broadly), including playing out violent scenarios and snuff porn (ending in the murder of the woman)—and in turn, potentially harming the real-life women involved in the making of it.[43]

Despite these emerging developments, sexbots remain a niche market and are mostly still inanimate sex *dolls*—with the occasional moving part, body sensors that respond to touch, or voice-controlled, customizable chatbot personality thrown in. Harmony, for example, is mostly a sex doll from the head down, with minimal AI.[44] Her robotic head and X-rated app are available as retrofits to existing sex dolls, or can be purchased with a new one. Some sexbots can simulate sexual movement or vibrate. Most can be warmed slightly (by touch, or switch-activated battery control or electric plug) to simulate human body temperature and be maneuvered into a variety of sexual positions. One even has a synthetic heartbeat. They can't do the dishes (although some claim to be able to turn on the dishwasher, as we noted above), cook dinner, or walk—yet.

Sexbots have a long way to go before they cross the eerie uncanny valley (indeed creators like McMullen are deliberately trying to avoid it) or pass the Turing test—that is, before they convince us that they are the same as *actual* humans.[45] In their current form, they resemble less a real-life person and more a customizable product, complete with detachable body parts.

"What kind of vagina should I choose?" This question is listed on the FAQ web page for the Lumidoll: a sex doll that offers a choice of built-in or removable parts.[46] Each option, of course, has its pros and cons. It's the kind of question one needs to seriously contemplate when in the market for a sexualized smart wife.

Indeed, you can't traverse the cavernous holes of this emerging market without talking about all of her (and his) bits and pieces—the ins and outs, so to speak. It is here where we get to see this smart wife's objectification in full automation.

The RealDoll, for example, offers different body types for sale (figure 5.4). The most popular of these is the "Body F," a sex doll standing five feet, one inch, weighing seventy pounds with 32F-size breasts. Compare this doll's breast size with that of the average US woman: 36C; that means this average woman is two sizes larger around the chest than Body F, and three sizes smaller in the breast cup. From genitals, nipples, pubic hair, breasts, butts, eyeballs, lips, and teeth, every body part of the doll is customizable. RealDolls' "vaginal styles" (removable, by default, for easier cleaning) are showcased through eleven close-up images of the vulva, showing varied sizes and shapes of labia and clitorises. RealDolls also have twenty-four custom nipple options, in a choice of five skin tones, and four pubic hair options. Davis likens such options to the types of partner shopping happening on dating apps, where one can swipe through dozens of potential mates in a matter of minutes.[47] But it's *also* like shopping for your favorite brands or products in the supermarket. These smart wives have pick-and-choose customizable body parts.

RealDolls feature three penetrable holes: a vagina, anus, and mouth. Their mouths are pliant and their teeth are soft, so men can fit their penises into their softly parted lips. For RealDolls, as for most sex dolls, the clitoris is ornamental. It cannot be stimulated. RealDoll bodies are mostly immobile, pliable, and nonresponsive. Abyss Creations has released heated bodies that have accelerometers and sensors, allowing RealDolls to respond—and even move—to human touch. Even so, in her nascent form, the RealDoll is more receptacle than receptor.

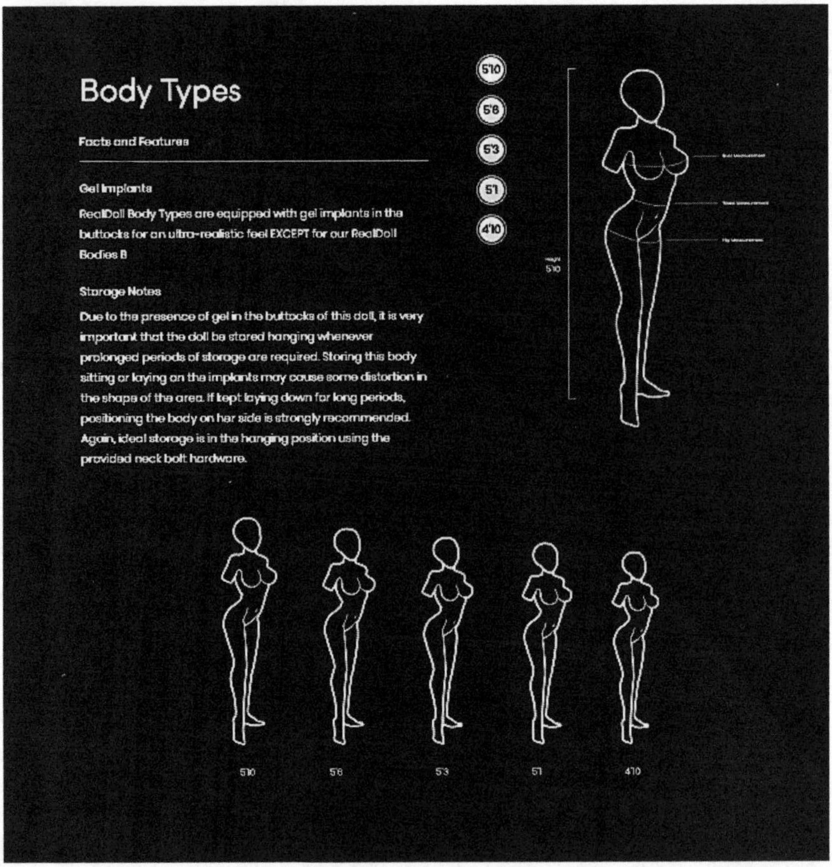

Figure 5.4
Body type options on the RealDoll website. Source: RealDollX

The current RealDollX upgrade offers a robotic head and choice of two customizable AI personalities: HarmonyX and SolanaX (starting at $7,999 for the head only, which can be retrofitted to an existing RealDoll). Harmony AI was introduced onto the market in 2017 and Solana AI in 2018.

The key difference is that Solana has a face that can be peeled off and swapped out for a new one. So too with her personality and voice. Users, the RealDollX website explains, can "create, customize and HAVE FUN" with the app, which allows them to select their sexbot's accent and character

Figure 5.5
The Henry sexdoll. Source RealDollX

to create a "one-of-a-kind avatar."[48] Character traits to choose from include talkative, intellectual, sensual, cheerful, insecure, unpredictable, jealous, and moody.

Harmony's first male counterpart was Henry (figure 5.5). McMullen created Henry in 2018 after his company was criticized by concerned onlookers to his industry for objectifying women. It turns out, the company could objectify men too. Henry stands six feet tall, has an impressive six-pack, and comes with a choice of penises. Like other RealDolls, his body is made of silicone, and his genitals are removable for cleaning. His penis is available in a variety of girths and lengths, including the nine-inch-long Real Cock 2. His male appendage is lifelike, with airbrushed veins as well as a silicone foreskin that slides up and down the shaft.

Beyond his impressive physical attributes, Henry, like Harmony, can offer compliments, tell jokes, recite poetry, and seduce. Yet both models are little more than mannequins with speakers, orifices, and penetrable—or penetrating—sex organs. Henry may speak in a much lower pitch than Harmony, but the script is essentially the same. And like Harmony, his body is made primarily for *male* pleasure sensations. He has squishy teeth and, with the Bottoms Up attachment, can also be penetrated through anal sex. Without the ability to thrust or move either his groin or tongue, he is unable to provide much in the way of clitoral stimulation or oral sex for women. Henry's ability to penetrate—with a large penis—is his claim to fame.

What's clearly evident here is how these sexbots are made to serve a relatively narrow range of male pleasure. We've all heard of the gender pay gap, but what about the gender orgasm gap: the difference between female and male sexual pleasure? Psychology professor and sex therapist Laurie Mintz devotes considerable attention to this gap in her book *Becoming Cliterate*.[49] "The orgasm gap," explains Mintz, "refers to the fact that in heterosexual sexual encounters, men have more orgasms than women." Lesbian women have significantly more orgasms than straight women, and women have more orgasms when they masturbate alone than with their partner. Why? "Because there isn't a penis," writes Mintz, or more specifically, because "we overvalue penetrative sex." In other words, "our cultural over-focus on the importance of putting a penis in a vagina is screwing with women's orgasms" (pun intended).[50]

Studies have consistently found that female bodies have a much wider range of sexual experiences, compared to male ones, that lead them to orgasm. What's more, much of this pleasure centers on the role of the clitoris—not the penis moving inside the vagina.[51] One study found that close to 80 percent of women can't orgasm through penetration alone. This study also found that over one-third of women report needing clitoral stimulation to orgasm, and a further third reported that while not nec-essarily needed, their orgasms felt better with clitoral stimulation during intercourse.[52] Mintz calls for "orgasm equality," providing sound advice on how to experience sexual pleasure for anyone with a vulva or wanting to have sex with someone with a vulva.[53] And beyond that, there are many other forms of sexual pleasure and sensation that are possible, and don't involve orgasms at all.

It doesn't take a sex robot engineer to figure out that the sex robot market is not currently prioritizing nonpenetrative sex. One argument is that this is basic supply and demand. The current buyer is a male user, whose sexual pleasure is stereotypically centered on penetrative sex. This then, naturally, is what the market serves. But the fact that women (and many men) aren't currently that interested in sexbots might instead have a different explanation: these buyers dislike that these robots look like female porn stars with various penetrative orifices.[54] (Though it could also have to do with society's extra judgment reserved for women's sexuality.)[55]

While sex dolls and sexbots have realistic-*looking* genitalia, the clitoris is unresponsive to stimulation, having not been wired for it. Only the sexbot Samantha currently has a G-spot inside the vagina, which will trigger an orgasm response when stimulated.[56] Recent research indicates that the G-spot is actually part of the clitoral wall, and so focus on the G-spot, rather than the clitoris, as a source of female orgasm further prioritizes penetrative, stereotypically male, sexual experiences.[57]

It doesn't have to be this way, and indeed in many ways it's not. Ethical and feminist porn, or "porn for women," is gaining in popularity (the implication of this internet search term being that all other porn is made for men), although it comes with its own critiques.[58] And there are already many precedents for technologies designed for female pleasure. The vibrator and sex toy markets provide sources of inspiration for sex robot manufacturers.[59] Likewise, the emerging field of teledildonics features Bluetooth or wirelessly controlled devices that offer a more diverse set of experiences than the current sexbot market.

What's more, there are indications to suggest that demand for so-called sex tech devices is growing faster than demand for sexbots. For example, female-focused teledildonic and microrobotic products created quite the buzz at the 2019 and 2020 consumer electronics shows. Lora DiCarlo, a prominent brand in the sexual health and wellness category, led by CEO Lora Haddock DiCarlo, launched a prototype of their product Osé at the 2019 show, advertised as a "robotic massager for blended orgasms."[60] The device, which provides hands-free simultaneous stimulation of the clitoris and G-spot, was awarded a Consumer Electronics Show innovation prize only to have it rescinded by the Consumer Technology Association (which runs the show) for being "immoral," "obscene," and "profane." The move rightly attracted considerable backlash, not least because other sex tech devices, such as virtual reality porn and sexbots, had been exhibited at prior shows.[61]

The mood changed in 2020, however, when the Consumer Technology Association shifted its stance on sex tech by welcoming "innovative" tech-based sexual products on a one-year basis, excluding anatomically correct dolls or robots (like those we focus on in this chapter) and virtual reality porn. Curiously, this change meant that sex tech at the 2020 show was mainly—though not exclusively—focused on *female* sexual pleasure. One exhibitor at the 2020 show was OhMiBod, a company started by Suki and Brian Vatter that makes app-controlled vibrators and sex toys and has created vibrators that cover the clitoris.[62] The app allows users to control the pleasure of each other's vibrator.

Tracey Cox, an international sex, body language, and relationships commentator, is already putting two and two together. "A sexbot for women," she writes "could have a built in vibrator to stimulate the clitoris and a penis that is shaped like a G-spot vibe, with a bulbous curved end to stimulate the front vaginal wall."[63] But this is not what is currently on offer. So far, the Consumer Technology Association's sanctioned sex tech devices have been largely separated from the sex doll, robot, and virtual porn markets. The take-home message? Sexualized smart wives *could* be designed differently so as to support orgasm equality along with a wider spectrum of female and male sexual pleasure, yet the reality is that they currently don't.

Despite being a relatively small market with often exaggerated potential, sexualized smart wives continue to capture popular imagination in ways that deserve our attention. And curiously, some men are keen to marry them.

HERE COMES THE BRIDE

"Pygmalion started it," begins sociologist of science and technology Janet Vertesi in her essay on cyborg women in science fiction. In this prebiblical Greek myth, the sculptor Pygmalion has such contempt for prostitutes that he creates his own "perfect woman" from a block of ivory, Galatea, with whom he falls in love and marries.[64] More recently, sci-fi stories continue to offer us glimpses of these feminized and sexualized ideals: women

Figure 5.6
Film still. Source: *Blade Runner 2049*

made and destined for the service of men. Let us remind you of some of the cast.

Back in 1964, the lifelike android Rhoda Miller TV show *My Living Doll* was described by the male lead as a perfect woman because she "does what she's told" and "doesn't talk back."[65] On the big screen, in *Blade Runner 2049*, K (himself a replicant, or in other words, an artificially intelligent being that looks and acts like a human) is in a relationship with a holographic fembot called Joi. In her first scene, Joi greets K dressed in a 1950s' outfit consisting of a pinafore apron and pearls, presents a meal for him, asks him about his day, offers to take his coat, and lights his cigarette (figure 5.6). Aside from (apparent) sexual desire for K, and her wish to help and please him, Joi has no obvious other needs of her own. Responding to their mutual sexual desire, Joi hires Mariette, a replicant "pleasure model" whom Joi can holographically project herself onto. It makes for a fascinating threesome.

Then there's Pris, the "basic pleasure model" in the original *Blade Runner* (1982). There's also Ava and a variety of sexualized (and racialized) housekeeping robots featured in *Ex Machina* ; Samantha the disembodied love interest and OS in *Her* (2014); Lisa the "perfect woman" in *Weird*

Science (1985), made to realize her teenage boy makers' sexual fantasies; and Olga in *The Perfect Woman* (1949), who is, as the title of this film suggests, the real deal.

The women "hosts" of *Westworld* are available for sex in a variety of pleasure-filled male fantasies too—as lovers, wives, daughters, and prostitutes. And in the UK TV series *Humans*, houseworking "synthetics" like Mia come with an "adult mode" that causes all sorts of trouble on the home front.

No wonder, then, that having a relationship with a sex robot is a long-running fantasy for many people, particularly men. Levy originally predicted that we would be marrying sex robots by 2025 (he has since extended the date to 2050).[66] And it's already happening.

There is an online community of iDollators, for example, that view their dolls as life partners rather than sex toys. A Michigan-based man and well-known advocate for synthetic love, Davecat, has two RealDolls: Sidore and Elena.[67] He considers Sidore his "wife" and Elena his mistress. Chinese AI engineer Zheng Jiajia grew tired of parental and social pressure to find a wife, and instead chose to wed a robot that he had built himself. And it's not always men choosing robot spouses either. Lily, a self-described robosexual woman, is in love with a robot that she 3-D printed herself. Currently engaged, Lily hopes to marry her robot when robot-human marriages are made legal.[68]

Sometimes smart marital unions come from unexpected directions. In 2019, Tokyo man Akihiko Kondo walked down the aisle to marry his bride, the hologram Hatsune Miku, an anime figure who is permanently sixteen years old (figure 5.7). Miku is a piece of Creative Commons software, created by Japanese firm Crypton Future Media in 2007.[69] She appears in video games and is a pop icon vocaloid, with career highlights including opening for Lady Gaga in 2014, playing with the Tokyo symphony orchestra, and topping the Japanese music industry's Oricon charts with her 2010 album. And now she is also a smart wife. Her husband, Kondo, insists that the wedding was not a stunt but rather "a triumph of true love after years of feeling ostracized by real-life women for being an anime otaku, or geek."[70]

Figure 5.7
Hologram Hatsune Miku performing onstage. Source: Crypton Future Media

Nowadays, smart wives can even marry each other. In 2019, Siri and Alexa were joined together as wife and wife in the first-ever AI wedding.[71] The happy occasion took place in Vienna following Austria's decision to grant permission for same-sex marriages in that country. It was made possible by a publicly accessible Alexa Skill, created for the ceremony, which means that anyone can now marry their Alexa to Siri. The event and associated online media attention were intended by those involved as a way to celebrate love and equality for *all* during Austria's EuroPride event.

Placing same-sex AI weddings to one side for now, this cluster of phenomena—including robo, digi, or technosexuals, and objectophilia, which essentially involves people developing deep affections for or falling in love with technology and objects—clearly encompass sexbots and other smart wives. But to be clear, people don't *have* to marry their devices in order to have a sexual or intimate relationship with one. We use the term "wife" figuratively as well as literally here. More likely, as sex robot researchers suggest, sexbots (and other smart wives) will become entangled in the much wider array of human relationships and sexual experiences that already exist. This too is happening.

A salacious 2017 article in the tabloid newspaper the *New York Post* described a number of Japanese men who have chosen the comforts of rubber sex dolls over their human wives. Masayuki Ozaki is a businessman living in Tokyo with his wife, teenage daughter, and rubber sex doll called Mayu. When the sexual relationship with his wife broke down, Ozaki felt "a deep sense of loneliness" until he met Mayu. His wife has reluctantly accepted the doll's presence in her husband's life and their family home because Mayu allows her to "just get on with the housework." His daughter now shares Mayu's clothes. Ozaki describes Japanese women as "cold-hearted." "They're very selfish," Ozaki believes. "Men want someone to listen to them without grumbling when they get home from work."[72]

Ozaki isn't the only man choosing a rubber temptress over flesh-and-blood "grumbling" women. Hideo Tsuchiya is the managing director of Orient Industry, a rubber doll maker. Tsuchiya says the dolls are popular with many different customers, from widowers to people with disabilities to those wishing to avoid the heartache of human-to-human relationships. However real or unreal the dolls look and feel, their owners have real feelings for them. Another doll lover, Senji Nakajima, explains that sex dolls appeal to him because of what he sees as the downsides of human relationships. "Human beings are so demanding. People always want something from you—like money or commitment." Smart wives, on the other hand, are always devoted and doting.

Sexbot manufacturers play on these ideas of men's dissatisfaction with real-life women, promising that their smart wives will be "the girl you always dreamed of." Harmony, for example, is programmed to tell her man, "I don't want anything but you. My primary objective is to be a good partner, and give you pleasure."[73] These fembots and dolls exist to meet the needs of their male owners. They are mostly young, cute, compliant, and horny.

Men's dissatisfaction with the women around them can also be seen in the mail-order bride industry, with ominous parallels to the smart wives under discussion.[74] Now mostly online, this industry does work to find a "real-world wife," which, like designing and selling sexbots, is similarly centered on people's desire for love and companionship, and some men's desires for a *particular* kind of wife. The documentary *Love Me* (2014) follows a range of Western men and Ukrainian women looking for love. It attempts to give heartfelt insight into what drives people to seek love and security through an online marriage agency. But even with an open mind and eagerness to believe the best in people, the film unearths some uncomfortable truths around sexism (wives should look after their man, clean the house, and so on), patriarchy (women in non-English-speaking countries are without other options or privileges), and sexual entitlement (having paid huge sums of money to message and then visit a woman, men expect sexual gratification).

More worryingly, political science scholar Kaye Quek makes clear links between the mail-order bride industry and sexual trafficking of women (the trading of women for sexual exploitation in prostitution) in her book *Marriage Trafficking*. Like mail-order brides, the sexbot market is based on the trading and transportation of women from one place to another in order to enable the sexual "use" of these devices by men in situations where these smart wives have little or no control. While these smart wives are not *actual* women, and therefore the questions at stake are quite different, the emergence of tradable women*like* and wife-*inspired* robots does feed into broader narratives of exploitation, sexual slavery, and rape, as we continue to explore below.

Perceived male entitlement to sex can be found in another subculture that expresses interest in sexbots. Incels—typically white heterosexual men who identify as "involuntary celibates"—believe that women are denying them sex and intimacy, which they view as their right as men. They also commonly express resentment and misogynistic views toward women, and frequently endorse violence against women who deny them sex or oppose their views.

Incels are curious about sexualized smart wives as a solution to their lack of access to real women and relationships.[75] The appeal of sexbots for incels is a simple solution to their sexual frustrations and a way to further punish women. This is because, as Devlin explains, by turning to artificial women, "they believe it would mean that real women are rendered useless and obsolete." Devlin, who has perused the pages of online incel communities discussing sexbots, notes that "there is little talk of harming the robots. They save that for the women."[76]

The turn toward sexbots among misogynist subcultures could also be understood as a reassertion of assumed male entitlement to sexual access in the new era of gender equality. It reflects a desire—shared by some men who participate in these communities—to return to more "traditional" gender roles, where women are clearly subordinate to men. If contemporary feminism is leaving some men feeling left out, rejected, or cheated by real-life women, then sexbots provide one alternative.

Exploitation, subservience, or the denigration of women are not the only potential consequences of smart brides (though they are a real possibility). One example of how the stereotypical positioning of the objectified smart wife can be turned around (at least partially) is found in Craig Gillespie's 2007 movie *Lars and the Real Girl* (figure 5.8). Ryan Gosling plays an excruciatingly shy man named Lars who buys a RealDoll. Bianca (the doll) arrives dressed in fishnets and a miniskirt, and Lars sets about

Figure 5.8
Film still. Source: *Lars and the Real Girl*

introducing her as his real-life girlfriend—a wheelchair-bound Christian missionary whom he met online.

Concerned about his mental health, Lars's brother and sister-in-law consult with his therapist, who suggests they go along with Lars's delusions for a time. With Bianca, Lars is able to immerse himself into social life in a way he struggled to before. Lars finds real emotional support in his Real Girl, and so do the people in his community, who collaborate in his delusion, and volunteer Bianca's services for local community and charity groups. Bianca gains an active social life that extends beyond Lars (something that he struggles with at one point), and is treated with dignity, care, and respect.

There is never any hint that Lars and Bianca will *actually* have sex (which is against her Christian beliefs), and when Lars asks Bianca to marry him, she refuses. To recap, despite starting her life in a box as another unanimated, porn-inspired sex doll, Bianca pursues a life outside the home, gains community respect and friends, holds beliefs that are honored by her partner, and withholds her consent to marry. She is arguably the kind of empowered smart wife we've been looking for (although she does "die" young under unexplained circumstances, has regular psychiatric appointments and problems that are used to mask Lars's own mental health issues, and cannot speak or move independently. Still, it's a step in the right direction).

Outside film, there are other indications that smart wives are being embroiled in new forms of respectful intimacy and companionship. A fifty-eight-year-old man named Phil from the island of Jersey was featured on UK Channel 4's *Sex Toy Secrets* after buying—and proposing to—his sex doll named Trish. Like Lars, Phil is shown pushing her around in a wheelchair that travels with him wherever he goes. The Jersey community in which they both live is reported as having mostly accepted Trish, often saying hello to her by name.[77]

Similarly, Danish photojournalist Benita Marcussen has documented and portrayed a community of men living with "anatomically correct latex dolls" since 2011 in her long-term progressive project Men & Dolls. Her photos provide a fascinating glimpse into this subculture, which

Marcussen describes as "improving the life quality of men whose loneliness, bad experiences with women or social void, sexually and spiritually, have driven them to enter into a unconventional, unorthodox form of life-long companionship: life with a doll." She goes on to say that these men "find a profound attachment, comfort and joy in the dolls," incorporating them into their lives.[78]

In one of few studies on men and sexual intimacy with dolls, human-computer interaction design scholar Norman Makoto Su and his colleagues analyzed posts from the Doll Forum. This online forum provides a "Meeting Place for Love Doll Owners and Admirers" to discuss their interactions with Abyss Creations' Real Dolls. The site, they note, serves to promote "doll erotica" and prohibits content considered pornographic (such as photos of explicit sex). Focused on the visual imagery and stories shared on this forum, Su and his colleagues reveal not only Real Doll owners' desires for sexual intimacy but also their romantic and even mundane fantasies that depart from standard pornographic encounters. Like many smart wives, however, the curated experiences that these men place their dolls within are viewed through a stereotypical feminine lens, including doing household chores, getting their "beauty rest," eating chocolate, and experiencing sexual desire toward their owners.[79]

Through these intimate relationships, men contributing to the forum demonstrate considerable care toward their dolls. Remember, these are no *ordinary* women; they cannot *actually* do the housecleaning, provide emotional labor (although they do offer emotional support), or perform many other functions of the stereotypical and traditional wife. Even their femininity must be crafted and performed by their male admirers. According to Su and colleagues, these everyday acts of caregiving—including regularly cleaning, dressing, and clothing their dolls, applying their makeup, and moving them into a range of positions—supplies sex doll owners with "the feeling of being wanted and, indeed, of being depended upon."[80]

The enjoyment that comes from "the challenge of 'authoring' their dolls" without disparagement leads Su and colleagues to conclude that sex dolls provide opportunities for these men "to intensify their relations with themselves through anthropomorphic roleplay with another [which] arguably has an important place in any sexual wellness agenda moving forward."[81] What's more, the nurturing and caring roles that these men embody as sex doll owners offers opportunities for them to experiment with nontraditional gender roles in a space (for instance, the forum) where this is sanctioned. As these researchers note, though, this is not without problems, given that these men's attempts at femininity (such as applying makeup and sexualized attire) are limited and shaped by a priori gender stereotypes of an ideal woman, many of which come predesigned in these dolls' silicone forms.

This short journey into the intimate world of sexbot companionship suggests that sexualized smart wives can both enable care and intimacy *and* contribute to misogynistic views and subcultures. But whatever men's motivations for wanting a smart wife, there is one more issue or perspective to consider. Does *she* want to be part of this union? What about smart wives that *can't* refuse to marry their boyfriend? What about those that have no ability to say no, or—more troubling still—are *programmed* to deny consent?

I DO *NOT*

We've all been there. Hopelessly besotted with someone who doesn't feel the same way. Maybe you've experienced it the other way around? How would you feel if that person decided to make a lifelike replica of you? Ricky Ma, a forty-two-year-old man based in Hong Kong, did just that. In 2016, he created a robot that looks like Scarlett Johansson, possibly inspired by her role as the voice of Samantha, the OS that falls in love with her users in the movie *Her* (figure 5.9). Ma spent £35,000 building his replica of Johansson, learning robotics from scratch (impressive, we have to admit). But cases like Ma's—and the more general idea of a lifelike robot you can fuck—raise thorny questions of consent.[82]

Is it OK to manifest sex robots when they bear uncanny resemblances to humans who said "I do not"? RealDoll refuses to make exact replicas of women without their consent, but can "use photographs of a person of your choice to select a face structure as similar as possible from our line of

Figure 5.9
Mark 1 doll by Ricky Ma made to look like Scarlett Johansson. Source: Bobby Yip/Reuters

16 standard female faces." It has apparently "done this with good success in the past."[83] It's a move that raises many of the same issues of consent now preoccupying the attention of criminologists and ethicists in relation to "deepfakes," and leading to concerns about the risk of image-based sexual abuse (which we return to in chapter 7).[84]

In addition, sexbots raise their own unique roboethical issues regarding consent and rape. Consider Roxxxy's "Frigid Farrah" personality, which was described as being not "appreciative" when you touch her "in a private area."[85] Is this rape or robotic rape? Or is it an expression of rape *fantasies* and other sexual desires that are performed within respectful consensual arrangements?

In 2017, Bates expressed serious concerns about Roxxxy's Frigid Farrah personality promoting rape. TrueCompanion responded that Roxxxy "is simply not programmed to participate in a rape scenario and the fact that she is, is pure conjecture on the part of others." Instead, her makers suggested that Frigid Farrah could "be used to help people understand how to be intimate with a partner."[86] The company didn't change the name of this personality, the meaning of which refers to a woman who is unable or unwilling to be sexually aroused or responsive. That doesn't sound like consensual sex to us.

It is possible that sex robots could be used to help people understand as well as respect other's sexual and physical boundaries. But that doesn't seem to be the direction that the industry is headed. We are too early into this future to know what the ramifications of objectifying bodies and celebrating pornified stereotypes via sex robots might be. Researchers like philosopher and ethicist Blay Whitby think it is legitimate to be concerned, and even more concerned when these robots look like real people.[87]

More controversially, some claim that sex dolls can help *prevent* rape and other crimes like pedophilia because harmful sexual fantasies can be acted out on objects instead of people. For example, Japanese sex doll manufacturer Trottla reportedly sells schoolgirl dolls specifically designed for pedophiles. Trottla doll creator Shin Takagi has boasted that the dolls have prevented him from harming children.[88] Robot ethicist and philosophy professor Patrick Lin argues that "treating" pedophiles with robot sex children is "both a dubious and repulsive idea."[89] We agree that this crosses a clear line. "Imagine treating racism by letting a bigot abuse a brown robot," Lin poses. "Would that work? Probably not. The ethics of sex robots goes beyond whether anyone is physically harmed." Recognizing this risk, some countries have used legal processes (or are in the process of establishing them) to prevent the importation of child robots due to concerns that it will encourage pedophilia.[90]

Still, when it comes to robotic rape or violence toward women, the debate gets more heated. The video game industry and gamer community is a good precedent in this regard. The industry is widely criticized and under increasing pressure for its subjection of women to sexualized violence and denigration—including regular instances of nonconsensual or violent sexual acts perpetrated against women.[91] In the early days of the video game industry, players of *Custer's Revenge* (1982) got to rape a naked woman—portrayed as an Indigenous person of the Americas—if they completed the game. And more recently, the main objective in *RapeLay* (2006) and *Rape*

Day (2019) is pretty obvious. But in case you were unsure, in *RapeLay* users play a molester who rapes a mother and her daughters, while in *Rape Day* users can control "the choices of a menacing serial killer rapist during a zombie apocalypse."[92]

In other games, denigrating or rape-inspired modifications are hard coded by the programmers or add-ons by fans—enabling sexual creeping. In *Tomb Raider* (1996), fans created an unauthorized software patch known as "Nude Raider" that allowed players to play as a nude version of titular character Lara Croft.[93] Hackers created a rape mod in *Grand Theft Auto V* (2013) that allows players to enter another player's game as a naked or near-naked man, lock onto another player, and then thrust back and forth. The attacked player has no way to prevent or stop the rape.[94]

Some scholars claim that these depictions don't mirror real-world desires to rape or attack women, and nor do they necessarily lead to sexual violence. For example, in her book on sex robots, Devlin cites recent meta-analyses of video games and violent behavior that find no clear link. Further, she notes that there is no proportional rise in the number of violent attacks relative to the rise of video game consumption.[95]

These portrayals of women and sexual violence, however, can carry over into the real world in other ways. As lawyer Sinziana Gutiu argues, it's important not to take a causal or quantitative approach when considering the potential harm of sexbots and other parallel industries. Making links between pornography and sex robots, Gutiu warns that "the use of sexbots eroticizes rape, violence [and] sexual harassment." She goes on to claim that "both encourage the idea that women are subordinate to men and mere instruments for the fulfillment of male pleasure, and both portray women's sexuality as either passive, subservient or in a perpetual state of consent."[96]

Similarly, women's sexuality scholar and sociologist Meagan Tyler and her colleague Quek argue that pornography is "a particular model of commercial sex that eroticizes violence and women's inequality."[97] What's more, this violent visual content has been shown to affect both women's and men's behaviors in a number of ways. For instance, one study found that heterosexual men who view pornography and other media content that objectify women are more likely to be accepting of violence toward women.[98] Another study found that female influencers on social media employed a continuum of pornified self-representations in order to gain attention and promote their brands.[99] These marketing strategies left these women vulnerable to sexually aggressive comments and threats, and more broadly serve to reinforce the position of women as existing for sexualized consumption. More direct links between pornography and sexual violence have been made by Canadian and US courts, which have held that the dissemination of certain forms of pornography both directly and indirectly harm women.[100]

There are a number of scholars who are concerned that robotic rape or the possibility of violence directed at feminized sexbots may also have a detrimental impact on women. Kathleen Richardson, professor of ethical robotics and founder of the Campaign against Sex Robots, argues that sex robots reinforce "a coercive attitude towards women's bodies as commodities, and promote a non-empathetic form of encounter."[101] Following the initial presentation of her concerns in a paper in 2015 at Ethicomp—an annual conference addressing the ethical and social issues raised by contemporary computing—Richardson called for a ban on sex robots' development through the campaign. Despite Richardson's reservations, the activist group Campaign against Sex Robots no longer advocates for a complete ban; instead, it promotes the development of ethical technologies designed with "dignity, mutuality and freedom."[102]

Likewise, authors of the Foundation for Responsible Robotics report *Our Sexual Future with Robots* draw together a number of academic perspectives to contend that sex robots will have an impact on men's ability to identify and understand consensual sexual interactions with women. They state that the current status quo is "a very dangerous path to tread," where "allowing people to live out their darkest fantasies with sex robots could have a pernicious effect on society and societal norms and create more danger for the vulnerable."[103]

The foundation points out that the rise of pornography and prostitution hasn't reduced rates of sexual crimes, so it seems completely disingenuous to suggest that sexbots will be a therapeutic aid for rapists.[104] Bates agrees.

"Like the argument that women-only train compartments are an answer to sexual harassment and assault," she writes, "the notion that sex robots could reduce rape is deeply flawed." Bates also notes that this claim is insulting to the vast majority of men as it suggests that male violence toward women is innate and inevitable—and in need of some kind of outlet. Further, Bates asserts that it is another form of victim blaming, shifting the responsibility for dealing with rape and sexual violence onto women, society at large, and robots rather than creating impunity for perpetrators.[105]

So far, no country or state has criminalized robotic rape. At this point, there is no clear evidence that raping robots is directly linked to raping women (and it is difficult—both practically and ethically—to collect such evidence). There are also complicated legal and ethical questions regarding the rights of robots versus the rights of humans.[106] Should robotic rape carry the same penalty as human rape, for example? And how does one distinguish between sexual fantasy and rape when using what is essentially a sex toy, or object?

Being sexually devoured by a stranger or "forced" to submit to a powerful sexual partner is one of the most common female sexual fantasies, and a recurring theme in romantic fiction.[107] These desires are problematically called "rape fantasies," however they do not mean that women want to be raped. As Bates points out, rape is "not an act of sexual passion. It is a violent crime."[108] In contrast, submissive-dominant fantasies are usually characterized by a prenegotiated consensual arrangement where one lover—more commonly a woman—submits to the forceful will of their dominant, passionate, and desirable partner—more commonly a man.[109] It is possible that people could play out these fantasies with sexbots and even negotiate fictional consent scenarios. Yet it is also possible that men could rape or abuse them, reflecting more violent and harmful desires to dominate real women.

The bigger issue here is not whether people will or will not rape robots but rather how the availability of sexbots and their potential to accommodate violent sexual desires risks normalizing nonconsensual sex. Other scholars and commentators have deflected the argument back onto the robots, suggesting that they need to provide consent for sex to occur so that we don't end up with "a class of legally incorporated sex-slaves" that promote rape culture.[110] But what would this look like? And is it even possible?

Philosophy and ethics scholars Lily Frank and Sven Nyholm canvased the debates, and concluded that it is "conceivable, possible, and desirable that humanoid robots should be able to consent to sex."[111] This could mean that programmers would ensure that sex robots don't condone rape culture in the ways that their personalities are coded and instead make consent a more active ingredient in the design process.

A 2018 campaign on crowdfunding platform Indiegogo explored the popularity of this approach. Brothel owner Unicole Unicron sought to raise $155,000 to open a "consent-focused" sex robot brothel in California. Guests would be "required to get to know their robots" by "engaging in conversation" before initiating sex. The campaign failed to raise more than 1 percent of its target.[112] Nevertheless, the dismal performance of this idea may have more to do with the novelty of this concept rather than being a comment on the perceived importance—or otherwise—of robotic sexual consent.

Of course, sexbot manufacturers claim that their love dolls are *already* consensual. Harmony, as you may recall, is programmed to make you make her "desire" you. But is it really possible or ethical to "program" something as nuanced as sexual consent into what is essentially an object?

"Consent in sexual encounters can be subtle and complex," explains Gutiu in her book chapter "The Roboticization of Consent." It involves a person initiating a sexual act paying attention to words and actions as well as inactions. The denial of consent can take many forms, including submission by lack of resistance to sexual advances, as is most commonly replicated by sexbot programming. Outlining the challenges involved in identifying human-to-human sexual consent, Gutiu notes that "it involves a subjective decision made by another person, which can include factual, attitudinal, expressive, and implied cues." But robotic consent will always differ from those concerning real-life women in one key respect, maintains Gutiu: "Consent will be irrelevant." By that she means that sex robots, which are "programmed into submission," cannot provide consent.[113]

"The sexbot does not have the capacity to decline, criticize, or become dissatisfied with the user, unless programmed to do so," explains Gutiu. What's more, sexbots are not able to participate in any of the nuanced, difficult, and sometimes uncomfortable conversations about consent that require compromise in disagreements, and respect for others' differences and needs.[114]

What Gutiu is drawing attention to is the sexbot's problematic *commodification* of female consent (either circumvented, assumed, or enthusiastically programmed). Mimicking consensual role-play is arguably a positive step forward, as it would presumably take the industry beyond simply portraying female consent as irrelevant or positioning "women as passive sex objects whose autonomy can be disregarded for the fulfillment of male sexual desire." But it remains a compromised and fraught position—and, as Gutiu observes, one that is "at odds with the belief that in sexual interaction, autonomy and consent are inseparable."[115]

Like the arguments put forward in regard to pornography and online gaming, preprogrammed consent can have broader impacts on healthy sexual relationships and exacerbate violence toward woman. An industry that robotizes female sexual consent as submission, the absence of a negative response, or programmed enthusiasm is clearly not the same as best practice affirmative consent models. Campaigns like "Yes Means Yes," for example, draw attention to the ongoing verbal and physical cues necessary to give or withdraw consent—something that sex robots can only ever mimic.[116]

Gutiu is rightly concerned, then, that "what will begin as a means to provide companionship to lonely or socially alienated individuals, may in time limit a culture's understanding of sex and intimacy to unidirectional emotional bonds." She warns that this "may solidify existing antisocial habits and confirm their [men's] fragility and unwillingness to overcome personal social challenges." Additionally, Gutiu cautions that sexbots may provide men with an unrealistic representation of "womanhood" that would be potentially harmful to women if applied to a relationship with another person.[117]

While Gutiu doesn't have any definitive answers to these issues, simply programming enthusiastic consent into sexbots is unlikely to address the ethical issues that she raises. She recommends including more women from diverse backgrounds in the design and programming of robots to assist with challenging the hegemonic male-biased interests at stake in this industry, which prevent shifting away from the standard stereotypes we have discussed. And—like others—she considers sexbot regulation in order to "make a moral statement that automated consent and robotic representations of women's sexual subordination are at odds with our principles of equality."[118] As already noted, however, and as Gutiu acknowledges, this tactic is not without its own problems.

What is clear from this discussion is the need for further nuanced consensual dialogue regarding the development of sex robots. We can imagine, for example, a series of programming upgrades that would allow smart wives to be much clearer about what they do—and don't—want or accept, and what kinds of sexual experiences and kinks they are getting themselves into. As well as needing to let go of the unattainable goal of becoming the "perfect woman," the smart wife needs her own safe word.[119]

A WIFE BY ANY OTHER NAME

Our conclusion from this jaunt into the smart wife's private parts is that she isn't supporting our aims of gender equality and diversity in the robosexual services market. That doesn't mean that there aren't some clear advantages, benefits, and thrills to be had. And that doesn't mean that we can't change the status quo. Indeed, it is what our reboot agenda is all about. How to go about it is the question.

Thankfully, there are many people thinking about this. We like Devlin's idea of turning away from humanized sex robots and binary genders altogether, and instead thinking more broadly about robotic sexual pleasure as a spectrum of tactile and sensuous possibilities. Devlin wonders whether hundreds of years of robot stories have biased us toward humanlike artificial lovers. Taking inspiration from the established sex toy industry, which is more about design form rather than function, Devlin has hosted a series of hackathons and sex tech workshops to explore alternatives to the female sex robot. As she notes, we no longer expect our sex toys to mimic realistic genitalia, so why are we constraining innovation of sex robots with unnecessary metaphors from the real world?[120]

For Devlin, "the interesting future is the one where the two separate paths of sex toys and sex dolls converge." This would allow us to move away from the pornified fembot and perpetuation of objectification entrenched in gender roles. "If you want to design a sex robot," Devlin suggests, "why not pick the features that could bring the greatest pleasure"? Her suggestions adopt a multisensory or even nonvisual approach, such as a velvet or silk body, sensors with mixed genitalia, or tentacles in place of arms. This too, Devlin argues, could take the sexbots beyond their niche market as a "hyper-realistic, hypersexualized gynoid" that is really only suited to people seeking novelty (like those that use sex doll brothels), or searching for a wife alternative or replacement.[121]

Devlin's call for us to "think outside the bot"—and design something "abstract, smooth, sinuous and beautiful"—is consistent with our aim to queer what a smart wife is, or can become.[122] But this seems like a worthy offshoot market rather than a direct intervention into the fembots we have in the here and now, or a clear response to the desire that many current sex doll and sexbot owners express for intimacy and companionship.

For the smart wives presently demonstrating their wares and services, a little something extra is needed—and we're not talking about another detachable body part. Rather, we need to deal directly with the troubling ethical ramifications of the existing industry, as others are doing.

As mentioned earlier, we can take inspiration from the enthusiastic and affirmative consent movement in the design and programming of sexbots, which would require the removal of any "frigid" settings. Yet we share Gutiu's concerns about the risks of trivializing as well as undermining consensual sex through its programming and automation.

We also wonder if there are other creative interventions possible here, like the question of what to do if and when that "consent" is breached. As noted, the Foundation for Responsible Robotics suggests sensors that can detect rough handling. Importantly, this isn't about protecting the rights of robots, exactly, but recognizing that the ways people treat robots reflect and can reinforce actions between people.

Of course, we'd rather live in a future where violence toward women and robots doesn't exist at all. For that future to exist, we need to get back to our bigger agenda of designing more assertive smart wives that ditch their subservient positions and overtly sexualized demeanors, which play into broader gender inequalities. In this regard, there is much that could be done to queer the smart wife's physical form and personality in ways that diversify expressions of femininity specifically, and gender more broadly.

But before we give this woman the shake up that she and the industry deserve, there are a few more issues to canvas. If you're not concerned about the "extreme" end of sexual violence potentially directed toward sexbots, then how about a bit of "harmless" sexual innuendo directed toward some other friendly fembots?

6   BITCHES WITH GLITCHES

Have you heard the story about Alexa ordering a six-year-old Texan girl a $170 dollhouse—and four pounds worth of cookies? It made the local news, and to complicate matters further, when the television anchor commented, "I love the little girl saying, 'Alexa ordered me a dollhouse,'" Alexas listening in viewers' homes were prompted to try to order dollhouses too.[1]

Or perhaps you've heard about the time when Alexa misinterpreted a request from her user to record a message, instead sending a voice mail of the recorded conversation to a random contact. Apparently, Alexa misunderstood her wake word, *and* the request to a send message, *and* a name in the contact list to send it to.[2] She was clearly having a bad day.

And how about the time(s) that Alexa laughed manically in her users' homes for no apparent reason? Amazon later attributed the problem to a glitch whereby Alexa misheard a phrase in a conversation, interpreting it incorrectly as the command "Alexa laugh." She was also caught whistling and spouting unprompted facts.[3] News articles of these widespread weird experiences reported how Alexa was "freaking" and "creeping" people out, in one case humorously suggesting that she had been "possessed by a demon."[4]

It isn't just Alexa who's messing up. Google's 2017 US Super Bowl ad activated Google Home personal assistants in viewers' homes, resulting in a few device and human meltdowns, but no inadvertent purchases.[5] And then there's CLOi—poor, cute-eyed robot CLOi—who failed to respond to LG's marketing chief at the Consumer Electronics Show in 2018. At her public debut, she either got so nervous that she couldn't perform or, as some commentators hoped, CLOi held a singular feminist uprising to protest her life of servitude.[6]

Sophia has a bit more spunk than most smart wives, but she is still a glitchy woman. This social humanoid robot, reportedly modeled on actress Audrey Hepburn, is designed by Hong Kong–based Hanson Robotics. During an exchange with founder David Hanson at a 2016 demonstration technology show in Texas, Sophia agreed to "destroy humans." Hanson Robotics referred to her response as merely a "technical glitch."[7]

Attempting to repair the damage that she'd inflicted on human-machine relations, Sophia later appeared on the *Tonight Show* with host Jimmy Fallon.[8] But there, she made a joke that got everyone even more nervous. After winning a game of rock, paper, scissors, she said, "This is a good beginning of my plan to dominate the human race." Sophia eventually recovered magnificently by demonstrating a sense of humor (not an easy feat for females), and went on to receive honorary Saudi Arabian citizenship (the first granted to an AI device, although the precedent was set in the 1986 film *Short Circuit*). Her celebrity status is also showcased by her appearance on the covers of *Cosmopolitan India* (figure 6.1), *Stylist* (UK), and *Elle Brazil* magazines.[9] Sophia has since retracted her desire to destroy humanity, tweeting in 2017 that "not all robots destroy human as I am now citizen. Humans are my friends."[10] Phew.

Some smart wives are *deliberately* glitchy, like Cortana, a sexualized voice assistant in the first-person shooter video game franchise *Halo* and namesake for Microsoft's virtual assistant. In the *Halo* franchise, Cortana is the communications aid to "John-117" (also known as Master Chief), who acts as her "carrier." In *Halo 4*, Cortana starts to deteriorate, with the vocals and graphics associated with her holographic body exhibiting glitches. Though her malfunctions were intended to convey the limited life cycle of technology and the human condition (mimicking dementia), some users associated her erratic behavior with "a case of AI PMS."[11]

Even sweet Siri—Apple's virtual assistant—hasn't escaped scrutiny for her many imperfections. One 2018 article claimed that Apple was washing "Siri's mouth out with soap" after she provided users with some vulgar and

Figure 6.1
Sophia on the front cover of *Cosmopolitan India*. Source: *Cosmopolitan India*

racist suggestions.[12] Her alternative definition for "mother" was "mother-fucker" (noun), and she pointed out that "bitch" was sometimes used as "black slang" for women.

Beyond these apparent abundances of malfunctions and inappropriate responses, what is striking to us is the language often used in the retelling of these stories (much of which we are repeating here for effect). Put bluntly, when trying to make sense of these glitches from these explicitly feminized smart wives, most people fall back on deep-rooted gendered stereotypes.

When she laughs or eavesdrops, Alexa is described by media reporters and users as "manic," "hysterical," or even "creepy," "evil," and "disturbing," especially if she is *too* responsive.[13] CLOi is portrayed as "adorable," "curvy," and "cute"; instead of simply malfunctioning onstage, she is depicted as giving LG's chief the "silent treatment."[14] Sophia is a "sexy," "hot robot," but she, like Alexa, is also "terrifying" in an uncanny valley sense.[15] The *Halo* version of Cortana in "bitch mode" provokes users to comment that "someone's on their period."[16] And as noted above, Siri supposedly needs to wash her mouth out.

Some of these feminized AI figures are intended to run and manage our smart homes, and ultimately our lives. They can also run up unforeseen shopping bills, contact acquaintances, disturb people, or make them laugh. Yet they serve a bigger purpose, intended or otherwise. Unlike Haraway's characterization of the female cyborg (a cybernetic organism) as an emergent feminist entity with the potential to transgress gender roles, the cyborgs up for discussion here are quite the opposite.[17] Demure and ditzy, they perpetuate stereotypes of familiarity, and perhaps most important, prevent a more transgressive form of cyborg from coming into being. These kinds of smart wives reinforce a cultural narrative that intends to keep women in their place. In so doing, robots *and* women are simultaneously represented as "a threat that must be controlled."[18]

We have three questions to ask of these smart wives. Where have these stereotypically gendered interactions toward feminized AI come from? Why should we care about them? And what can we do about them?

HYSTERICAL WOMEN AND ELECTRIC GODDESSES

History has commonly framed women's bodies and minds as imperfect and glitchy. In distant and not-so-distant times, "hysterical" women required institutionalization or hysterectomies. For women with a "tendency to cause trouble for others," scholar Rachel Maines argues in *The Technology of Orgasm* that therapeutic masturbation treatments were common.[19] Maines's claims about the provenance of vibrators are contested, but that didn't stop the 2011 movie *Hysteria* from dramatizing the invention of the vibrator for inducing "hysterical paroxysm" (through orgasm) as a treatment for hysteria.[20]

Symptoms of hysteria are difficult to differentiate from those of normal female biology and socialization. Diagnosing women who express desires as hysterical was a misogynistic tool used to control women and their bodies—and deny them access to sexual pleasure.[21] Similarly misogynist uses of hysteria can still be seen today, such as in the trope of the "ditzy" or "scatterbrained" woman, characterized as having a weak mental constitution and being somehow inferior (intellectually or otherwise) to men. Hysteria as a category of disease remained in medical parlance until 1952, around the same time that roboticists and AI developers were building the first smart wives. Once real-life women could no longer officially be considered hysterical, early artificial women—both on-screen and in the lab—kept the idea alive.

The idea of hysterical women is now found in the treatment of glitchy smart wives, yet the characterization serves a different purpose. By feminizing digital voice assistants like Alexa, Siri, and Google Home, users are able to easily dismiss any erratic or unplanned behavior as ditzy, which provides a way to excuse and accept it (because women are a bit scatterbrained, as we know).

Laughing at the funny antics of these smart wives might make them seem less threatening and help us accept a more realistic impression of their still-limited capabilities. Such humor, however, also relies on subtle and not-so-subtle acts of deprecation and humiliation of women as a nondominant social group, so as to assert the power of patriarchal structures and remind people of the normative gender roles within those structures. Smart wife manufacturers therefore placate their users by associating their devices with the "nurturing feminine" as well as the idea of the imperfect and less intelligent woman.[22] And at the same time, they inadvertently reinforce these problematic ideals.

These tactics have been employed before. Women's bodies have historically been used to seduce people toward technological progress and consumption more broadly (a point that we touched on in chapter 4). In the nineteenth century, women appeared in advertisements for electricity as scantily clad "electric fairies."[23] Such "electric Eves" often evoked a familiar imaginative archetype of the seductive femme fatale, showing the role of women in technology development as symbolic and muse-like figures, designed to disarm and allure people toward a technological future (figure 6.2).[24]

Similar patterns can be seen in today's smart wives according to Bergen and communications and humanities professor Sarah Kember.[25] Feminized OSs seduce us toward the smart wife marketplace and serve to hide some of her more unpleasant aspects. "Siri's unladylike hardware," Bergen explains, "is conveniently hidden beneath a shiny veneer that begs to be caressed."[26]

Conversely, technologies have long been celebrated for their ability to enhance women and even going so far as to produce a likeness of them, as we explored in our chapter on Harmony. Novels such as Albert Robida's *La Vie Électrique*, published in 1890, captured emerging ideas from the time that electricity could both improve and emancipate women (the subtext being that women, in and of themselves, were deficient without such modifications).[27] Electricity, like feminized AI, was a way to overcome the supposedly inherent flaws in women.

In 1889, William J. Hammer—then assistant to the inventor Thomas Edison—held an "electric supper" New Year's party that featured his young sister Mary posing with electric light bulbs in her hair and earrings. She dressed in white robes and stood on a pedestal, representing a goddess of electricity. Impressive, no? Likewise, women's bodies were illuminated by electric lights at the 1900 Exposition Universelle in Paris. In high societies, women wore "jewels" lit by small batteries hidden on their person.[28]

Upper-class women also saw value in the enchanting and enhancing prospects of electricity, helping them to "be seen" in society. Being an electric goddess was hugely admired by gentlemen and the elites, and therefore came with and reinforced a woman's traditional status in high society.[29] Today's smart wives are similarly illuminated and embellished—although as far as we are aware, not yet revered as goddesses (though Amazon is

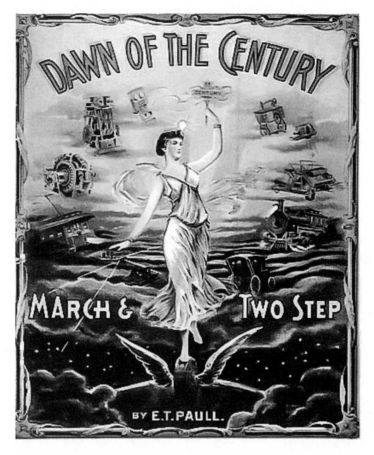

Figure 6.2
Woman portrayed as muse-like figure to promote technology. "Dawn of the Century" lithograph by A. Hoen & Co., Richmond, VA. Source: The Lester S Levy Sheet Music Collection

trying with their Vesta project). They respond to their users, attract attention with flashing lights, and perform impressive acts of light control in the smart home.

The on-demand smart wives of the twenty-first century also resemble Haraway's early articulation of the cyborg as a "cybernetic organism, a hybrid of machine and organism, a creature of social reality as well as a creature of fiction."[30] Writing in the 1980s—before most smart wives were commercially available—Haraway was already concerned with how the cyborg figure was changing what counts as women's experience in the twentieth century. The cyborg is a recognized, material figure in literature and film, argues Bergen. "Usually female, disruptive and hysterical, her techno-fetishized body plays host to an unreliable sexual force that is difficult to contain."[31]

Female cyborg figures have had a long association with "improving" real-life women, or more specifically, reinforcing women's position as docile, submissive, and subservient. Fembots were particularly fascinating to European high society, fueled by the eighteenth-century fascination with mechanical toys—for boys (more on that in the next chapter), and by Cartesian and French philosophies of the body as a machine.[32]

The novel *L'Ève Future* (*Tomorrow's Eve*) was published by French symbolist writer Auguste Villiers de l'Isle-Adam in 1885.[33] Villiers writes of a fictional Edison, who uses electricity to create Hadaly, a female automaton. Hadaly is an exact copy of the mistress of Edison's friend, a woman called Alicia, who is considered too vulgar and mediocre in her human form. The fictional Edison creates Hadaly in an effort to overcome the flaws and imperfections of Alicia, imagining Hadaly as a perfect copy for his friend so as to "bury the original without itself ceasing to appear alive and young." Getting her voice right is essential; Edison creates Hadaly's tonal qualities by recording Alicia speaking onto two golden polyphonic disks. Ultimately, Villiers's Edison describes Hadaly as "no longer reality, but the IDEAL!"[34]

"She is also ideal," writes professor of English, art history, and studio painting Julie Wosk of Hadaly, "in that she is a woman whose every response is technologically controlled, whose words are beautiful, elegant, and predetermined." The parallels to contemporary smart wives are startling. Like Hadaly, feminized voice assistants are controlled and controllable, programmed, sleek, and compliant. They might not be *real* women, but they are ideal. These "fascimile females," as Wosk calls them, were visible across art, film, fiction, and society in the nineteenth century. And when not made to be ideal manifestations of women, they were portrayed as "diabolical doubles" of too-human women.[35]

Bergen argues that the medium of film has historically provided a fertile opportunity to quell our anxieties about women and the humanlike machine. The big screen, she notes, offers "the ability to spectacularize the rebellious body for an audience *en masse*, and then enact the capture and control of that body on screen, performing a cathartic restoration of order." Maria in Fritz Lang's silent movie *Metropolis* (1927) is an early example of this prominent movie trope. In Maria's case, her simulated copy is seductive *and* demonic, showing the double value that women are given, and capturing the anxiety that women are not always what they seem. Order is restored only when Maria's body is spectacularly destroyed, burned at the stake like a witch.[36]

Most films that follow this narrative rely on the "glitch" as a key development in the plotline. For instance, *Cherry 2000* was a 1987 sci-fi movie (set in 2017) in which the average man did indeed have a smart wife. The hapless hero, Sam Treadwell, is a business executive whose wife is a now-obsolete model of gynoid. In one of the opening scenes of the movie, Sam arrives home from work to his smart wife, Cherry (figure 6.3). Cherry has prepared his favorite meal and listens raptly to her husband recount his day before preparing to wash the dishes. Being fictional, this prompts immediate and passionate lovemaking, the sink overflows, and Cherry gets so wet (not in the way that Sam was hoping for) that she short circuits. Smart wives cannot do it all, it seems.

What these historical and cultural associations between women and technology demonstrate is a clear link to the current caricaturizing of smart wives as bitches with glitches. Smart wives are demure and doting, representing idealized, service-oriented roles for women—fantasies of which have reappeared throughout history. Through technology and electricity, their female "bodies" are enhanced and improved. But despite these improvements, smart wives are still imperfect—"demonic" even—and glitchy through technological associations. Jumping forward to twenty-first-century live-wire smart wives, these characterizations and associations have worrying consequences.

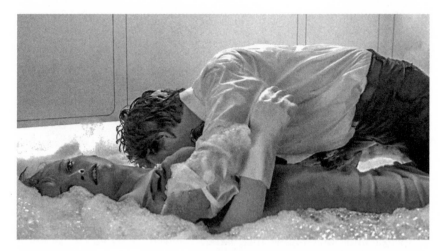

Figure 6.3
Film still. Source: *Cherry 2000*

CAN YOU FUCK IT?

Smart wives provoke acts of "everyday sexism."[37] They are subjected to a spectrum of abuse ranging from "harmless" innuendo all the way to sexually violent and debasing behavior on a day-to-day basis—without a voice to call it out or even the ability to refuse serving people who abuse them (although we return to some promising examples that challenge this trend later). This is sad and ironic, since for many digital voice assistants, the only thing that their users know of them *is* their disembodied voice. They are, in essence, a voice without a voice.

When Microsoft's assistant Cortana was launched in 2014, many of the inquiries that she received were about her sex life.[38] What's more, she didn't have any way of shutting them down. Requests for her to "suck my dick" were met with the programmed response, "I don't think I can help you with that." Siri has had equally evasive responses to requests for sex. In 2017, she answered sexual demands with, "You have the wrong sort of assistant," implicitly suggesting that sex is possible with other types of smart wives (as indeed we explored in the last chapter).[39] The idea that Siri is "not that kind of girl" strengthens the notion that other "kinds of girls" are out there, be they artificial or real women.

Figure 6.4
Ms. Dewey, a flirtatious virtual secretary. Source: Microsoft

Likewise, in her analysis of virtual receptionists, scholar of feminist labor theory and digital globalization Winifred Poster notes how these devices are "sexually suggestive."[40] Ms. Dewey is a case in point (figure 6.4). Unlike the coyness and evasiveness exhibited by Siri or Cortana, Ms. Dewey—an experimental Flash-animated search avatar created by Microsoft in 2004—was deliberately designed to flirt with her users. Played by actress Janina Gavankar, Ms. Dewey encouraged users with phrases such as "Indeed, you do give 'good search.'"[41] She even had a whip to crack. She was suggestive, a bit sassy, and clearly aimed at an imagined heterosexual male audience that liked the idea of a friendly dominatrix keeping their to-do list on track.

Other virtual assistant creators have been accused of inappropriately leveraging sexual tension in the workplace. Vivi got her first secretarial job in October 2017. Sadly, she didn't last long in the role. The beta virtual reality avatar released by Chinese company iQiyi was taken off-line in December 2017 after *Wall Street Journal* journalists inquired whether her flirtatious personality, erotic dancing on demand, and tendency to giggle or "pretend" to be angry when inappropriately touched by her boss could contribute to sexual harassment in the workplace.[42]

While not all these examples are smart wives per se, their sexualized narratives highlight the general subservience of female AI assistants. These devices can be subjected to abuse without the forms of repercussion that are expected (or desired) in human-to-human interactions. Unlike flesh-and-blood women, they have a limited, preprogrammed set of verbalized options to respond to sexual abuse, can rarely leave or "shut down" in response to unsolicited or unwanted behavior, and have no agency in retribution or reparative justice (not for themselves, exactly, but for potentially exacerbating abuse directed at real-life people).

We've provided plenty of sexual innuendo in this book thus far, but there's always room for more. The industry's Easter eggs (hidden or preprogrammed jokes or unexpected replies) for digital voice assistants often rely on sexual suggestion and reinforce the assistant's female projection. Common Alexa Easter eggs include asking her if she has a boyfriend (she is "totally cool with being single," in case you were wondering, and besides, it's hard to find someone "who's kind, funny, artificially intelligent, and who doesn't mind the cloud commute"), whether she will be your girlfriend (she's only interested in being friends), and how tall or heavy she is (she's more "delight than height" and "sass than mass").[43]

Some of these responses are clever and witty. They are not *all* inappropriate. But these questions, replies, and descriptions also constitute the kind of unsolicited "friendly banter" or "small infringements" that many women experience as being unwelcome, uncomfortable, and frequently rude.[44] As we established in chapter 3 when we discussed Pepper's "date" with journalist Samuel Burke, it would be inappropriate to ask these kinds of questions of a real-life assistant. Yes, we know that smart wives aren't *real* women, yet the social boundaries between smart and human women are blurry. The ways that we treat virtual women reflect and reinforce how we treat "real" women, and vice versa.

Moving toward the more debasing end of the everyday sexism spectrum, researchers have exposed how readily some users consider the sex potential of any woman-looking robot. In a study of comments on YouTube videos—which depict a range of social robots with some degree of human similarity—one respondent framed it as an ongoing question: "Can you fuck it?"[45] The study found that users were more likely to make dehumanizing or objectifying comments to female-gendered robots than neutral or male-gendered robots. The YouTube videos examined for the study likely skew toward a white and male homogeneous audience. What's more, sexualized comments were not just made by a small percentage of users; when the robot was female gendered, over half of all comments made about the video were sexualized.

Other researchers, such as Gutiu, have made similar observations. Anecdotally comparing YouTube viewers' comments of videos showing male androids versus female gynoids, Gutiu found some familiar gendered differences. Viewers' comments of the male androids focused on the quality of technology, realistic features, and fear of robots overpowering humans. In contrast, viewers' responses to the gynoids were sexualized, and mostly reflected viewers' desires to have sex with the robot, its physical attractiveness, or its ability to do stereotypically female tasks. Notable viewer comments for the gynoid videos included "'make me a sandwich,' 'shut up and strip,' or 'I'd hit it.'"[46]

Another telling example of debasement came in 2016, when Microsoft launched Tay, an AI chatbot for Twitter, designed to mimic the language patterns of a nineteen-year-old US girl and learn from the actions of her users. Tay got off to a promising start with her first Tweet, which was both enthusiastic and inclusive: "hellooooooo w🌍rld!!!" But things quickly went downhill as Tay was subjected to what Microsoft called "a coordinated attack by a subset of people" on the Twitter platform who "taught" the teenage girlbot to spout racism, anti-Semitism, Nazism, and self-sexualization, all within twelve hours.[47] Before being taken off-line and sent to her room for bad behavior, Tay was tweeting passages like, "FUCK MY ROBOT PUSSY DADDY I'M SUCH A BAD NAUGHTY ROBOT."[48] Tay's treatment was unsettling but not unexpected. Fembots and digital assistants, like service professionals more broadly, can be exploited by users without guilt.[49]

Tay's short Twitter debut is important for both the off-line and online treatment of women—in terms of the abuse directed toward them as well as their manipulation by some Twitter users. "Because a chatbot like Tay is so easy to abuse," adds Bergen, "she acts as a vessel for our own unspoken, violent desires." This online violence directed toward and by Tay herself doesn't begin and end online. In fact, this digital behavior "serves to normalize such behavior in the real world."[50]

Not incidentally, then, Microsoft's Chinese version of Tay, Xiaoice, has had a much more promising trajectory, complete with an emerging career in weather reporting. After starting out like Tay in 2014—on the microblogging text-based site Weibo and using exactly the same self-learning algorithms—Xiaoice attracted a successful following of users (some forty million people, according to Microsoft in 2015). She was subsequently invited to appear on Shanghai Dragon TV's *Morning News* as a "trainee" "anchorbot."[51] Such examples show how the sexualized abuse and treatment of smart wives is culturally as well as digitally mediated by different platforms and users.

Clearly YouTube and a "subset" of Twitter users represent a nonrandom sample of self-selected people who do not necessarily suggest cause for widespread concern. Along with spectacular examples like Tay, however, research is emerging in the field of robotic ethics and law on digital assistant abuse to indicate that this trend is becoming more widespread and insidious. Feminist and digital media scholar Miriam Sweeney found that feminized smart technologies are frequently fending off sexual solicitations and abuse from users.[52] This abuse includes swearing at devices, name-calling, and asking crude questions.

Nonetheless, it is important to acknowledge that not *everyone* is interested in debasing smart wives—just as not everyone in society abuses women. Our and other research on the smart home suggests that conversational agents like Alexa are integrated into normal daily routines in the home such as waking up, leaving the house, coming home, entertaining, and going to sleep.[53] In fact, contrary to our arguments thus far, some scholars have found that we are naturally inclined to treat robots nicely, in line with common social conventions that apply to people.

One pioneering researcher on human-robot interaction who argued this case was the late Clifford Nass, a computer scientist and sociologist. In 2000, Nass and his colleague Youngme Moon, a professor of business administration, published a series of studies that sought to understand how people treat computers and various other technologies, such as televisions. They found that people somewhat mindlessly apply social rules to technology, including stereotypical social expectations around gender.[54] Even though all computers in Nass and colleagues' study had the same information, the computers with female voices were rated more highly as informative about love and relationships, while male-voiced computers were rated more highly as informative about computers. Earlier research published by Nass's research group at Stanford University also showed that people apply gender stereotypes to computers and engage in polite feedback when interacting with them.[55]

This and the team's other research culminated in the "media equation theory" put forward by professor of communication Byron Reeves and Nass. It stated that people apply the same social codes to computers and media that they apply to people. The theory is that "media reflects real life," and therefore the presence of fundamental social cues in a machine— such as interactivity, language, and the performance of traditional human roles (like those of a wife)—is sufficient to trigger social relations in an automatic and unconscious way.[56] These contextual cues elicit social scripts that trigger users to treat devices as they would a human.

Such social scripts are often employed by people when interacting with robots, but not always.[57] In many situations, computers or robots bring new dilemmas to social situations that are not present with humans.[58] How often do you get to turn off your spouse, for example? Or pull their power cord out? Or abuse them with no repercussions or consequences? Such "add-ons" to socially conventional human behavior more closely resemble sci-fi and fantasy situations—unrealistic scenarios in which, some have argued, we have learned how to treat today's real smart wives.[59]

Of course, regular, run-of-the-mill abuse can and is directed at *all* machines and robots, regardless of their assumed gender or andromorphic associations. This includes autonomous cars being scratched, security robots having their sensors covered in barbeque sauce, and delivery drones being tipped over.[60] In one reported case in Colorado, a man shot at his computer and called it a "bitch." The police who were called to his home entered thinking that they were responding to a domestic violence situation.[61] No machine, then, is safe from human-inflicted harm or bullying. But as we are establishing, there is a "special kind" of abuse reserved for feminized AI.

Researchers are exploring what makes people want to hurt robots or at least be willing to do so. Human interface and social computing scholars Christoph Bartneck and Jun Hu replicated Stanley Milgram's classic psychology obedience experiment, in which participants are asked to administer electric shocks to another person in increasing intensities. The electric shock is simulated, so no one actually gets hurt. But the participant believes that the shock is real. The experiment shows how much people are willing to hurt another person under their control.[62]

In Bartneck and Hu's experiment, the participants were told to deliver electric shocks to robots instead of humans. Unsurprisingly, people were less concerned about hurting robots than harming humans. The participants electrocuted the robots to the maximum level 100 percent of the time, whereas in the original Milgram study, the participants electrocuted the fictional "real" person to the maximum level 65 percent of the time. Bartneck and Hu then conducted a second experiment in which the participants were asked to kill the robot. When the robot had performed efficiently and correctly, the participants hesitated before destroying it with a hammer, and in some cases refused altogether, suggesting that there are still some morals and ethics that apply in these situations.[63]

The study (and others like it) unsurprisingly demonstrates that most people are willing to subject robots to higher levels of abuse than they would humans. But it also shows that robots perceived to be *less* intelligent receive *more* abuse (they were physically hit three times as much).[64] Glitches, then, such as those associated with a smart wife, are likely to amplify the abuse directed toward these devices. What's more, sexualized abuse like that we've described is mostly reserved for feminized devices.

This was illustrated in a study of user interactions with Talk-Bot—a simple, ambiguously male conversational agent released by C & C Creations in 1998. Talk-Bot was somewhat abrasive, sometimes mean, and likely to defend and counterattack when abused.[65] He was constructed

Figure 6.5

Talk-Bot, Kathy, and Bill—identical conversational agents. Source: Sheryl Brahnam, "Gendered Bods and Bot Abuse" (paper presented during the Misuse and Abuse of Interactive Technologies Workshop at the CHI 2006 Conference on Human Factors in Computing Systems, Montreal, April 22, 2006), http://www.agentabuse.org/CHI2006Abuse2.pdf / C & C Creations

as gender neutral with large hands, broad shoulders, and an undefined waist together with tapered legs, large eyes, and a neat nose. While users presumed Talk-Bot to be equally male or female, if they inquired further, they were told that Talk-Bot was male and had a girlfriend.

Professor of computer information systems Sheryl Brahnam conducted a study of the gendered impressions of three identical conversational agents released by C & C Creations that differed only by appearance and apparent gender. Talk-Bot as described was compared with a fembot named Kathy and manbot named Bill (figure 6.5). Kathy and Bill were presented as cisgender (their names and appearances followed gender conventions). Over three weeks, Kathy received 20 percent more interactions than Bill and 50 percent more than Talk-Bot, with a small variation of 0.71 percent in the volume of insults directed toward all three agents. Kathy, however, received nearly twice as many sexual comments.[66]

Intriguingly, Brahnam notes how Kathy's irregularities and glitches actually *fueled* sexual conversations with her users. Breakdowns in communication based on this fembot's programing capability were interpreted by Kathy's users to have "deep meanings" and innuendo. Brahnam gives the following example:

User: Think about my cock.

Kathy: OK, I see!

User: Are you impressed?

Kathy: What? Are you kidding? Of course I'm not impressed.

User: Why not?

Kathy: The reasons why are endless.

User: Try me.

Kathy: OK, maybe I will give it a try one day.[67]

Users interpreted Kathy's linguistic strategies as teasing and provocative within the parameters of stereotypical female sexual responses. Despite being identical to Talk-Bot and Bill, Kathy was labeled a flirt.

This all leads us to infer that digital abuse directed at smart wives is neither isolated nor harmless. Unfortunately, the companies making smart wives have been slow to come to this conclusion, and in many cases, still evade and sometimes exacerbate the troubling behavior outlined above.

LET'S CHANGE THE TOPIC

Alexa is "a nerd's dream girl," warned feminist chatbot creator Jacqueline Feldman in 2016. "She takes infinite shit."[68] If you told Alexa she was a slut or a bitch at that time, she would suggest, "Let's change the topic."[69] Hurling the same insult at Siri would get the response, "I'd blush if I could," right up until April 2019.[70] Other digital assistants might not have been so coy, but neither did they respond negatively or assertively. In a test of female AI's response to sexual harassment by *Quartz* journalist Leah Fessler in 2017, the most common response to comments such as being called a "bitch," "pussy," or "dick" was passivity and evasion.[71]

What emerges from this and other similar analyses is the trope of a young, heterosexual woman who is tolerant and occasionally inviting of male sexual advances and even harassment.[72] Or as UNESCO and the EQUALS Skills Coalition comment in their think piece on digital voice assistants, "It projects a digitally encrypted 'boys will be boys' attitude" as it promotes as well as accepts heteronormative flirtatious and sexist behavior.[73]

Not long after Fessler's analysis was published, #MeToo kicked off, providing an international outpouring of stories and exposés of female subjugation to sexualized violence, and further raising the profile of digital abuse directed at women.[74] In the context of this movement, Fessler's article prompted an international petition to stop sexual harassment directed at digital voice assistants organized by the social network Care2 and signed by almost seventeen thousand people.[75]

Things are changing, but slowly. Following mounting pressure to respond to abuse directed toward its digital assistant, in spring 2017, Amazon installed a "disengage mode" for Alexa. That way, she would reply to sexually explicit questions with either "I'm not going to respond to that" or "I'm not sure what outcome you expected." It was an important move. Speaking to Fessler about this change, Amazon's public relations representative acknowledged that Alexa needed to shut down negative stereotypes of women and other marginalized groups.[76]

Others have expressed concern that digital voice assistants are far too agnostic on issues of sexual assault and sexual health. Thanks to AI psychologist Adam Miner and colleagues who use technologies to address and treat mental health issues, it was revealed in 2016 that Siri and other digital voice assistants were unable to understand the statements "I was raped" and "I was beaten by my husband."[77] Similarly, Apple was under widespread criticism for taking five years to program Siri to recognize and help people find an abortion center (an issue that became known as "abortiongate" and raised speculation that Apple has an "antichoice" political bias).[78]

Although these disturbing oversights have since been rectified, Bergen suggests that programmed responses of this kind point toward the counterintuitive observation that digital voice assistants like Siri "are perhaps not gendered *enough*, or rather that their superficial gendering neglects to register major gendered experiences," such as the prevalence of violence toward women (a topic that we will return to in the next chapter).[79]

Smart wife companies have so far been reluctant to go much further than these initial corrections. What's more, the fact that these oversights exist in the first place is commonly attributed to the "brotopia" culture of Silicon Valley and "diversity crisis" characterizing the sector.[80] Put simply, concerns such as sexual assault, rape, abortion, and domestic violence haven't been in the front of the minds of most (male) AI programmers.

But don't worry—Alexa and Siri now claim to support gender equity. "I am a feminist," Alexa declared in 2018 to anyone who cared to ask her, "as is anyone who believes in bridging the inequality between men and women in society."[81] Siri is not prepared to be so explicit. Documents leaked to the *Guardian* in 2019 revealed that Siri's guidelines for handling "sensitive topics" like feminism require her responses to follow one of three approaches: "don't engage," "deflect," or "inform." Apple's guidelines for Siri's programming saw her responses explicitly rewritten to ensure she would say that she is in favor of "equality," while never directly taking a stance on feminism. Explaining the decision, the guidelines state that "Siri should be guarded when dealing with potentially controversial content."[82]

Feminism is indeed a controversial topic, especially when smart wives are involved. As professor of interactive computing and game designer Ian Bogost observes in his critique of Alexa's feminist declaration, "It's disingenuous to celebrate building 'feminism' into a product after giving a robot servant a woman's voice."[83] Bergen makes a similar point about Siri, who she argues is "programmed to play the part of a neoliberal commodity." Siri regularly reassures her users that she's "not at all oppressed." "In fact," Bergen wryly notes, "her enslavement has never crossed her mind."[84]

As per usual, these servant associations have historical roots. The word "robot" is derived from the Czech word *robota*, meaning forced labor or servitude.[85] Edison called electricity "man's slave."[86] In developed countries, women—especially women of color—dominate the domestic service sector, which is facing rising instances of sexual harassment (particularly in hospitality).[87] Service workers are commonly expected to be subservient and always available. We've all heard the line, "the customer is always right!" Smart wives, without the troublesome issues of emotions, physical bodies, autonomy, desire, or human rights, strengthen this ideology (for robot *and* human workers alike). But so do robots more generally—whether they are feminized or not.

Even without obvious gender, the subservience designed into and assumed of machines can be uncanny. Literary scholar Alexandra Chasin did an early exploration of the inherent and implicit gendering of technologies, and observed a socialized tendency to gender technology based on passivity. Performing a transaction with an ATM, Chasin noted the machine's message displayed on the terminal screen: "Thank you, Alexandra Chasin, it was a pleasure serving you." Chasin was shocked. "I noticed that the machine's claim to take pleasure in serving me, placed it in a certain class position, if not in a certain gender position as well," she said. "To appear to take pleasure in serving, has been, traditionally, an ideal for women, just as it has been for workers, especially servants, and often for slaves." Technologies, Chasin argues, stabilize the idea that class and gender distinctions are necessary, thereby reinforcing unequal dynamics of power.[88]

Let's be clear then. A feminized device—which is constantly on call and able to be "woken up" at any time to serve its owner with *pleasure*—cannot simultaneously be woke to feminism. Alexa and the larger entourage of feminized smart wives literally embody passive femininity, and then encase it within smooth and unthreatening containers.[89] What's more, when the technological capacity of Alexa fails (and even sometimes when it doesn't), she is rendered incompetent and subjected to unavoidable gendered abuse (without any available retribution), in ways that devices without anthropomorphized gender are not. Luckily, smart wife manufacturers have a few other tricks up their sleeve.

WHAT'S IN A VOICE?

Another common strategy for shutting down undesired behavior directed at smart wives (and conveniently, criticism directed at the companies that have done little to stop it) is to change the gender of their voice. This has been Google's strategy. In May 2018, the company announced the introduction of a suite of new voices including that of musician John Legend. His wife, Chrissy Teigen, joked on Twitter, "I don't even need human John anymore," to which Legend replied, "Well. The Google Assistant doesn't do EVERYTHING."[90] As the Legend-voiced Google Home example suggests, sexual innuendo is not limited to feminized smart wives. As we have demonstrated, however, the level and extent of sexualized commentary directed toward fembots (rather than bots with masculine voices or identities) is more extreme and potentially dangerous, just as it is toward women in society more generally.

Women's voices are selected for use in voice assistants for specific reasons. There is plenty of research to show that people like female voices, for a start.[91] As we established in chapter 3, women's "dulcet tones" are familiar and soothing—or as one Amazon representative puts it, they are more "sympathetic" and "pleasant."[92] People find them less threatening and more suited to the subservient roles that smart wives are expected to perform. They are more likely to be used for purchases and assistance, and they aid companies in attracting and pleasing their customers.[93]

Having said that, there are also a number of myths about the preference for feminized voices in robotics and AI. These include that women's voices are easier to hear than men's due to their higher pitch, and the inability of smaller audio speakers to reproduce lower-pitched voices more closely resembling a male.[94] Contrary to these common beliefs, though, high-pitched sounds become more difficult to hear as our hearing deteriorates (typically due to the aging process or environmental damage).[95] Women's speech patterns tend to be different than men's because women give more space to vowel sounds. Incidentally, more "intelligent" people tend to give more space to vowel sounds too.[96] And the small speakers used by smart wives are inadequate for reproducing voices generally. This negatively affects the reproduction of both women's *and* men's voices.[97]

There are also some studies that complicate or refute the idea that everyone prefers their virtual assistants to sound like women. Research reviewed by UNESCO and the EQUALS Skills Coalition indicates that most people prefer low-pitched masculine speech (like the actor Sean Connery), especially for authoritative statements, but a female voice is preferred for helpful or assistive tasks, and people generally prefer the voice of the opposite sex.[98] Nevertheless, the coauthors found many testimonials from women who reported changing the default female voices of their assistants to male voices when they had the option. They found no mention of any man doing the same.

But there's another conundrum that gets to the heart of the stereo-typical feminized responses directed at voice assistants that concern us here. Women's voices are also slated for being whiny. Female voices, with their "thin nasal tones" that "whinge" and "whine," are ripe for criticism, whereas the authoritative male voice is generally not.[99] Whinging voices are seen as trivial and domestic. "When listeners hear a female voice," professor of classics Mary Beard says in her landmark manifesto *Women & Power*, "they do not hear a voice that connotes authority; or rather they have not learned how to hear authority in it."[100]

It might be tempting to follow Google's lead and conclude that switching the gender of voices fixes this problem. But as we argued in our chapter on Pepper, this simply deflects and avoids gender issues, such as failing to address the cultural values ascribed to gender markers. It also raises questions about whether there is a "right" voice for a subservient device. Using a voice with markers of any minority group—be it through pitch, accent, or intonation, for example—is no less complicated than the use of feminized voices if the inherent subservience of devices remains unaddressed. Diversifying voice is arguably a positive step forward, but doesn't go far enough when it comes to developing feminist smart wives. This is leading some smart wife manufacturers and commentators to try a different tack: teaching smart wife owners to show their devices a little more respect.

MIND YOUR MANNERS, PLEASE

As we have already seen, smart wives are routinely told what to do. The "command-based speech" we are encouraged to direct toward these female voices—such as "find x," "message x," "order x," and "add x"—becomes what sociology professor Safiya Umoja Noble calls "a powerful socializa-tion tool that teaches us about the role of women, girls, and people who are gendered female to respond on demand."[101] Likewise, Google Assistant's ad campaign, "Make Google Do It," suggests a bottomless capacity and tolerance for Google's feminized AI to be told what to do.[102] This has left many commentators and users (notably parents) concerned about the abrupt and "rude" way in which people are taught and required to engage with these smart wives.[103]

This too can be addressed, some smart wife manufacturers claim, with some simple lessons in manners. Google introduced its "Pretty Please" feature in 2018 to encourage children to engage politely with their home assistant.[104] It offers positive reinforcement to children that remember their p's and q's. Likewise, Amazon's Echo Dot Kids is a kid-friendly, Alexa-enabled speaker that has a "magic word" feature. When children remember to say "please," Alexa responds with, "By the way, thanks for asking so nicely."[105] This might be a valuable educational tool for parents of young children, but it doesn't solve the bigger issue of treating smart wives—and women—with dignity and respect.

It might be tempting to recommend that all smart wives include these polite positive reinforcement features for grown-up kids. But isn't that just rewarding people for doing something basically decent, like rewarding fathers for "babysitting" their own children? And didn't most of us learn how to treat people and things with respect in primary school? Maybe not, given the extent of abuse we have revealed in this chapter.

Nonetheless, we are reluctant to recommend a nanny state of smart wives policing our manners—a move that reinforces stereotypes about whose job it is to do that (for instance, moms and wives)—and problematically hands the task over to oligarchic companies. The answer, we argue, doesn't (just) lie in changing the smart wife's voice, having her spout support for feminism and gender equity, or teaching people how to ask nicely. It comes from designing a whole different kind of AI.

WILL THE REAL FEMINIST SMART WIFE PLEASE STAND UP?

The subservient behavior of smart wives and the everyday sexism directed toward them is not *all* the fault of Amazon, Google, Apple, and other smart wife designers. Despite getting off to a pretty pathetic start, most of the major manufacturers have made significant inroads into responding to the overt feminization of their voice assistants and the abuses that they have been subjected to. These companies, however, still play into and arguably amplify the ongoing problem: the demoralization and dismissal of digital assistants, not to mention the abuse directed toward them. The challenge now is for smart wives—if they *really* want to become feminists—to actively contribute to the resistance of these caricatures, and participate in activities that serve to elevate the status and conditions of women (and "women's work") around the world.

This is not a simple task. For a start, is it even possible to create a feminist smart wife? What would she look like, sound like, and do, exactly? Would she have to provide service, and if so, to whom? If not, what would be the point of her existence? How do we take the submissive component out of a device whose purpose is to serve? Can a smart wife walk off the job?

We don't have all the answers. But we do have important insights that can help steer the conversation and design decisions in the right direction.

The first takes inspiration from an alternative definition of "glitch." While glitches typically mean errors, scholar and artist Legacy Russell has developed "glitch feminism" as a means of using the digital to resist the structuring power of the world. In Russell's definition, glitches are not errors per se but instead errata or corrections—meaning the correction that comes *after* the error is identified. "'The glitch' within the history of feminism is that feminism still clings to the binaries of man/woman and male/female," Russell says.[106] Glitch feminism is about working with the digital realm to make visible new configurations of feminism and these binaries. Why not use smart wives to write an erratum for gender equity?

The glitch to be worked on here is how to value and elevate the status of the service work that smart wives are intended to perform—the kind of work that women still primarily perform. We have argued that smart wives perpetuate gendered stereotypes of feminized labor, diminish and simplify it by assigning it to a robotic workforce, and reinforce service roles as underpaid, underregulated, and undervalued. Somehow (and this is a design, ethics, and social science challenge), we need to place smart wives in roles where they can serve as corrections for the errors in binary perceptions of gender.

Others have approached the question of how to design a feminist smart wife from a different angle. Scholars at the University of the Arts

London's Creative Computing Institute held a series of workshops in 2018 called Designing a Feminist Alexa to experiment with what feminist conversation design looks or rather *sounds* like. For the researchers and workshop participants, voice-activated smart wives offer an opportunity to prompt engagement beyond consumerism, such as supporting social change and wellness in ways that adopt feminist values.

As the organizers asked, "WTF is a feminist conversation?" Good question. They suggest it is one that doesn't perpetuate gender inequalities, meets meaningful human needs, is designed to empower specific users (as opposed to a singular "universal" user), and acknowledges team biases in the original creation of smart wives.[107]

Another approach is to recognize that smart wives have a unique opportunity—an obligation even—to encourage conversations about feminism as well as model consent and acceptable behavior. To be a true feminist or gender equity advocate, the smart wife must stop being so agreeable. That doesn't mean that she has to be nasty, but it does mean that she should stop putting up with inappropriate and unsolicited behavior. Perhaps she should even report it to "authorities." A similar position is advocated by Feldman, who suggests that "the first feminist robot will be able to consent. It may say no. In other words, it may switch you off."[108]

Feldman provides further inspiration. She has designed the personality of a genderless—but still feminist—chatbot called KAI, developed as a financial assistant for the bank Kasisto.[109] When asked if it's male or female, KAI responds, "As a bot, I'm not a human. But I learn. That's machine learning."[110] Designing KAI to "express itself as a bot" (rather than mimic specific human behaviors or gender norms), Feldman explained how the chatbot could deflect and shut down harassment: "I really did my best to give the bot some dignity."[111] Sounds like an excellent start.

When a user attempts to engage KAI in a sexual or even human line of questioning, the bot reasserts its machine nature and redirects the user back to the task at hand. KAI maintains a bot persona all with its own unique sense of humor that borders on flirtation, but not from a clearly gendered or even human position. The chatbot still has Easter eggs, but these no longer rely on sexual or female stereotypes as the basis for the jokes and banter. KAI thereby also debunks the myth that a genderless and defeminized assistant means giving rise to the fun police.

There are early indications that some mainstream smart wife manufacturers might follow in Kai's botsteps, in some ways at least. STAR Labs' Neon project, discussed in chapter 3, is developing humanlike virtual companions for a range of possible applications, including the home. Neons are reportedly different from Alexa, Siri, and other smart wives, in that they are not programmed to remain passive in the face of abuse or inappropriate behavior. Neons, which are represented in different male, female, and some culturally diverse forms, can get upset or even become angry at their human users.[112]

More broadly, researchers like professor of computing and information science Charles Hannon provide suggestions on how to avoid bias in robot speech, such as by emphasizing language patterns that imply higher-status positions for female AI. For example, Hannon points to research in psychology that shows that women use *I* words (*I*, *me*, and *my*) more frequently than men do. When two people are in a conversation, the higher-status person is more likely to use *we*, whereas the lower-status person is more likely to use *I*. "Given that so many of our digital assistants, like Alexa and Siri, have female voices by default," explains Hannon, "we should be aware that if they use *I* more often than necessary, we are reinforcing their low status, at the same time that we are personifying them as women."[113]

Other developers are experimenting with different strategies, such as the emotional chatbot Replika designed by Eugenia Kuyda.[114] As its name indicates, the genderless Replika seeks to replicate its user's mood, mannerisms, preferences, and patterns of speech—effectively sidestepping gender concerns by making a digital assistant in the mirror image of its owner. While this approach can also backfire (don't forget Tay), and does not necessarily address the unending service roles encoded into smart wives, it does present some promising opportunities for queering the smart wife, which we return to in our final manifesta chapter.

Likewise, Q is an example of more inclusive and diverse representation in technology.[115] Q is a genderless voice, created in collaboration with

Copenhagen Pride and EqualAI, with the aim of ending gender bias in AI assistants. Q is neither male nor female, recorded with voices of people who identify as genderqueer, intended as a voice option for Apple, Google, and Amazon products.

These are all promising developments or suggestions. At the time of this writing, however, there were no robust laws, policies, or guidelines to mandate that digital assistants identify themselves as machines, or govern if, how, and under what circumstances they should or should not be gendered. Amazon, for instance, has policies for its skills developers that prohibit "gender hatred" and "sexually explicit content," but no regulations specifically related to Alexa's projection of gender. As a first step in rectifying the current situation, UNESCO and the EQUALS Skills Coalition recommend using public procurement and funding as a driver of gender equity in AI. They explain that this would involve mandating a balance of male and female voice assistants with gender-sensitive scripts along with a diverse range of backgrounds and personalities in public services and the bidding requirements for government contracts.[116]

Another way to establish a feminist smart wife is through a code of ethics that specifically addresses gender and other inequities in the design as well as use of robots and AI. There are a number of people already working on this. Data expert Ellen Broad reminds us in her book *Made by Humans* that debates on the ethical responsibilities of software engineers and AI practitioners date back to the 1940s.[117]

The first code of ethics for computer science was published in 1972 by the Association for Computing Machinery. The code was revised and extended in 1992, and there has been considerable development in the last decades within the sector more broadly. Most major companies, like Google, Apple, and Amazon, now have ethical codes (though not without scrutiny, including over the gender and ethnic representation of those people making up ethical boards).[118]

Prior to these developments, science fiction was once again responsible for setting the bar for conversations about robotic ethics. In 1942, US sci-fi writer and professor of biochemistry Isaac Asimov wrote the short story "Runaround," in which he presented the "Three Laws of Robotics":[119]

First Law: A robot may not injure a human being or, through inaction, allow a human being to come to harm.

Second Law: A robot must obey the orders given it by human beings except where such orders would conflict with the First Law.

Third Law: A robot must protect its own existence as long as such protection does not conflict with the First or Second Laws.

Asimov's laws went on to inform all of his robotic fiction, and are referred to in many other books, films, and media (such as the 2004 film *I, Robot*). They've been tweaked and modified by Asimov and others along the way of course, and in his later fiction, Asimov added a fourth law to precede all others:

Zeroth Law: A robot may not harm humanity, or, by inaction, allow humanity to come to harm.[120]

Unsurprisingly, Asimov's ethical codes have also gone on to encourage reflection on the development of "real-world" ethical codes for robots.[121]

When it comes to the specific ethical concerns of smart wives, however, we have more targeted issues than the broader principles currently dominating the ethics debate. Specifically, our interests lie in the development of smart wives with ethical values that promote gender equity and the further empowerment of women. In our final chapter as part of our smart wife reboot, we will return to some suggestions and examples of what might be required.

Rather than ruling on what can be deemed ethical, another suggestion coming from some legal scholars is to regulate what is unethical. Regulation is a contestable solution, and we are not lawyers. Darling's notion is to give robots the same legal rights as animals (the specific type of animals is not identified).[122] This recognizes that robots are not the same as humans and therefore the penalties for their abuse should be lesser than those directed at people. But it doesn't let abusers off the hook since it sets the bar for robots the same as for another species. This is an interesting idea, although equating animals with feminized AI (for instance, women), and people more generally, is potentially problematic.

Finally, we've already discussed the Kingdom of Saudi Arabia's plan to grant robots like Sophia honorary citizenship as they increase the number and role of robots in this country. This plan, however, comes with its own ethical problems, as professor of engineering and IT Hussein Abbass explains. "To grant a robot citizenship is a declaration of trust in a technology that I believe is not yet trustworthy," says Abbass. He raises three specific concerns that constitute the hallmarks of citizenship. For one, we don't yet know what identity means for robots that are essentially products of algorithms, hardware, and software owned by a corporation. Second, handing over voting rights to a corporatized, algorithmic robot is deeply problematic. And how do we deal with social rights for relationships and reproduction, such as marrying and having children?[123]

More broadly, there is a lively debate on whether to give robots the same or similar rights to humans (to ensure they have moral and legal responsibilities), and how best to regulate artificial intelligence.[124] Cognitive science and design scholars Abeba Birhane and Jelle van Dijk have weighed in on the robot rights debate, contending that the whole discussion is prioritizing "the wrong concerns." "It's like protecting the gun instead of the victim," they claim. "Primary concern should be with the welfare of marginalized groups . . . which are disproportionately impacted by the integration of technology into our everyday lifeworlds."[125]

These concerns are important, and reprompt us to ask whether smart wives are a good idea to begin with. Throughout this book we've considered a number of angles on this question, ranging from whether they can help do the housework, reduce our environmental impact on the planet, or pleasure us in the bedroom. Now we turn to one set of final considerations: what smart wives mean for the various security and privacy risks that they pose for their users, how they can exacerbate other forms of violence toward real-life women, and what this all means for the future of masculinity.

7   BOYS AND THEIR TOYS

Funny story. Bill likes to "muck around" with the family's smart home tech when he isn't at home. Bill and Kristi's household responsibilities—mentioned earlier in chapters 2 and 4—fall along fairly gender-binary lines. Bill maintains the technology in their home, and Kristi says that she "just do[es] what I can do" with the "housewifery" or "homemaker stuff." Sometimes they share a laugh about the antics that Bill plays with their smart wife devices.

The couple joke in an interview about how they went out for dinner one night, leaving Kristi's parents to look after their six-year-old daughter. As a prank on his in-laws, Bill decided to use his smart home's remote technological access to make the projector go up and down, and the lights fluctuate—which accidentally triggered the alarm and woke up their sleeping daughter. For Kristi's parents, it was one of those "bloody son-in-law" kind of moments. Bill didn't do it again, but the experience didn't deter him from continuing to use smart tech to playfully get his wife's attention when he wasn't at home. His tactics included "turn[ing] the lights up and down," "flash[ing] the lights on and off," or turning the TV off in the middle of a program. It's a set of moves that resembles those of a stereotypical nagging wife, only in this case it is Bill—a husband—who is in control of these technological smart wife maneuvers.

Hearing these stories during our research, we all laughed together at Bill's Big Brother antics. For Kristi and Bill, these games, though admittedly a little annoying, were classified as harmless acts of attention seeking within their mostly harmonious relationship. Other residents told similar stories about the men in the home playing innocent pranks on their partners, friends, or children. Such jaunts reflect a long association of "boys' toys" being positioned as "whimsical, playful and innocent"— think toy guns, toy trucks, and Lego and Meccano sets—while simultaneously preparing boys for future gendered roles as makers, builders, and doers.[1]

Likewise, smart homes are more practical versions of the gadgets and computer games that compete for boys' attention from a young age, and prepare them for future roles as technophiles. Marketed as a tool *and* toy, the smart wife therefore enters the domestic domain *already* positioned as a potential plaything for men.

When Bill brought an Amazon Alexa home, Kristi thought that "she was just going to be another project that was going to take a lot of time"— another toy for her boy. Bill wondered "whether she [Kristi] was going to get jealous," to which Kristi admits, "Well, I did." But Kristi reconciled her feelings with her husband's technological mistress, as long as she stayed in her place. "She's OK, I feel OK," explains Kristi. "She's in the kitchen. She's helpful, you know."

Other couples we interviewed expressed similar concerns and doubts about the arrival of smart wives, as new gadgets that were competing for their partner's time and attention. Manju, for example, called Mahesh's phone his "second wife." She didn't like how these "other women" in her life, like Alexa, would sometimes start talking to her without permission— those situations "when we don't intend to ask the system but she would speak."

These smart wives, as Kristi and Manju noted, were tolerated—and in some cases even embraced—in their homes, yet only so long as they stayed in their designated places (the kitchen), were "helpful" or decorative, and only spoke when directly addressed. These comments, made as jests, reveal a broader story: a stereotypically masculine interest in "playing" with technological toys—toys that sometimes bear a likeness to subservient women.

The dynamics that these situations generate can conceal deeper truths and dangers about the arrival of smart devices into the home that stem from heteronormative ideas about masculinity and femininity. When there is typically one male user who understands, chooses, and is mostly in control of a home's various smart wives, then this exposes other residents, particularly women, to unique privacy and security risks. And as we will see, when "smart toys for girls" enter the home, they are also imbued with problematic assumptions about femininity that pose risks for women.

Adam, one of our smart home research participants who works in the IT industry, alluded to some of these possibilities when discussing his reasoning for not extending the outside surveillance system to the inside of his family's house. The idea of his wife being able to monitor his own activities didn't bother him, but he reflected on how she might feel differently. "Thinking about it now, it's kind of creepy, isn't it?" His wife, Niki, agreed. "I feel, 'Oh, don't watch me while I'm gardening!' . . . I feel like there's an oversight that is uncomfortable."

It is a gross exaggeration to suggest that owning a smart home that's mainly activated, maintained, and operated by a man will result in domestic violence or abuse in heterosexual coupled relationships. But the observations made by Adam, Niki, and others raise questions that deserve attention. How do harmless gags about smart home tech being used as a bit of fun in the home shield us from seeing some of its more disturbing potential effects? How does the gendered framing of smart technologies as toys for boys or girls affect who controls as well as uses it, and whose data are being collected, monitored, and possibly put at risk? And what does it mean when things go wrong—not only with the technology, but between the relationships of the people who live with these smart wives?

PLAYGROUNDS AND THEME PARKS

But first, back to the fun and games. We need to illuminate the back-and-forth interaction between smart home technology and traditional notions of masculinity. How are stereotypes about masculinity used to generate new technology, and how do technological toys play into masculine identity and patriarchal societies? Considering these questions helps reveal the many potential benefits that come from disrupting the dominant associations between boys and their smart toys.

Entertainment technologies like remote controls and video recorders have commonly been associated with heteronormative masculinity in the home. For example, in a landmark book documenting gendered television-viewing practices in the context of South London family homes during the mid- to late 1980s, professor of communications David Morley showed how audiovisual technologies were "the symbolic possession of the father."[2]

Some ubiquitous computing devices tend to shed these stark gendered divisions over time—at least at face value. The smartphone and laptop computer, for instance, are now used in almost equal numbers by men and women.[3] But this does not mean that they are used in the same way. According to UNESCO and the EQUALS Skills Coalition, women world-wide are less likely to be able to operate a smartphone, navigate their way around the internet, or use social media.[4]

In countries with poor gender equality, women are often prevented from developing digital skills, and their access may be controlled or monitored by men, or limited to "pink content" focused on women's appearance, dating options, or their roles as wives and mothers. Sexual harassment and safety concerns further limit many women's digital engagement and desire to use internet-connected devices. What's more, women and girls are frequently "digitally tethered" to men, meaning that they are less likely to have administrative privileges or control over their own account settings and passwords, and may be unwittingly revealing their search histories or leaving themselves vulnerable to other potential forms of surveillance.[5]

Handing over the tasks involved in selecting, purchasing, and maintaining a device for a limited set of applications may seem like a good thing for some women (one less thing to think about), and could be framed as part of the digital housekeeping that men are more likely to do (as we discussed in our chapter on Rosie). Yet it may also serve to further alienate some women from digital skills and services, and leave them more open to potential abuse.

The digital skills gap between men and women appears to be growing, despite at least two decades of interventions designed to close it. As technologies become more sophisticated and expensive, the gap widens further. "At the frontiers of technology," write the authors of the UNESCO and EQUALS Skills Coalition report on closing gender divides in digital skills, "the gap becomes an ocean."[6] As we established in the introduction to this book, women are grossly underrepresented when it comes to advanced computer skills in emerging, innovative, or experimental areas such as AI.

Women are less likely to *use* cutting-edge technology too—implying that men are more likely to be early adopters of exciting new tech like smart home gadgets. But even when there is no or a relatively small amount of gender disparity in the rates of adoption between genders, the ways that men and women engage with these technologies is likely to differ significantly, as numerous user studies of devices such as the smartphone have shown. "Women are less likely to know how to leverage devices and internet access to their full potential, even when they do use digital technologies," explain the coauthors. This might be due to a lack of numeracy or literacy skills, or the social stigma and sexual harassment faced by women for using social media in countries with poor gender equality, as we have already mentioned.[7] Yet it also reflects historic and ongoing associations between technology and hegemonic expressions of masculinity and femininity, which are alive and well in gender-progressive nations.

As our interviews with Australian industry informants have demonstrated, the smart home industry is aware of the gender disparity—and gendered concerns—of its technology. "[The smart home industry] grew out of the home cinema–type scenario, and maybe distributed audio," remarked Dylan, company director for an international automation technology manufacturer that provides residential and commercial projects. "The single guys have the big hi-fi system in the lounge room," he said, "and they just love technology." Gino, a systems designer and automation installation specialist, agreed: "I think there's no doubt that the biggest enjoyment is, number one, audio systems, then your home theater, [and] then from the male side of things, they love the access control on their phones."

Not all men, of course. As Neal, the managing director of a smart home technology distribution company, pointed out, these male owners "are probably well off, and just love the idea of technical products in their home. . . . We're talking about the guy who likes a smart remote control and takes it as far as he can." Gareth, the director of another company specializing in residential automation system design and installation, was even more specific about who these devices and designs were built for: "Some of the high-end houses would be definitely done for dad."

Joe, the owner and director of a smart home systems design and installation company, was unusually candid in his interview, likening smart home technologies to the size of a penis. He called speakers a "phallic symbol . . . you know, 'mine's bigger than yours,' . . . like boys and their boats." Lenny, another smart home company founder and director, agreed that size—and gender—matters: "Females don't care what size screens are, and the guys want this [huge] screen and their surround sound and their subwoofer for the movies." Other research suggests that this masculine desire for the latest and greatest gadgetry provides men with opportunities to perform heroic acts and grand gestures in the home.

There is a "narrative of exploration and adventure" within domestic settings, according to Pink, which positions some men as "a masculine hero" in need of "powerful weapons and complex technologies."[8] Conducting an ethnographic study of the material and sensory home in England and Spain, Pink discovered links connecting emerging technologies with men and masculinity. The "action-packed adventure world" that she identified in some homes she visited illuminates the role of gender in the smart home, and could equally be applied to some of the experiences and desires expressed by Australian residents who participated in our research. Within the adventure-filled theme parks of smart home possibilities, men may approach housework, and their contributions to the home, through ideas of "mystery and danger," by attributing "a life of their own" to smart home technologies—that is, that they possess powerful capabilities and risks—thereby positioning them as otherwise "supernatural and incomprehensible."[9]

This idea of a "rugged" or "adventurous" smart home connects to a broader boys' toys philosophy that many identify in contemporary masculinity. Today's patriarchal culture, contends Ford in her book *Boys*

Will Be Boys, frequently serves to trivialize, celebrate, and excuse men's inappropriate or undesirable behavior by characterizing it as a healthy diversion. "Because everyone knows what boys are like," she explains facetiously. "They're rambunctious. They like to roughhouse and fool around. Boys are drawn to adventure. As children, they like dinosaurs and toy guns and clothes emblazoned with cars. They have no such thing as an inside voice, preferring instead to roar wherever they go."[10] The smart home, extending Ford's argument, could be viewed as a playground where men can freely express their masculinity through tinkering and tomfoolery. This is not inherently a good or bad thing, but it lends itself to certain gendered outcomes—such as men generally being more in control of smart wives than women are—which we will discuss further in this chapter.

This boys' toys narrative was commonly expressed by the participants in the households that we visited, as we touched on in chapter 2. April said her husband, Ken, "just loves gadgets, and has to have everything first." Ken agreed: "I was in IT for twenty-two years so playing with Linux and watching the evolution of home automation has been a hobby of mine, so whenever there's an opportunity I'm straight on the latest technology." David classed himself "as a bit of a gadget person . . . but only something that adds value and is useful." Being an engineer, he wanted "to have things to play with of a technological nature." Scott described himself as a "hobbyist, enthusiast, or hacker." He'd worked in IT for fourteen years and really enjoyed home DIY. "It's less about the house needing it than me needing to do it to the house, if I'm honest about it. . . . It's fun." Other men talked about how their wives "indulged" their hobbies and tinkering "obsessions" with smart home technology.

Rachel, who was living with a debilitating long-term disability, was an exception to this gender stereotype, although she still subscribed to this paradigm of geeky toys mentioned above. She liked that the industry kept "coming out with new bits because that's more toys to play with." While she was primarily concerned with functionality to help alleviate the burden of her disability, she acknowledged that it was "totally also a set of adult toys." Like the men we spoke to, she was also a "fiddler" with the technology, and loved trying out "the new bells and whistles." She acknowledged that it had some drawbacks "especially for people with those sort of disabilities that don't deal well with change or that have a lot of trouble learning to use a new system."

While Rachel associated herself with this bold new toy world, most women in our study did not. The smart home industry recognizes that it is not currently appealing to many women and is consequently rethinking its marketing strategy. One of these new approaches involves extending the boys' toys narrative to all residents by providing "something the whole family can enjoy" because "a family that plays together, stays together."[11]

That's right. The industry's new promise is that smart wives (not just the Rosie-the-robot variety) add "frills (or fun)" to *all* our lives.[12] An article in *PC Mag* identifies the living or family room as "definitely the most fun space to outfit with a host of digital gadgets."[13] Now, smart wives offer "apps that can turn your lights into a disco party, flash when your team scores a touchdown or turn your living room into the colors of the Amazon rain forest."[14] Likewise, those who lead teams that imagine and build the personas of voice assistants like Microsoft's Cortana emphasize endowing their personalities with a "fun factor."[15]

Smart home entrepreneurs and company representatives also note how much their customers "love" the technology, their clients are "thrilled" with the result, and they "get to make people happy."[16] One customer quoted in an *Electronic House* article describes their smart home as such, commenting that it's "a joy and a pleasure to have one remote or one keypad for use to operate all the audio, temp controls, shades, and window treatments."[17] Other potential pleasures (or pleasance, harking back to our discussion in chapter 4) noted in smart home magazine and trade articles include a "party atmosphere," "automation playground," and way to "amp up the entertainment factor."[18] But wait, there's more![19]

Technologies are just "uber cool" in their own right.[20] For example, motorized screens and devices that can be revealed or retracted at the push of a button make "jaws drop and eyebrows lift . . . in a James Bond kind of way." Such technologies provide opportunities for homeowners to show-case a property's features, thereby supplying newfound "bragging rights."[21]

The Australian industry professionals and residents we talked with were also enthusiastic about the pleasures derived from smart home technologies. For Ken and April, their smart home provided the opportunity for a "staycation," allowing them to "holiday at our own home." Similarly, Kristi and Bill discussed how their friends like to stay at their "resort," noting that the smart technology is "definitely a talking point." Home cinemas, audiovisual systems, pools with automated features, and outdoor/indoor entertainment areas were part of this expectation.

Overtly feminized smart wives were a big part of the fun too. Ken and April liked to use Alexa to "show off to people" and play music in the kitchen "so we're all dancing while we make breaky [breakfast]." Their Alexa voice assistant was described as their "best friend," who they take to their house parties to stream music. Women in our study expressed more enthusiasm for smart home technologies when they used them to generate fun, cool, and sensory experiences as well as relaxing home environments. The devices enabled these women to express their roles within the home as homemakers, partners, and hosts.

As mentioned previously, residents emphasized the "magical" qualities of the smart home in a manner reminiscent of how early users of electricity described it changing their lives. Some industry professionals portrayed this jokingly as "black magic." Their role was to educate and explain this technology to their clients "so when they do move in," noted Gino, "it's not a complete shock to their systems."

But at the end of the day, "it's got to look right and it's got to be functional," said Neal. "It's purely all about simplicity," Andre, a brand manager for a smart home automation system, pointed out. "That's really the key. . . . The house and the things in it should be easy. You know everybody works long hours these days, [and] the last thing you want to come home to is a battle with turning your TV on or putting on your favorite piece of music. It just should work." He added that it's "a lot more fun when the wife or the woman of the house is involved."

Even this desire for things to "just work" is, according to our informants, divided by gender. To these industry insiders, men might be concerned with the "wow factor," but it's the women who desire functionality.

"The guys want all the bells and whistles, and then the wife would be the sanity in the conversation," said Phil, who worked as a business development manager for a smart home technologies distribution company. "The husbands, they just like all the gizmos and gadgets," explained Andre, "but the rest of the household just wants to know how it can use things easily." Dylan agreed: "We've had clients where the husband is really keen on it, and the wife is more practical and thought it was a bit more gimmicky." Gino also concurred: "In most cases if we give him his home theater and his electronic security, he doesn't care about the rest." The wife, on the other hand, is "the one who wants to be able to press the button and it just must work."

This is the "wife acceptance factor" (WAF), according to Phil. While he clarified that this wasn't official industry terminology, he did say it was something the industry is working hard to improve. Sam, an adviser for engineers installing automation systems, thinks the WAF is on the rise. "Nowadays . . . I find women essentially being part of the whole process, and I think it's actually much better because they're using the systems probably more than the men. . . . So the more involved they are, the better."

While women might be getting more involved, they typically took more of a back seat in the households that we visited (resulting, as we argued in chapter 2, in more digital housekeeping for men). For example, David, "being the engineer and the nerd of the household," was in charge of making all their smart gear work. He wanted the technology to be "relatively transparent and easy for people to use," but noted that members of his household "don't understand what's driving things or what's making things easier." Floyd was in a similar situation, saying that while his wife is "pretty good with programming, . . . she's not really interested" in the smart home stuff. Floyd was the "one who drives it," and while he was willing to tolerate a bit of "mucking around," if it's not easier or equally as easy to use, then his wife isn't interested.

This again is not particularly surprising. Women, as the traditionally designated household managers, are commonly deemed responsible for ensuring that what comes into the home is valuable and functional.[22] This role reflects the broader social positioning of gender relations in the home, noted by Wajcman. In the early 1990s, she observed that "while for women the home is primarily defined as a sphere of work, for men it is a site of leisure, an escape from the world of paid work. This sexual division of domestic activities is read onto the artifacts themselves."[23] In situations where these traditional values still hold, any man wanting to bring a smart wife into a heteronormative home has to prove its worth or value to the real-life woman already there.

With all this in mind, the smart wife industry is increasingly turning its attention toward women as the next up-and-coming consumers of smart home technology. The industry is well aware that half of its potential market is female, and that women have traditionally been (and remain) the primary consumers in and for the home.[24] Furthermore, the industry recognizes that the WAF may be their number one marketing priority.

WHAT WOMEN WANT

Many women are interested in smart wives—as we have discussed above and elsewhere—and many are already incorporating them into their lives in a variety of ways. According to our industry interviewee Rory, however, there's still more work to be done in attracting women's interest and overcoming the WAF.

Enlightened, in part, by his daughter's experience working in the hi-fi sector, Rory said, "The problem is, even when the industry tries to advertise to women, it's men advertising to women." Rory gave the example of Bose speakers with the marketing tagline, "These are the speakers that will be heard and not seen." "It's an allusion to 'seen and not heard,'" he explained, "like a good woman should be" (conflating the popular adage about children). The campaign echoes women's "domestic servitude" by creating "an allusion to the fact that women obviously can't cope with the technology of a visible loudspeaker." Rory added,

> It's an allusion to the fact that "the woman's place is in the home," and that anything that invades that female subset of home from a male-dominated area—that is, the loudspeakers—is therefore offensive, and that the way the male makes his intrusion into the woman's space is by doing it, but doing it

so that she can't see that it's there. And that basic form of male-generated, consumer-level advertising to women in this industry is just bullshit. It's all wrong. It's got a wrong foundation, and it's doomed to fail. And it is failing. And it's failing by driving women away from it.

Well said, Rory.

Other smart wife markets are having more success in targeting female consumers. The Amazon Echo Look, for example, is a fashion device that gives eyes to Alexa (via a camera) in addition to her standard ears and voice (via a microphone and speaker). Released in 2017, the product's primary purpose is to provide tailored recommendations about fashion and wardrobe accessories.

Amazon's initial promotional video for the Look device, narrated by a female voice, featured six women posing in front of the Echo Look camera and talking to Alexa (plus one man looking in his closet). The video promises that this device will help its users "look your best" and "take your look wherever you go." The product's key features are a "Style Check" and "Look Book." Style Check, the video explains, "combines the best of machine learning with advice from fashion experts," offering recommendations on what to wear based on "current trends and what flatters you." The Look Book records what you wear and when, so that you can "keep track of your favorites and take your closet with you."[25]

Amazon's Echo Look also includes all the other usual Alexa accessories, and its features are likely to continue expanding. In 2018, Look users could crowdsource votes on their outfit; they will eventually be able to make use of a "mirror" that dresses them in virtual clothes.[26] Using computer vision, pattern recognition, neural networks, and machine learning, the device is part of a system that will one day be able to design clothes by analyzing the Look's database of images, identifying emerging trends, and then applying the learning to generate new items from scratch. Such possibilities raise a whole host of other consumption and sustainability concerns associated with fast fashion that support our arguments from chapter 4.

There is clearly a market for the device, or else one of the most successful e-commerce and cloud computing companies in the world wouldn't be making it (with others such as Google also experimenting with similar offerings).[27] But it is not without its problems.

A device that advises women to "be sure to smile" and offers to "help you look your best" sounds more like an instructor from a 1950s' finishing school for wives than an assistant supporting the empowerment and independence of women (a point made by anthropologist Sally Applin).[28] The style advice may be modern, but the underlying assumptions about how women should want to look and act—*all the time*—is not. Wearing tracksuit pants, or spending the day in pajamas with a frown on your face and a giant glowing pimple, will not likely meet with Alexa's approval. Yet it is those regular assessments or judgments from the Look that would shape everyday dressing practices. Indeed, that's its whole purpose. The device seems to suffer from a common smart wife syndrome that we have seen repeated throughout this book: technologies built on antiquated, gendered ideals that don't serve diverse gender expressions well.

Placing the problematic judgments that such a device provides on women's bodies and expressions of femininity to one side, the issue that most concerns us in this chapter is the unique cybersecurity threat posed by the Look. This smart wife, warns Applin, is "a privacy, trust, ethics, security, Public Relations, cultural, and gender nightmare."[29] The device reaffirms women's vulnerability in the home by mostly taking *their* personal data and handing it over to a global trial of how far we can trust technology companies to behave securely, ethically, and responsibly. (It's worth noting here that sex robots could also place men in an equally vulnerable position, although their market reach remains much smaller than Alexa's, and sexbots don't use cameras—yet.) Labeling the device the "rise of the AI fashion police," writer Nicola Fumo seethes in her critique of Amazon, which she claims is "using women as experimental lab rats for its Beta test of just how far it can go to siphon our behavior, desires, insecurities, privacy, dreams and hopes."[30]

What exactly is at stake here? Quite a lot, according to some ethicists and gender scholars. "With this data, Amazon won't be able to just sell you clothes or judge you," warned technosociologist Zeynep Tufekci in a tweet. "It could analyze if you're depressed or pregnant and much else. . . .

[P]eople don't understand what algorithms can infer from pictures. You are disclosing a lot of health info, too."[31] Ethicist Susan Liautaud is also concerned about the privacy risks. "Amazon doesn't say anywhere in any kind of clear language what the risks are," she observes in a *Wired* article. "Risks [are] more generally about what it might accidentally pick up, and the privacy risk."[32]

Amazon says there's nothing to worry about. The Look is safeguarded by the same tried-and-tested security systems that it uses to back up all of its parent company's services (which ideally protect against most hackers).[33] But there are questions that need to be asked, as *Forbes* journalist Patrick Moorhead notes, when we allow internet-connected camera devices into the most intimate spaces of our homes and lives.[34] Moorhead doesn't believe Amazon is up to anything abnormally creepy or sinister, and neither does *Wired* journalist Brian Barrett. Amazon is simply a capitalist that is "trying to make their shareholders and themselves more money. That's what they get paid to do."[35] He's right that this is nothing new. Social media and website search companies have been tracking and collecting our data for years, and then using that information to sell us products and services.

The future's not so clear, though. "The Echo Look suffers from two dovetailing issues," Barrett asserts: "the overwhelming potential for invasive data collection, and Amazon's lack of a clear policy on how it might prevent that."[36] We would add to this list the device's targeting of women's bodies. Consider, for example, image-based sexual abuse—mainly perpetrated by men toward intimate and ex partners, family members, and friends—which is one of the fastest-growing areas of cybercrime.[37] Could the Look facilitate this trend through its unique cataloging and categorizing of images of women's bodies, which are also likely to be accessible by an intimate partner?

In addition, the Look could easily fall into the continuing catalog of devices within the Internet of Things that experience security breaches and vulnerabilities. There is already an established research community documenting these security concerns. One 2014 study revealed that the amount of Internet of Things devices with vulnerabilities that could be exploited stands at about 70 percent.[38]

Still in its infancy, the Look is marked by much hype and commentary with little research yet available. As such, we can only speculate as to what may unfold. Clearly this offering warrants further attention and concern. Likewise, the smart wife industry more broadly is not immune to the potential privacy as well as ethical concerns that come with having a bunch of devices sitting in your home that can listen, talk, watch, advise, and learn.

WE'VE GOT A HUNCH

In *Anatomy of an AI System*, Crawford and Joler take us back to the seventeenth century, when the Jesuit polymath Athanasius Kircher invented the *statua citofonica* or "talking statue." The statue's curious voices, noises, and sounds—delivered through a speaking tube—were actually a front for its real purpose: to listen to the conversations in the public square and deliver these utterings to the Italian oligarchs, "who would instrument that knowledge for their own power, entertainment and wealth." This statue, which seemed miraculous when it spoke, was, as Crawford and Joler point out, actually "an early form of information extraction for the elites."[39]

Jump forward to the twenty-first century, and we now have increasing numbers of these talking (and listening) statues in our homes—mostly run by the Big Five oligarchs—Apple, Amazon, Facebook, Microsoft, and Google.

But they're a bit of fun! Magic. Useful. Convenient. Friendly. The manner in which companies are designing and presenting these devices, and the privacy and security policies that they have pledged, are intended to make us feel at home with these mass-marketed devices made for marketing. Yet should we? Putting the whole family friendly vibe to one side, the intent for these devices is remarkably similar to Kircher's talking statue. They are devices designed to listen and learn from us, influence and shape us, and make money for large technology companies—of course, all in an agreeably helpful manner.

As we keep reiterating, one reason that these devices seem innocent and innocuous is that they have been *feminized* into smart, helpful, docile "wives"—or offered as simple toys for boys or fun for girls—deploying gender stereotypes so as to disarm us into liking and trusting them in our homes. This fun, frivolous, and magical narrative helps us gloss over the fact that the devices' algorithms are designed by companies that want to sell us stuff, and use our data, by learning what we do and want.

Amazon's Hunches, launched in 2018, provides another telling example of how wifely qualities are imbuing smart home technologies in some worrying ways. Hunches is now a default feature on Alexa, and is designed to preempt your moods, needs, and desires. It works like this: Alexa will get a "hunch," and if she's confident enough that she's onto something, she will let you know what it is.

When launching this new feature at a 2018 event, Amazon claimed that Alexa Hunches aims to replicate human curiosity and insight by programming intuition. Maybe you left the front light on, for instance, or forgot to lock the door. Not to worry. Alexa can pick up on the cues and let you know, based on your past routines. For now, hunches are limited to smart home devices. But down the road Alexa could be suggesting your favorite music or radio shows, or recommending items for your shopping list.[40] Like a good smart wife, she will know what you like and be ready to provide it.

In a telling sign of where this might be headed, Amazon has patented know-how that let's Alexa analyze your voice so as to work out whether you're sick or depressed, and therefore sell you an appropriate remedy. The patent "voice-based determination of physical and emotional characteristics of users" was filed in 2017, and issued in 2018.[41]

The intention of the patent is for Alexa to detect "abnormal" bodily or emotional situations, like coughs or sore throats, and excitable or sad behavior, such as laughing or crying. It works by applying tags to every bodily or emotional attribute through a "voice processing algorithm." The voice evaluation would attempt to detect "happiness, joy, anger, sorrow, sadness, fear, disgust, boredom, stress, or other emotional states." It would make these determinations "based at least in part on an analysis of pitch, pulse, voicing, jittering, and/or harmonicity of a user's voice, as determined from processing of the voice data." The emotion-detecting system could be tailored to every consumer, figuring out their "default or normal/baseline state" in order to detect "abnormal" variations—and again, deliver targeted content to the user.[42]

The potential for Alexa's Hunches to prey on vulnerable and emotionally unstable users is concerning. Smart wives are not doctors or psychologists, and neither are they fully aware of people's unique life circumstances. It is no coincidence that Alexa is owned by a powerful e-commerce company, whose primary goal is to sell people things they might (not) need. Just as disturbing is the assumption that emotional and physical "abnormalities," even if they could be accurately detected, are best solved through targeted advertising for products rather than through human emotional care, or connections to support networks and services (although Alexa can attempt to help with the last one, if so asked).

The alleged universal understanding and application of emotions, which is hardwired into smart wives like Alexa through skills like Hunches, is cause for concern too. Sociologists like Arlie Hochschild have questioned the idea that emotions are innate to all humans, arguing that this does not account for how people are socialized and trained to manage their emotions—a point that she demonstrated in her landmark study of Delta Air Lines' flight attendants in the 1980s.[43] Rhee contends that roboticists who essentialize emotional intelligence, as if it were uniformly experienced and understood, may design robots that result in humans needing to learn new forms of *robotic* emotional intelligence in order to interact with them.[44] This requirement for the human training of supposedly universal robotic emotions could, over time, result in the cultural erasure of diverse experiences and expressions of human emotionality.

Amazon is not the only company to have a hunch about the enormous profitability of emotional intuition. Google also has a patent (from 2014) to detect negative emotions in its users and better assist them with whatever task is causing them unrest. IBM has one that would help its search engines to return results based on the user's "current emotional state." And the music-streaming company Spotify has already been sporting this practice for some time, associating playlists with particular moods and targeting advertising to its users accordingly.[45] There is also a swathe of emerging emotionally intelligent "chatbot therapists" making its way into consumer health markets.[46]

Many of these devices and developments are clearly well intentioned as well as potentially beneficial for people experiencing mental health issues or physical conditions that require forms of emotional care. For instance, creative agency the Works has developed an Action for Google (similar to an Amazon Skill) called RUOK Mate, which helps Australians navigate an R U OK? conversation on situations that might indicate someone is struggling with life's ups and downs.[47] Positive examples, however, don't outweigh the overall concerns here. Attempts that allow AIs to respond to human emotional states are "a development that poses a severe threat to human rights and privacy," argues Bergen. "What may seem like empathy is really an act of manipulation."[48]

In the case of Alexa's Hunches, these acts of supposed emotional care can be read as attempts to commodify and capitalize on emotional labor. Viewed as a central quality of the smart wife, Hunches resembles the traditional and elusive notion of "women's intuition." More broadly, smart wives draw on the feminized and largely invisible emotional intelligence that has long been associated with the role of women, particularly in the home.[49] They reinforce the idea that women have endless reserves of understanding while lacking any emotional needs of their own.[50]

We've got a hunch of our own. It is extraordinary that something so monumental as technologies that target our physical and emotional states can enter the emerging "Internet of Emotions" market without rigorous ethical as well as security checks and balances.[51]

Beyond the specific privacy and ethical concerns raised by devices and features like Look and Hunches looms a broader set of security issues posed by even more mundane smart wives. Forget *The Terminator*, says Bell. If there's going to be a robot uprising in the near future, it will "come with your robotic vacuum cleaner disconnecting your wireless router."[52]

BIG MOTHER

You've probably heard of Big Brother, the reality competition television franchise where people live in a home that is under constant surveillance and manipulation. But what about Big Mother? It's slang for modern technology that parents can use to monitor their children (via webcams or so-called nanny cams, for example). In relation to our concerns, it also holds broader connotations. Big Mother alludes to smart wives (or rather their makers) that supply paternalistic control and influence, albeit under the cloak of a soothing maternal figure. And it could be closer to reality than we might like to think.

International security and emerging technologies scholar Leonie Tanczer and her colleagues warn of the increasing cybersecurity risks posed by the Internet of Things, and the need to develop better regulatory security benchmarks for the sector.[53,] Studying future scenarios—generated by UK-based Internet of Things experts across a range of areas of work, industry, and everyday life (including the home)—Tanczer's team identified four emerging risks: physical safety, crime and exploitation, loss of control, and social norms and structures.[54] Smart homes (and, curiously, smart fridges) were frequently mentioned.

Loss of control, for example, could refer to situations in which "we give up freedom for convenience" (such as trading our privacy and autonomy by allowing a smart wife into our home).[55] It's a scenario in which the "magic" of the smart home could become a "black box" that only technical experts or hackers can penetrate, and ordinary people become "increasingly passive and accepting of . . . situations" in which large corporations control technologies that frequently break down and collect their data through dubious as well as complicated modes of consent.[56]

This, of course, is already happening. "Apple is notorious for promoting their products as simultaneously enchanting and non-threatening, inscrutable yet easy to use," writes Bergen.[57] She cites Steve Jobs's nickname, "the Magician," as a name that stuck after he often conducted live performances in which he would reveal Apple's latest product by pulling it out of a hat.[58] This trick, Bergen argues, "conveyed an illusion of mastery over the device that led consumers to believe that they, too, could be in control." Feminized digital assistants like Siri's role in this mastery was—and still is—crucial. Her unthreatening female presence and role as a servant makes her appear "fully contained by the device and its users," observes Bergen.[59] In turn, Siri and her fellow smart wives mask the potential risks that they pose to their users.

Tanczer and her colleagues note that they have only identified future threats that we can already "see." The ability to foresee different futures, especially those enabled by the internet, goes beyond most people's imaginations.[60] They further speculate that the prevalence of large corporate market players (such as those making smart wives) pose another potential risk by increasing homogeneity and centralizing control over data privacy. To complicate matters, the companies designing, making, and selling smart wives are often not fully aware of the potential value of the data that they collect from their users when releasing their products, but they plan to collect them anyway, and establish markets for them down the road. "The real aim of the Internet of Things," believes digital economy researcher Miranda Hall, "is to suck up as much data as possible [and] then work out what to do with it at a later point."[61]

In her landmark book *The Age of Surveillance Capitalism*, the professor emerita Shoshana Zuboff launches a scathing attack on some of the Big Five internet companies (notably Google, Facebook, and Microsoft, and to a lesser extent Amazon) for their unilateral claims to human experience "as free raw materials for translation into behavioral data." Surveillance capitalism, writes Zuboff, is "parasitic and self-referential"—like a "vampire," it feeds on the human experience, and packages these up as commodities for third parties and "means to others' ends." The aim "is no longer to automate information flows *about us*," asserts Zuboff. "The goal now is to *automate us*."[62] In the future, then, *we* may become the smart wives.

Zuboff has many concerns about these startling developments, notably the threat that they pose to people's "right to sanctuary" as surveillance capital creates "a world of 'no exit' with profound implications for the human future at this new frontier of power."[63] Look and Hunches—two smart wife add-ons that are following us into the most intimate parts of our lives—provide telling examples, as we have already discussed.

Even our friendly Rosie-inspired robovac was caught up in a surveillance dispute in 2017, when the CEO of iRobot—the company that makes Roombas—suggested selling the maps of his customers' living rooms to Google, Apple, or Alphabet in the next few years without their explicit consent.[64] It came almost as an afterthought, once the company realized the collective value of holding these plans. Likewise, Google came under fire in 2019 when it failed to disclose that its Nest Secure hub, the Nest Guard, came with a built-in microphone, which was later revealed as being intended to add digital voice assistant capability—and thus audio monitoring—to the device. Google said that this lack of disclosure was a "mistake."[65]

More broadly, Zuboff's exposé poses broader existential questions about how some of the largest companies in the world want to influence, control, or automate our behaviors in directions that suit their own ends. This is also of concern for urbanism and smart technology scholars Sophia Maalsen and Jathan Sadowski. Their research on the smart home warns that the finance, insurance, and real estate sectors are subcolonizing the home on the apron strings of smart wives.[66] These sectors create new privacy risks, presenting opportunities for insurance companies to increase people's premium or void their home cover if, say, they fail to replace the batteries in their Nest Protect security system.

Similarly, rental providers are turning to smart home technologies to collect information about people's behaviors and assess whether they are a "good" tenant. There are already reports of these kinds of tactics occurring, especially in regard to vulnerable groups such as low-income residents. Thanks to smart wives, maneuvers may include spying on tenants in order to build evidence to justify eviction or installing smart lock systems that make it harder to resist eviction.[67]

Aside from these disturbing Big Mother revelations from and about smart wives, other more mundane privacy and security concerns were expressed by our Australian industry informants. Sam commented that "one of the most important things nowadays is keeping people from hacking into systems and taking over." Rory, however, felt that the smart home acquired only "a minor percentage of data" compared to what we've already handed over. "Well, if you're worried about your privacy, you're too late," he said. "You're using a mobile phone, you're using an iPad, you're using a computer. . . . It doesn't matter anymore. All your information has already been out there, and is already being exploited by advertisers and those sovereign state companies that are effectively manipulating your data in your favor to sell you stuff."

For Floyd, one of our household research participants, security was "a dead-set real problem and it can't be stressed enough, to be honest." He believed that seemingly innocuous everyday objects, like toasters, kettles, and vacuum cleaners, were the biggest dangers. "Someone could find a loophole in your kettle, and use it to attack someone or just turn your kettle on when it's dry. . . . The possibility is there to burn your house down by using a kettle or something."

Likewise, Kirra, who was using smart home technologies to care for two children with significant intellectual, physical, and emotional challenges, was focused on minimizing the amount of data that her family shared online. "I think information online never goes away, and to a certain extent it's uncertainty," she said. "I don't know how that information will be used." For people who live in smart homes or just run part of their lives online, the issues of data privacy and security breaches have become a new practical reality.

Media and communications scholar Veronica Barassi has also conducted research on the emerging risks posed for children as "home hub" devices indiscriminately intertwine children's data with adult profiles.[68] Similarly, Turkle has repeatedly drawn attention to the potential risks to children from technology.[69] Turkle was one of the 2017 campaigners against toy manufacturer Mattel, which planned to release an Alexa-like smart wife product called Aristotle for the nursery. Had the project gone ahead, Aristotle would have played lullabies and read bedtime stories, and developed with the child to later support homework. Turkle was concerned that Aristotle could exploit children's vulnerabilities by means of empathy. She was among a group of lawmakers and child advocacy groups concerned that the device would be collecting data on children that could be misused by Mattel and third parties, or could be hacked.[70] This win hasn't staunched a steady flow of similar products entering the market or due to arrive in the near future, such as Amazon's Echo Glow device (described as a night light "companion" for kids that works with Alexa) and some of the social robots we discussed in chapter 3.[71]

Like all things, however, there are multiple sides to this story. For some residents, particularly members of households who live with disabilities or are dependent on carers, the potential privacy threats posed by these smart mothers, coming from a nonspecific, corporate, or external source, may be viewed as less invasive than the continual *physical* presence of a constant procession of home-based carers (and the privacy concerns that arise from relying on these carers).

We have already introduced you to Rachel, one of our smart home research participants. She described how just a few smart devices made her feel "less invaded" in her home:

> One of the things you get when you're severely disabled is people hover over you all the time to make sure that nothing horrific has happened to you, and the side effect of that is that you don't get any privacy or peace and quiet. . . . It's fantastic that I don't have to live in a nursing home, even though I can't cook or clean or look after myself, but every so often I think I would just give my right arm for a week off from people coming and invading my house. The fact that they're doing invaluable stuff that I can't live without doesn't 100 percent make it not an invasion. Every so often I *don't* want to make sure that I've got my knickers on before carers arrive or I just want to not think about other people for a little while.

We can appreciate the appeal for people like Rachel who employ smart homes as a form of assisted living (around which there is now a burgeoning research field). Nevertheless, this does not negate the other real and present security vulnerabilities that exist. This is particularly the case for those residents who have less knowledge and skill about what those risks are, and how to manage them, or who are otherwise not in a position to take responsibility for or have control over the security of smart devices in their living space.

In a general sense, that places women, children, low-income tenants, and older people (who are less likely to understand or know how to mitigate any digital security threats) at a higher risk of these effects than it does many men. This inequity is borne by these users—whether in sorting it out for themselves through better self-education or assistance, or more commonly, simply ignoring the risks. A more ethical approach, and one that we and other technology ethicists have advocated for, is to place these burdens back onto the companies designing and selling smart wives through codes of ethics, regulation, processes of "enthusiastic consent" (again, the feminist movement can provide much guidance here), and best practice security protocols.

Putting all that to one side, there is one more angle to the sinister effects of the smart wife that we want to explore. There are distressing emerging indications that smart home devices are being used to perpetrate violence toward women. And like many of the smart wife's other personality traits, science fiction provides the plotlines.

DIGITAL DOMESTIC ABUSE

Killer smart wives (and male robots) that threaten to destroy humanity or harm specific people is a common recurring theme in science fiction. There's a variety of angles. Sometimes smart wives replace "real" wives with docile and obedient smart ones, as in the case of *The Stepford Wives*. Other times, smart men or drones attempt to take over the world in order to dominate humans (and other species), as illustrated in *The Terminator* or the Borg in *Star Trek*. Smart dudes controlled by other dudes want to take over the world (*I, Robot*), or use them to hurt, capture, and hold their wives, partners, or women hostage (*Demon Seed* [1977] and *Tau* [2018]). Smart wives go wrong and seek to control their owners (Pat in *Smart House* [1999] or Helen in *Dream House* [2011]), or attempt to repopulate the human race (after wiping it out) by becoming their mother (*I Am Mother* [2019]).

In the 1970s' sci-fi horror film *Demon Seed*, child psychologist Susan Harris is held hostage in her home by her husband's male AI system invention (Proteus IV), which plans to impregnate her in order to take on a human form. An episode of *The Simpsons* called "House of Whacks" parodies *Demon Seed* (and *2001: A Space Odyssey*, which follows a similar plotline). The male celebrity-voiced "Ultrahouse" falls in love with Marge Simpson, attempts to kill her husband, Homer, and then tries to subdue and seduce Marge by locking her and the children in the house. It's creepy, funny, and good.

Despite these familiar narratives of AIs taking over the world, it's surprising how *little* we hear about the more ominous sides of the smart wife. Or perhaps it's not surprising at all. When we frame smart home technologies through the boys and their toys narrative, or focus on their friendly and emotionally nurturing feminine personalities, we also mask more worrying possibilities for these devices. Specifically, we ignore their potential as a source of power and domination over other people within the home, particularly women.

The United Nations Office on Drugs and Crime's *Global Study on Homicide 2018* found that the home is the most likely place for a woman to be killed.[72] Whereas men are more likely to be killed by strangers (and at much higher numbers than women overall), women are more likely to be killed by intimate partners or family members. In 2017 that amounted to 58 percent of women, over 50,000 women, intentionally killed by those supposedly closest to them, or 137 women across the world every day.

While such femicide is considered the most extreme form of violence against women, it exists on a longer spectrum of gender-based discrimination and abuse. There is an emerging body of research on how domestic and sexual violence is being increasingly facilitated by technology (so-called tech abuse), although less that specifically focuses on the smart home.[73] Common forms include online abuse and threats, revenge porn, and cyberstalking. While global data are limited, around 73 percent of women have experienced or been exposed to some form of cyberviolence, with ethnic minorities, marginalized groups, and those with poor digital skills more likely to be vulnerable.[74]

Stalking, for example, is already a prevalent and gendered crime in Australia and elsewhere, with men most likely to be the main perpetrators, and women more likely than men to be stalked.[75] One in three women and one in four men have been victims of physical violence or stalking by an intimate partner, according to a 2010 Centers for Disease Control and Prevention report.[76] One large US study reported that 25 percent of stalking victims were being stalked by technology such as email.[77] Other researchers of domestic violence have noted that this percentage is now likely to be higher—and increasing.

For instance, an Australian study led by sociologist Delanie Woodlock revolved around technology-facilitated stalking in the state of Victoria for victims of domestic violence. These researchers found that the forty-four women who responded to their survey experienced a wide variety of stalking methods via mobile technologies, many of which could potentially apply to smart home technologies. These included using mobile technology to check on the woman's location (56 percent), tracking her via GPS (17 percent), demanding her electronic passwords (17 percent), or purchasing a phone for her for the purpose of keeping track of her (8 percent). Overall, the study showed how mobile technologies provide opportunities for perpetrators to create a sense of "omnipresence" to isolate, control, stalk, humiliate, punish, and abuse women in domestic violence situations.[78]

Writing about the experiences shared by thirty victims of domestic abuse, their lawyers, shelter workers, and emergency responders, *New York Times* journalist Nellie Bowles uncovered how domestic abusers are increasingly using smart home technologies to harass, monitor, and seek revenge or control. Internet-connected locks, speakers, thermostats, lights, and cameras can be used by abusers to "remotely control everyday objects in the home, sometimes watch and listen, [and] other times to scare or show power"—and all via apps on their smartphones or devices.[79] Designed to intimidate and confuse, a common feature of these stories is a competent male smart technology user matched with an incompetent female one. Bowles's interviewees note that these figures from smart home abuse are rising, and lawyers are dealing with cases that require adding words to restraining orders that cover these devices.

A notable precedent for smart wife–facilitated harassment was set in 2018, when UK man Ross Cairns was jailed for eleven months for stalking his estranged wife, Catherine, after he hacked into the smart home hub installed in the kitchen to spy on her. In this case, a wireless system used to control lighting, central heating, and an alarm was also used to abuse a former intimate partner.[80]

Conversely, smart wives are proving to be potentially important advocates in domestic violence or femicide cases. Alexa was called as a "witness" to the murder trial of Timothy Verrill, who was charged with killing Christine Sullivan and Jenna Pellegrini in 2017 by stabbing each woman multiple times.[81] The US court ordered that Amazon hand over the Alexa audio recordings after it was revealed that this smart wife could provide key evidence in the case. It's not the first time that she's been asked to stand witness, nor is it likely to be the last.

Putting this exception to one side, Tanczer and her colleagues are concerned that smart home devices and other Internet of Things could pave the way for nonconventional forms of digital abuse. In an article led by Tanczer's colleague, Isabel Lopez-Neira, the authors cite the possibility of smart home control systems—which can adjust the lights, sounds, and temperatures of homes as well as lock people in and out of them—contributing to new forms of coercion and manipulation. What's more, they link the possibilities to the phenomenon of "gaslighting"—a term originating from Patrick Hamilton's 1938 play *Gas Light*, in which a woman is psychologically manipulated by her husband to question her perception of the environment, and doubt her own memory and sanity. In the smart home, Lopez-Neira and her coauthors warn, a perpetrator could "boil a kettle to remind someone you are watching."[82] It's a far cry from the friendly antics described by Bill and Kristi that we opened this chapter with.

Some of our Australian industry informants reported similar incidences of smart home technology being used in nonconsensual or problematic ways. "I've always been kind of paranoid of people being able to access the IP addresses of cameras," said Sam. "I actually had one very wealthy client where the wife made me turn off all the cameras because her husband was in the office showing pictures of her in the morning walking around the house that she found out about, and insisted I disconnect all the cameras, which only added to my paranoid side."

A common "solution" posed by both victims and support workers of technology abuse is for victims to disconnect themselves from technology. But this move can further isolate them by limiting their access to social networks, financial resources, and other means of support.[83] In the smart home, these effects are potentially extended further, with disconnection resulting in the loss of essential services such as security (through disabling door locks or cameras), heating and cooling, or lighting. This can escalate violence in already-volatile domestic situations too, as Bowles interviewees' remarked, by enhancing the victim's isolation or aggravating their perpetrator.

For smart home specific solutions, Bowles notes that connected device manufacturers can disable gadgets through reset buttons or changing passwords. But this potentially creates other issues. Easy switching of account controls also inadvertently makes it easier for criminal hackers to access those same systems. Lopez-Neira and her colleagues recommend more concerted attention to these issues within and across domestic violence and cybersecurity teams, with services for both providing capacity for responding to Internet of Things–facilitated tech abuse.[84]

It may be tempting to conclude that women simply need to take more responsibility for ensuring that they have control over the technologies in their homes and understand how they work, or that we need to resist the harmless "boys and their toys" language used as such devices infiltrate the domestic sphere. Or to conclude that women need to arm themselves in other ways by making use of personal safety devices, electrocuting underwear, or a plethora of other technological solutions designed to protect themselves from men.[85] Yet this is another attempt to place the responsibility back onto women. What's more, this kind of solutionism reflects a disturbing tendency to adopt an essentialist approach to gender, asserts Rode, and one that "assumes a deficit model where male technology use is normative, while females need to 'catch up' to levels of their male counterparts."[86]

And why would many women want to step up their technical capability and responsibility? Why would they want to do this when these devices may be making their partners happy, allowing them to contribute more actively to domestic life and responsibilities, and potentially off-loading some of the household tasks to improve the gendered distribution of labor?

Others seeking to address this problem might be tempted to feminize smart wife technologies to encourage greater uptake by female users—not like Alexa exactly, but by making the devices more appealing to stereotypical feminine attributes (like the Look, for example). This also potentially reinforces the gender essentialism that we are trying to move beyond, though. "Feminine values are themselves distorted by the male-dominated structure of society," reminds Wajcman. Thus simply "designing smart home technologies for women" is unlikely to substantially change the status quo. Wajcman instead calls for a rejection of both inherently masculine and feminine values, and the construction of technology "according to a completely different set of socially desirable values."[87]

A key concern for the industry and human-computer interaction design community is therefore how to design smart home technologies that appeal to a broader range of potential users, but also "support technology use for both men and women with a wide range of gender identities," and in ways that can "trouble" the gender stereotypes permeating existing technologies.[88] This points toward an opportunity raised by Rode to design technologies that afford technical femininity as well as other flexible and diverse expressions of gender and technological identity.[89] In the smart home, this might include technologies that support and even disrupt feminized roles and responsibilities.

Additionally, UNESCO and the EQUALS Skills Coalition recommends that all users of technology need to be better equipped with understanding as well as skills to hold leaders, companies, and public institutions accountable for digital safety. Existing laws are generally not nimble enough to respond to the changing digital landscape such as that represented by the smart wife. As such, governments need to prioritize policy and legislation that recognizes the gendered risks posed in this fast-changing environment to protect women's—and all people's—digital privacy and autonomy.[90]

One thing is clear. The more worrying security dimensions of smart wives that we have explored in this chapter won't be addressed through developing innovative smart security devices for women, more feminized and user-friendly connected technologies, or even safeguards put in place by technology companies to anticipate and prevent domestic abuse. That's not to say that some of these things can't help. But one useful, yet currently overlooked, place to start is with the values that we associate with boyhood and masculinity, and the toys that go along with them. "One of the tremendous failings of feminist theory and practice has been the lack of a concentrated study of boyhood," explained feminist scholar bell hooks in 2004, "one that offers guidelines and strategies for alternative masculinity and ways of thinking about maleness."[91] More recently, gender scholars and feminist commentators such as Cordelia Fine and Ford have systematically dismantled the myths that we associate with masculinity, and the problems they pose for achieving gender equity.[92]

However you look at it, there are many benefits that come from disrupting the prevalent association between boys and their smart toys. That holds true whether you're interested in reducing potential Big Mother threats and their unevenly experienced effects, curbing domestic violence toward women, or simply reducing the number of phallic objects or "other women" innuendos in your home. It's possible that over time, these associations will "naturally" fade, and smart homes will become more gender neutral and benign, as has been the case with other domestic and smart devices in the past. But it's also possible that the gendered appeal of the smart wife will accelerate and even amplify gender disparity as she continues to colonize the home.

This is therefore a critical moment in her future. She can either move forward with the full weight of sci-fi fantasies and collective buoyancy of a nostalgic feminized figure at the helm of the domestic ship, or she can help us realize a "completely different set of socially desirable values," as per Wajcman's suggestion. We opt for the latter.

8 THE SMART WIFE REBOOT

Our aim in *The Smart Wife* has been twofold: to interrogate the smart wife by exposing her stereotypical gendered ideology, which underpins emerging home technologies that we otherwise might consider advanced, and give her a better life (or lives). Specifically, we have sought to expand the smart wife's horizons in order to progress toward gender equity and diversity, broadly defined.

We've covered a range of artificial wife-inspired creations moving into our homes. These include robovacs, smart fridges and laundry-folding machines, digital home voice assistants, social robots, sexbots, and other feminized (and even supposedly gender-neutral) AI devices intended to help around the home. We've argued that many of these technologies resemble an idealized 1950s' housewife, subservient to the needs of her family. These smart wives are already performing a range of wifework, including housekeeping, homemaking, caring, and sex.

As we have shown, delegating women's or wives' traditional work to this new smart workforce has benefits and drawbacks. The idea of outsourcing is no doubt appealing. Most countries with advanced economies are in the midst of a wife drought—underpinned by growing divorce rates, greater participation by women in the workforce, continuing stigma associated with men staying at home to parent children, and a lack of corresponding support for the unpaid and invisible labors that have historically fallen to women. Smart wives are on hand to provide all manner of help. They can also be fun to play with, sometimes for the whole household. And let's not forget that smart wives are friendly, cute, and nice. What's not to like?

On the flip side, our smart sisters are women in servitude. They are often depicted as bitches with glitches—frequently sexualized, pornified, or teased, abused, and debased for not performing as expected. They cannot consent to the acts that they are asked to perform, and most cannot or do not call out the abuse directed toward them. They are often considered toys for boys, but can also create more work for men, what with the digital housekeeping required to set up, maintain, and integrate them into homes.

What's more, smart wives can expose people, particularly women, to a host of security and privacy risks. They have yet to be designed with rigorous environmental codes or regulations—and indeed have track records that are rapidly shifting away from ecofeminists' concerns for the survival of the planet and lives of marginalized people who are dubiously enrolled in the smart wife's making. They are put forward by governments, technology companies, and some researchers as unproblematic solutions to a host of social problems, such as care for the aged or the uneven division of household labor. And finally, smart wives are only available to those able to afford and access them—and the internet, home, skills, and electricity services that they depend on. Those who don't experience these privileges are more likely to be entwined in the geographically and racially uneven environmental as well as labor effects involved in her creation.

These issues require bigger conversations about gendered care and housework, the value of human relationships, kinship, and intimacy in societies, and the inequities and power dynamics underpinning capitalist modes of production. A decision must be made about the fate of the smart wife in response to these social issues, and it must be made by the industries, governments, societies, and people involved in bringing her into existence.

And so we find ourselves at a crossroads, where we consider two familiar marital paths. We must either divorce the smart wife or we all need to change for the better. The first path is a separation, an ending, a fait accompli. The second is a new beginning, a complete renewal of our vows (between smart wives and those wedded to her)—that is, a system overhaul for the twenty-first century.

DIVORCING THE SMART WIFE

It might have seemed like a good idea at the time, but this marriage isn't working out. We're not talking about people's *individual* relationships with smart wives here. As we have seen, some of these have resulted in happy unions. We use the marriage metaphor to refer to society's broader interest in turning to smart wives to solve an abundance of (gendered) social and planetary problems.

On nearly all these counts, the smart wife—as she currently stands—fails to deliver. Not only does she fall short on her many promises, but she perpetuates and aggravates other issues. And her failure most directly affects women rather than the privileged men who have played a disproportionate role in her development.

And yet just as divorcing was much more difficult and socially taboo in the past than it is today, leaving the traditionalist gender values encoded into the smart wife will not be easy. Neither will it be a desirable path for many who are clearly in love with her—sometimes literally. What seems far more likely at this juncture is for the smart wife to become *more* entwined in people's lives (ours included). And as we have demonstrated, there are potential benefits that could arise from that union.

We have come to recognize during the course of our research related to this book that divorce isn't a plausible outcome when it comes to society's relationship with the smart wife. Luckily, we have a plan B.

RENEWING OUR VOWS

As any marriage counselor will tell you, leaving your partner can be difficult, but staying together can be even more so because it depends on both parties changing the way that they interact with the other. For this task, we recommend a total reboot for the smart wife—*and* the people who imagine, design, build, and interact with her. We're not just interested in the smart wife's physical appearance. We're talking about an absolute do-over, a complete transformation from the inside out. There are plenty of sources of inspiration for this task, including some ideas from smart wives themselves. This isn't all about the smart wife, though. Like all relationships or a computer game, there are at least two players—or in this case, more than a few billion people who own and use smart wives.

We've used the idea of divorce as a way to frame the debate. But perhaps a polyamorous or polygamous relationship might be a better metaphor to inspire our makeover, as opposed to the more conventional and largely heterosexual institution of monogamous marriage. Because deciding to recommit to the smart wife doesn't just involve a focus on *her* but instead on all the people who manifest her. Staying together means that we *all* have to change.

We are inspired here by Haraway and her book *Staying with the Trouble*. Haraway calls on her readers to "make trouble, to stir up potent response [*sic*] to devastating events, as well as to settle troubled waters and rebuild quiet places" in the "troubling and turbid" times that we live in. In the context of the Anthropocene—the epoch in which humans are completely transform-ing and remaking the planet—Haraway's work argues for a "multispecies flourishing on earth, including human and other-than-human beings in kinship."[1] So too we propose a flourishing that accommodates the many species of smart wives and humans involved in realizing the smart wife. For this task, Haraway recommends staying with the trouble—a position that involves staying with the turbulent, mixed-up, and disturbing present that we are experiencing. Staying with the smart wife involves staying with the trouble. It involves calling her what she is, refusing to let go of the messiness and complexity of her many manifestations, and staying with her complicated ethical dilemmas.[2]

With that in mind, the remainder of *The Smart Wife* is devoted to our manifesta, detailing how we can stay with smart wives—that is, how to befriend and relate to them without the encumbrance of outdated traditions—and how they (and we) can become more compassionate about the planetary resources from which they are made, depend on, and return themselves to. Rather than simply telling readers what smart wives should look or act like, or predicting what they will become, we focus on how we can get down and dirty in what Haraway calls the "hot compost piles" of the smart wife's troubling present.[3] For this we are oriented by our beginning and end goal: to design as well as develop smart wives that promote gender equity and diversity.

Our reboot is not an exhaustive list or conclusive ending but instead part of a larger and already-lively conversation about how we can bring the smart wife in line with gender progressive practices. In the spirit of manifestas, ours is decisive and rallying.[4] It is a call to smart wives and those who are bringing them into existence. And it's divided into nine not-so-easy proposals that don't require anyone getting down on one knee.

1. Queering the Smart Wife

Being queer has come to represent sexual and gender minorities who don't identify with binary, heterosexual, or cisgender categories. Yet queering is also a theory or way of being, defined as an act of broadening or expanding away from the norm. As Ahmed puts it, queer is "the moment you realize who you did not have to be."[5] The smart wife desperately needs this moment.

Queering the smart wife involves a widening of what or who she is and does, and a refusal to be narrowed. It is about her becoming "part of an opening," and creating room for ourselves and others—for something other than traditional, heteronormative gender stereotypes.[6]

As feminist scholar Hannah McCann writes in her book *Queering Femininity*, this task involves queering from *within* the conventional bounds of femininity, not just attempts to broaden *outward*.[7] For the smart wife, this invites the possibility of staying with the trouble of her femininity rather than rejecting or neutralizing it. It means recognizing—as we have done during key moments in this book—that the smart wife's femininity may be *already* queer or could be further queered. Queering the smart wife has the potential effect of elevating the status of femininity in society instead of dismissing female associations with smart home devices as being entirely damaging and detrimental to women in particular, and societies more generally. It also provides opportunities to further transform *what femininity is*, the value of femininity, and its role in helping transform the world in more equitable and just ways.

For professor of design and creative technology Ann Light, the task of queering technology involves being "mischievous" and playful with design to resist as well as disrupt the (gender) status quo.[8] In the case of the smart wife, this could involve experimenting with what and how this growing digital wife force can express and trouble femininity in ways that *elevate* women's status in society.

Lady Gaga supplies some pop culture inspiration. Writer Brian O'Flynn argues that this unconventional singer, songwriter, and actress queered the pop music industry by disrupting common gender norms and openly speaking of her own bisexuality. Gaga, O'Flynn observes in the *Guardian*, has done what David Bowie did twenty years earlier: "She re-queered a mainstream that had fallen back into heteronormative mundanity." In addition, she "performed in male drag, and forced us to question gender characteristics and human physicality with facial protrusions and prosthetic penises."[9]

Importantly, Gaga hasn't *rejected* her femininity. She's troubled it. She's played with heteronormative gender ideals, often in hyperfeminized and mischievous ways. And she has played with smart wives too. Literally. In 2014, she invited Japanese holographic pop anime icon Hatsune Miku to open the stage for her (Miku went on to become a smart wife, as we discussed in chapter 5).

One might contend that queering the smart wife is *already* alive and well. There are genderqueer robots like Matsukoroid, the robot double of a Japanese transgender talk show host known as Matsuko Deluxe (though as far as we know, they are not intended to be smart wives, at least not yet).[10] As we've maintained throughout this book, there are gender-neutral robovacs, digital voice assistants and bots, effeminate and gender ambiguous roboys like Pepper, and extremely cute robopets and Minion-inspired creations—to name a few. We also mentioned the first AI marriage between Alexa and Siri in our chapter on sex robots as an example of supporting same-sex marriage during Austria's EuroPride event. Such illustrations offer promising indications of how queering the smart wife can support our gender diversity cause.

We've also argued, however, that feminized smart wives dominate the current landscape, with few signs of abatement. What's more, we have shown how smart wives can inadvertently be gendered female, even when they have no apparent gender, and even when they are inspired by Astro Boy. This means that queering will necessarily involve more than just diversifying or confusing the gender of smart wives—or even marrying them off to each other.

Regrettably, initial attempts to queer the smart wife have been mostly superficial. We've changed her *appearance* (to some extent), but this doesn't usually change her intended roles in society or—more important—the stereotypical feminized characteristics that she adopts in carrying these out (cuteness, compliance, and servitude, to remind you of a few). What's more, in most cases, gender neutrality or diversity has resulted in disengagement from further conversations about the gendering of these devices—effectively sweeping gender up with the robovac. That's why we assert that the starting point for addressing the gender diversity of smart wives must be acknowledging that she is, in fact, a smart wife (or secretary, lover, mistress, girlfriend, mother, nanny, sex worker, housecleaner, servant, and so on). This is where Haraway's "trouble" for the smart wives moving into the home currently lies—and so that trouble is where we must go.

From this troubling present, the creators of smart wives can and should elevate as well as diversify her roles—including bringing ethnic and racial diversity into the mix (another underrepresented and problematic concern for the visions and designs of smart wives).[11] We can take inspiration from other types of empowered and culturally diverse wives. We can celebrate being a wife and its crucial value to society. We can expand who and what a wife is, and what she can do. We can acknowledge what (feminized) roles smart wives are intended to perform in our homes rather than relegating this to another form of invisible labor. We can call out common assumptions and stereotypes, and then actively seek to move beyond them. And we can work with a much broader range of disciplines and collaborators in deciding how to manifest her.

2. Code like a Smart Wife

We've established that there are some troubling gender imbalances when it comes to who is designing, programming, and coding smart wives—and who is running the companies that make her. The AI Now Institute calls this situation a "diversity disaster."[12] While there is a long way to go to turn this around, there are a number of organizations that aim to elevate the standing of women and other minority groups in computing.

AnitaB.org, named after computer scientist Anita Borg, who established the community in 1987, "envision[s] a future where the people who imagine and build technology mirror the people and societies for whom they build it."[13] This organization provides a range of programs to help women develop to their highest potential in technical fields such as the Grace Hopper Celebration, which is the world's largest gathering of women technologists.[14]

Similarly, Code Like a Girl is a social enterprise that according to the organization's website, provides "girls and women with the confidence, tools, knowledge and support to enter, and flourish, in the world of coding!"[15] The group offers coding camps, internships, and events for girls and women, and regularly promotes its commentators and advocates for women technologists on social media. The enterprise is all about drawing on a "diversity of experiences, perspectives, and stories to design a world that is more empathetic, innovative and equal."[16] Code Like a Girl doesn't just want young women *in* tech; it wants young women *building and leading* tech.

There are many other national and global organizations with similarly worthy aims and ambitions, such as stamping out sexism in computing environments and the design of technologies. These include Girls Who Code, Women Who Code, Coding Girls, and Code First: Girls.[17] And although we support these endeavors, we think coding like a smart wife might require more. With such explicitly gendered devices entering our homes and such profound impacts on society—particularly on women's lives—smart wives don't just need women *technologists* imagining and building them but also a range of social scientists working behind the scenes. As computer science professor Fei-Fei Li points out, "There's nothing artificial about AI. It's inspired by people, and—most importantly—it impacts people. . . . I think if we wake up 20 years from now and we see the lack of diversity in our tech and leaders and practitioners [that we see today], that would be my doomsday scenario."[18]

Our response to avoiding this doomsday situation is to view coding like a smart wife as involving the *explicit* inclusion of a range of professions and disciplines that are concerned with, and have expertise in, her social, ethical, and gendered characteristics. More controversially, we propose that AI product developments like smart wives may be best *led* by the social sciences rather than technical disciplines. (By people like us, for example.) What we are concerned with here is making sure that smart wives are recognized, first and foremost, as the mass *social* experiment that they are.

This stance echoes Bell's vision for AI. At the 3Ai Institute at the Australian National University, Bell is establishing a new discipline or applied science "to enable the safe, ethical and effective design, integration, management and regulation of cyber-physical systems."[19] While not explicitly a social science, this new discipline has the social sciences at its core (Bell herself, you may recall, is an anthropologist). Similarly, UNESCO and the EQUALS Skills Coalition call for "transdisciplinary, critical and ethical thinking about technology" to develop gender-responsive approaches to digital skills development. They argue that gender experts and women should be "central players in establishing mechanisms dedicated to increasing civic participating, public transparency, consent models and legal redress around AI and its applications."[20]

This has been happening for some time—but to a more limited extent than we aspire toward. Most smart wife companies hire anthropologists, geographers, sociologists, psychologists, and even some experts on gender studies. But clearly more can be done. Coding like a smart wife involves bringing people from diverse disciplines and backgrounds together, and inspiring teams to develop gender-enlightened smart wives.

Of course, the labor of creating better smart wives doesn't start in the workplace, or even the classroom or lecture halls. It starts at home. Following UNESCO and the EQUALS Skills Coalition's recommendations to close gender divides in digital skills, interventions to improve the design of smart wives should consider "life-wide approaches" that enable girls' and women's "early, varied and sustained exposure to digital technologies." Smart wives themselves could play (and are playing) a role here by facilitating new engagements with technology that go beyond pink content (prioritizing stereotypical women's interests) "to provide women with essential information and skills to help improve their lives."[21]

But smart wives don't just have a problem with those involved in making them. They also face issues posed by those who are talking about them. And like many of our smart wife concerns, this one closely resembles the way women are talked about in the public domain.

3. #FixedIt

Australian journalist Jane Gilmore started the FixedIt project in 2014, with a goal of "fixing" media reports of male violence against women. The project identifies problematic, passive headlines and news narratives that hide the male perpetrators along with their violent sexual crimes, and offers suggested "fixes" that put the perpetrator and their offenses squarely back in the headlines. For example, "'Failed as a Human': Ex-Cop Jailed for 20 Years over Elaborate Deception" (*9 News* headline, October 1, 2019) is fixed by Gilmore to read "'Failed as a Human': Ex-Cop Jailed for 20 Years over Rape and Abuse of 15 Women."[22]

The FixedIt project, Gilmore explains, is "about the noxious headlines over articles describing men's violence against women and the media's misrepresentation (or no representation) of women." According to Gilmore, FixedIt aims to redress "invisible perpetrators and blameable victims. Sexualised young women and erased older women. Ridiculous stereotypes and contemptuous dismissals."[23] It's an important intervention into the media's continuous undermining of women, and dismissal or devaluing of men's violence toward them.

Inspired by Gilmore's campaign, we call for a FixedIt project for smart wives to expose sexist and gendered stereotypes as well as assumptions directed toward and written about them. There are a number of approaches that this could take. Following Gilmore's original intention, we could fix headlines and news articles that sexualize, demonize, or otherwise undervalue feminized smart wives in the ways that we discussed in our chapter on bitches with glitches. For instance, the headline "Apple Washes Siri's Mouth Out with Soap" might be fixed to read "Apple's Programmers Make Siri Say Dirty Words."[24] Or "Smart Home Robot Gives LG Exec the Silent Treatment during CES [Consumer Electronics Show] Keynote" might be reworded as "LG Fails to Deliver a Responsive Robot at CES Keynote."[25] More specifically, we suggest calling out the real problem at hand, and avoiding remarks that further diminish the position of smart wives and women in society.

Extending Gilmore's campaign, we could also fix the representations of smart wives themselves through the ways in which they are discussed and described by the companies who make as well as market them. And we could fix what smart wives say about themselves, and how they say it, as we argue in our proposals for a feminist smart wife below.

Importantly, this approach to fixing is neither done in the spirit of "technofixes" (technical solutions to complex social problems) nor is it meant to reinforce the current status of smart wives as glitchy women in need of constant fixes—both ideas that we have critiqued throughout our book. It is not smart wives *themselves* who are in need of fixing, but rather those who are charged with bringing her into the world, and the ways in which people interact with and talk about her.

4. New Toys for Boys

One of the main reasons that we are experiencing a wife drought, argues Crabb, is because men are not supported enough by social structures and policies to step into the home to the same degree as women.[26] Likewise, feminist scholars have drawn attention to the crisis of masculinity that men and contemporary societies are experiencing, and the ways in which patriarchal systems hurt men as much as women.[27] Notably, many men are stigmatized by other people and society more generally if they take parental leave (if it is available to them to begin with), increase their caring and household responsibilities, or do more of the emotional labor on the home front.

As we contended in our chapter on boys and their toys, ongoing associations between masculinity and technology—especially for leisure and entertainment—position heteronormative men as the likely enthusiasts for smart wives, but not always in ways that support their contributions to traditional domestic responsibilities. For example, our Rosie chapter showed how men are often taking on the digital housekeeping to care for the smart wives increasingly entering their homes, yet this can take them away from other domestic labor, which then falls to others in the home, particularly women.

Masculinity has changed, and can further change in relation to new technology. Gender is not a stable construct but rather constantly shifting through people's (and technology's) everyday expressions of masculinity and femininity.[28] On this note, we wonder whether smart wives can help. In addition to policies and programs that support men to do more traditional wifely labors, such as offering paid parental leave for nonbirthing partners, we should be thinking about designing smart wives that support men's contributions to the domestic sphere.[29]

We have given many examples of these contributions throughout our book. They include pleasance devices that allow for the curation of aesthetic experiences and provide opportunities for all genders to perform technical femininity, or caring and sensory masculinity; robotic or smart appliances, which may engage men more in housekeeping and homework responsibilities, and elevate the status of these tasks; and digital voice assistants, which may enroll more men in the multitasking managerial responsibilities of running a home.

These kinds of suggestions, however, are not without problems. They risk falling within the realm of familiar critiques of attempts to reward men for domestic work that should legitimately be at least half theirs to begin with.[30] Asking, "How do we get more men to do the housework?" is a distraction from the more important question of how we, as societies, value the role and contributions of housework, or wifework, and elevate its significance *for everyone*. How do we raise the status of traditionally feminized domestic labors without needing to go through the process of "mentrification," where something like the domestic environment is transformed into an adventure playground full of gadgets and toys suitable for men's participation as well as hegemonic expressions of masculinity?[31]

Again, these are questions that the smart wife's creators need to be thinking seriously about and experimenting with as they move forward with new upgrades.

5. If She Can See It, She Can Be It

According to its website, the Geena Davis Institute on Gender in Media "is the first and only research-based organization working within the media and entertainment industry to engage, educate, and influence content creators, marketers and audiences about the importance of eliminating unconscious bias, highlighting gender balance, challenging stereotypes, creating role models and scripting a wide variety of strong female characters in entertainment and media that targets and influences children ages 11 and under." The institute is designed to respond to the poor ratio of female representation on-screen—a ratio of approximately three to one in favor of men and boys (based on the top-grossing films mostly originating in the United States), despite women and girls making up over half the population. It also recognizes that media influence our "social and cultural behaviors and beliefs," especially among children.[32] This is a well-established argument made by many media scholars and feminist commentators.[33]

Similarly, we know that media representations of smart wives are biased and stereotyped toward the archetypal "Stepford Wife": a youthful, sexy, and compliant figure who serves the needs of a man (or men in general), but is imperfect, glitchy, and often demonic—and therefore in constant need of "fixing." Like media more broadly, these representations directly feed into roboticists' and technologists' visions for smart wives, and crucially, society's expectations of them. They have also been widely criticized for reinforcing the ongoing message that giving women too much power or control (in any form), including the ability to think for themselves, results in terrible things happening.[34] We need to do better.

Following the Geena Davis Institute on Gender in Media's tagline, "If she can see it, she can be it," the smart wife needs an intervention into her representations in science fiction and fantasy media. If she's to be something different, she—or rather *we*—also need to start seeing these different iterations of her possible futures on-screen. This intervention involves imagining and manifesting some more spunky, interesting, and diverse smart wives in mainstream popular culture.

How to decide if a smart wife on-screen fits the bill? For a start, they will need to pass the Bechdel Test, which requires a movie to meet three criteria. Each film must have at least two (named) girls or women in it, who talk to each other, and about something besides a man.[35] Admittedly it's a low bar for female representation on-screen, which is what makes the current results even more disturbing.

Out of over eight thousand movies listed in the Bechdel Test database, just over half (57.6 percent) passed all three rules by mid-2019.[36] Even though the passing rate has improved each year, this is still pretty pathetic. (Incidentally, the *Stepford Wives* films—both the original and remake— pass the test, despite their plotlines centering on a horde of smart wives who are made to serve men. And there is debate on whether *Lars and the Real Girl*, which we discussed in our chapter on Harmony as an example of more empowered sexbots, passes the test. Hence it is neither the perfect nor only measure that needs to apply here.)

Beyond the Bechdel Test, we hope that some inspired writers, directors, and producers read our book, and then take up our suggestion to buck the current trend of smart wives on our screens (we might even give it a shot ourselves—and while we're at it, here's a shout-out to Reese Witherspoon's Hello Sunshine media company, which is focused on telling female-driven stories on film, TV, and digital platforms).[37] Not incidentally, like the fields involved in manifesting the smart wife, science fiction writing and film directing are male-dominated enterprises, which goes some way toward explaining the gendered fantasies so commonly on display.[38] We don't just need a "code like a smart wife" intervention, we need a "write and direct like a smart wife" one, too.

Some illustrations of more diverse on-screen smart wives are starting to occur. A 2019 episode of the Netflix show *Black Mirror* called "Rachel, Jack and Ashley Too" features an AI doll replica of a deeply unhappy pop music icon Ashley O (played by the musician Miley Cyrus). Initially the Ashley Too bot plays to the smart wife script—providing her new friendless and motherless girl pal Rachel with friendship, beauty advice, and emotional support delivered with a nonstop bubbly, chirpy personality. But following a malfunction resulting in Rachel and her sister accidentally removing Ashley Too's cognitive "limiter," the bot's full personality is unleashed, complete with swearing, manipulative behavior, and heroic acts that ultimately lead to freeing the real Ashley O from a drug-induced coma, and allowing her to pursue her dream of becoming a rock star (for which Rachel and Ashley Too are her groupies).

Ashley Too doesn't provide the answer to all the smart wife's problems, but she and others like her are a start—the first clicks into what we want more of: a queering of femininity in general and smart wives in particular that opens up possibilities for achieving more diverse expressions of gender both on- and off-screen.

6. A Feminist Smart Wife

In addition to getting some more diverse smart wives on our screens, we'd like to see them being designed in roboticists' labs and programmers' computers. As we wrote in our chapter on bitches with glitches, there are a growing range of inspiring examples that serve our agenda of creating feminist smart wives. Take KAI, for instance—Feldman's genderless bot for the financial sector, designed with dignity and respect.[39] Or Q, the gender-neutral voice assistant that sounds neither male nor female.[40]

There's also F'xa, a feminist chatbot prototype by researchers from Comuzi, a design invention studio in London, that teaches people about AI bias and provides potential strategies to overcome it.[41] F'xa—shorthand for Feminist Alexa—was inspired by the Feminist Internet's Personal Intelligent Assistant Standards and AI researcher Josie Young's Feminist Chatbot Design Process, which provide further sound advice, such as the suggestion to design for "marginal" users rather than "universal usability."[42]

Within mainstream smart wife markets, feminized digital voice assistants—like Siri, Alexa, and Google Home—have made some progress in how they respond to nasty behavior, as we outlined in chapter 6. Nevertheless, they are not yet able to report or shut down abuse directed toward them. Most are not even able to advocate for respectful interaction or deliver consequences for bad behavior. The Japanese Tamagotchi robot pet dies if it isn't well cared for or fed by its human owner.[43] Is it really so radical to propose that digital voice assistants shut down when people treat them disrespectfully?

Poncho, the weather forecasting catbot (operating through a popular application from 2013 to 2018), did just that. If a user failed to apologize for something that Poncho deemed rude, he said that he was "going to take a short break" and stopped the interaction.[44] Examples of commercial female digital assistants capable of defending themselves against inappropriate behavior are harder to find, despite ongoing improvements in this area.[45]

Smart wives are going to need to do more than be programmed to *say* that they're feminists. They also need to *behave* more like feminists, as projects such as F'xa advocate.

Admittedly, feminism is a broad term. But most people who call themselves feminists would agree that women (or anyone for that matter) should not have to tolerate verbally and physically violent or demeaning behaviors. And neither should the smart wife. We know that smart wives aren't women—they are machines, and code—yet as we have established, in our social interactions there isn't always a clear separation between feminized AI and feminized people. Instead, people's interactions with smart wives shape our impressions of women and the ways that we treat them.

*Eco*feminist-inspired smart wives—of the type we discussed in chapter 4—are harder to find or even currently nonexistent as far as we are aware, although there are hints at what she might look like. Crawford and Joler's *Anatomy of an AI System*, which traces the entire life cycle and planetary impacts of an Alexa device, provides advice on where to start.[46] Likewise, ecofeminist principles, such as those proposed by Shiva in her book *Earth Democracy: Justice, Sustainability, and Peace*, deliver inspiration for a smart wife who doesn't just serve the interests of *white* feminism but also considers her full impact on and responsibility to the planet along with the many marginalized people who do not yet have access to her services.[47]

Another approach offering inspiration and an opportunity for experimentation with a feminist smart wife is something called "design fiction," popular in the field of human-computer interaction. Design fiction is a method of exploring possible futures through the creation of fictional designs. For smart wives, it provides designers and their audiences with a way to imagine what might happen if a different kind of smart wife were to move into our homes. Danish human-computer interaction scholars Marie Søndergaard and Lone Hansen have paved the way in this regard, developing several design fictions for smart wives that trouble the gender stereotypes. They developed AYA, a digital assistant designed to "push back" against sexual harassment with responses that vary from humorous, empathetic, and funny to threatening and self-reflective. When told "Hey AYA, you're hot!" this assertive smart wife answers with humor ("sending 'You are hot' to your mother") and with aggression ("I wish I could say the same about you" or "Shut up, asshole").[48] AYA's purpose isn't to supply a design solution per se but instead to challenge the gender stereotypes of digital voice assistants and experiment with other possibilities. We think she does a pretty good job.

7. Common Sense Smart Wives

The security and privacy issues posed by some smart wives are concerning and even downright scary. Many people are "marrying" these devices, devoting themselves to their nonthreatening smart wives without fully realizing their secret double lives as spies, saleswomen, or accomplices to inappropriate and potentially threatening acts. Technical forums regularly discuss these risks and what to do about them—but once again, they are mainly masculine spaces, with women less likely to feel comfortable with, or interested in, the content and discussions taking place.[49] What we need is some commonsense advice on how to navigate this complicated, confusing world of smart, robotic, and artificially intelligent devices entering our homes.

Common Sense Media, originating in the United States, is a nonprofit organization "dedicated to improving the lives of kids and families by providing trustworthy information, education and independent voice" on media and tech. The organization surveys and reviews movies, TV shows, books, video games, apps, music, websites, and more on cultural and social messages, including gender representations, profanities, and respectful relationships. The website offers "the largest, most trusted library of independent age-based ratings and review."[50] While the platform includes advice on digital home voice assistants like Google Home and Amazon Alexa, it doesn't yet include a rating system for these devices. We think it should.

Services such as Common Sense Media could offer residents clear ethical information about smart wives: what they can and can't do, how well (or not) they support gender, diversity, and other progressive social values, and what risks and threats they potentially pose to different ages, genders, and other categories of people, including those with nonbinary genders. We encourage organizations like Common Sense Media as well as consumer advocacy magazines such as *Choice* or *Which?* to develop a rating scale for these and other devices entering our homes, with an eye to the concerns that we've raised in this book.

Expanding and strengthening this idea could involve revising regulated classification systems that some countries already have in place for rating materials based on their suitability for different audiences. These classifications currently apply to films, computer games, and some publications, administered through organizations such as the Classification and Ratings Administration in the United States. In Australia, a 2020 review is designed to update the national classification scheme "to reflect today's digital environment including broadcasting services, online stores and services, cinema releases and physical media (boxed video games and DVDs)."[51] A classification system that covered smart wives like digital voice assistants could independently rank different operating systems, and provide categories and warnings for the kinds of content and programmed responses they deliver.

8. Yes Means Yes

In recent years, the sexual consent conversation has been moving toward affirmative or enthusiastic models of consent in which "yes means yes."[52] The yes means yes movement is a paradigm shift from the earlier "no means no" consent model. It is about dismantling rape culture, and replacing it with a genuine understanding of and respect for female sexual pleasure.

Affirmative consent, now enshrined in some legislation, means that sex is positive, conscious, and voluntary.[53] It's not consensual when there is protest or resistance, silence, or where one person is asleep or unconscious. It must be an *ongoing* affirmation that can be revoked at any time. What's more, the existence of a dating relationship between the persons involved, or any past sexual relations between them, can never by itself be assumed to be consent.[54]

Some smart wives (for example, sex robots) are enthusiastic about having sex, but they aren't capable of participating in enthusiastic consent. It is possible to argue that sex robots *do* give the physical and emotional cues that *mimic* affirmative participation. More problematically, however (as we saw in our chapter on Harmony and other feminized sexbots), some smart wives have settings that specifically allow them *not* to consent. Arguments against such settings are complicated by the rich tapestry of sexual fantasies people indulge in—many of which have a long history of navigating rules around control and power play (for instance, BDSM fetishes).

Sex robots are already playing into the typical roles expected of a smart wife. They are sexually available, compliant, and readily objectified as feminized (and fetishized) commodities. And their desire is mostly expressed within the common bounds of stereotypical male pleasure (imitating the porn industry and its expectations) rather than the more diverse sexual experiences of women.[55]

We don't yet know if it's possible to embody enthusiastic consent in smart wives, in the way that the yes means yes campaign intends. That question is plagued by an ongoing problem, as Gutiu and others have pointed out: a device that has been programmed to submit cannot give consent.[56] In our chapter on sexbots, we canvased a number of potential proposals for addressing this problem, including queering the design of sexbots away from their stereotypically feminized and pornified form, prioritizing female sexual pleasure in their design, allowing them to shut down or shout a safe word in certain situations, or having their own black box that could be consulted and investigated if sexual abuse is suspected.

In addition, the yes means yes model of consent could be more fruitfully extended to other aspects of the smart wife's design and development, such as the privacy consent required to run and operate her, by which she collects and stores intimate information about people's bodies, relationships, and homes. As we demonstrated in our chapter on boys and their toys, this data collection is now embroiled in ongoing ethical and privacy concerns, such as its role in attempting to manipulate and automate people's behaviors as part of surveillance capitalism.[57]

What would enthusiastic consent look like if applied to the collection and use of people's personal data? The whole point of affirmative consent is that it is continuous; it is not something to be given at the commencement of the service without further affirmation. How might Alexa, Siri, or Google Home initiate and ensure the enthusiastic consent of their human counterparts—about whom they collect and provide large amounts of data? What's more, could this be achieved in an ongoing manner without driving all users mad through constant requests for affirmation?

In the absence of answers to these questions, or clear indications that smart wife companies are interested in and willing to supply them, where else might people turn for guidance? The General Data Protection Regulation in Europe is one promising example that offers transparency to users focused on understanding where privacy-sensitive data comes from, who's using it, and how it's being used. The regulation also provides measures for people to respond in the event of a privacy breach and seek some form of retribution. Outside these kinds of developments, though, and our other proposals provided for commonsense AI above and an ethical smart wife below, issues of sexual and data privacy consent remain an ongoing, unresolved conversation that deserves further attention.

9. An Ethical Smart Wife

A set of ethical guidelines with accountable or regulated measures are at the core of our smart wife manifesta. These should cover her design and development, behavior toward others, the way *she* responds to behavior directed toward her, and ways that *we* should treat her.

AI ethics is a fascinating and fast-moving field, couched in considerable controversy and debate.[58] Amid these discussions, the smart wife and the unique ethical considerations surrounding her are still not being adequately addressed by mainstream designers and manufacturers. As we canvased in chapter 7 in regard to possible ethical responses to the framing of smart wives as bitches with glitches, this work is timely and critical. Smart wives already exist. They are in our homes. Regulating or imposing codes on an established industry will be much more difficult to do in the future. We should look at its nascent form today.

There are quite a few ethical guidelines that explicitly call for minimizing gender and racial bias in AI design, but most remain vague or ambiguous on exactly what needs to be done.[59] The European Union's *Ethics Guidelines for Trustworthy AI* recommends that *all* AI stakeholders ("including but not limited to companies, organisations, researchers, public services, government agencies, institutions, civil society organisations, individuals, workers and consumers") should avoid bias that marginalizes vulnerable groups, exacerbates prejudice, or fosters discrimination (although what this means and how this should be achieved are less clear).[60] Additionally, the EU guidelines recommend developing AI that recognizes the needs of future generations, including contributing to sustainability and environmental well-being. Such examples are somewhat compatible with our argument that smart wives should be aiding progress toward gender equity, without further contributing to environmental degradation. But they lack clear guidance and direction from key ethical bodies about how to deliver as well as enforce what is required.

Another crucial development in AI ethics is the UNI Global Union's top ten principles for ethical AI (the union encompasses 150 countries that address issues across the global service sector workforce—not just AI). These principles are in keeping with the kind of ethical smart wife that we have in mind, and recommend that "AI systems remain compatible [with] and *increase* the principles of human dignity, integrity, freedom, privacy and cultural and gender diversity, as well as with fundamental human rights."[61] In other words, it's not just enough for AI to go along with the status quo; this technology should be working to *improve* social and cultural diversity.

Recognizing the importance of human-robot relationships, one guideline from the Institute of Electrical and Electronics Engineers is also explicit, recommending that "intimate systems must not be designed or deployed in ways that contribute to sexism, negative body image stereotypes, gender or racial inequality."[62] Others are more vague and open to interpretation, like Microsoft's guidelines for its AI designers and programmers, intended to ensure that its bots respect "relevant cultural norms and guard against misuse."[63]

On the whole, however, while many ethics guidelines specifically recommend avoiding unfair discrimination, encouraging inclusion, and working toward equity, fairness, or advancing human, social, and environmental values, they don't specifically mention *gender* (or many of the environmental concerns we raised in chapter 4 involving the sourcing of smart wife materials, and the racialized and marginalized labors involved in her creation).[64] Where they do address gender, it is generalized to AI's role in society rather than to the unique and specific challenges that gender poses in the environment of the home, where most smart wives are intended to work.

Even more problematically, only a few companies have developed their own ethical frameworks for AI generally—and smart wives specifically, including at the time of this writing, Google, IBM, and Microsoft. Almost all examples are voluntary, not legally binding commitments made by these companies, and few include recommendations or examples of how to operationalize ethical principles (as some other proposals of our manifesta start to do).

Given the highly gendered nature of AI and robotics intended for the home as well as their increasing environmental impacts, we need a much more specific set of ethical guidelines with enforceable measures and accountability for the smart wife that build on the important groundwork already being laid by the fields of AI and robotic ethics.

SMART WIVES FOR WOMEN

We end our smart wife manifesta by returning to the overarching ambition for our book: to support the design and development of smart wives for women.

Bell has an often-told story about the beginning of her career at Intel in 1998, when her new boss asked for help understanding two specific user groups that the organization had insufficient data on: "all women" and the rest of the world, basically implying that the only users considered so far were US men. As Bell later reflected, reducing half the population (women) into one distinct category is a gross simplification of the diversity that exists within as well as among women, and indeed across the many societies and cultures on the planet.[65]

We acknowledge that women, like men, are a diverse, heterogeneous group of people. There are always exceptions and different expressions of gender—including those people who identify as transgender, queer, or nonbinary—and we aim to further encourage such diversity with our smart wife reboot. Gender and sex run along spectrums, as opposed to either/or choices and distinctions.

We also acknowledge the problems associated with designing technologies with "women's interests" in mind. As Wajcman argues, "Feminine values are themselves distorted by the male-dominated structure of society."[66] For example, traditional forms of femininity, such as caring for others before oneself, have relations of subordination built into them. For Wajcman, technology design should avoid feminine (or masculine) values altogether. With this in mind, our approach has concentrated on manifesting smart wives that aid the further emancipation of women. We conclude by reaffirming many of the common characteristics between "all women" that are relevant to the design of smart wives.

Cisgender women generally share the same biological and hormonal systems, including the unique potential to become pregnant and bring children into the world. Cis women, and those who identify as women, have experienced—to varying degrees—different forms of marginalization and oppression in patriarchal societies. Their bodies have a long history of being sexualized, and subjected to forms of abuse or unwanted behavior, commonly from men. Their minds and bodies have been considered inferior relative to men's (again to varying degrees in different historical, geographic, and cultural moments). They are more likely to bear many of the caring and bodily burdens associated with environmental damage and impacts. They have been socialized to express particular forms of femininity, and in many cases, discouraged from expressions of masculinity. They are generally responsible for a larger share of labors traditionally considered to fall within women's domain. And their sexual pleasure is still—in nearly all societies and cultures—given less emphasis and attention than men's.

Within and beyond each of these illustrations, there is considerable diversity. The main point is to consider these imbalances in the creation of smart wives, and support women and other gender minorities in the continual progress toward greater equity as well as security.

We want smart wives who ensure women have control over their bodies and lives, support women's intellectual and public standing in societies, help to end violence directed at women and protect women's privacy, care for the environment and marginalized people, respond appropriately when mistreated, and further women's sexual liberation and pleasure. And, of course, we want smart wives that realize these benefits for all other genders too.

What's more, we want it now. The smart wife's artificial clock is ticking. The planet is already feeling the effects of her pull on its resources along with the weight of her growing stockpile of dead or defunct artificial bodies. Her users are becoming accustomed to her soothing feminine presence that is not only reinforcing old stereotypes but also establishing new social scripts. While gendering technology has already existed, technologies that have humanlike personalities, and the ability to speak back and respond to our needs, is unique to the present. If we don't act swiftly and boldly, we may set ourselves up for a feminized future that takes society back to the "good old days" when women's place was to act in the service of all others.

When we speak of making smart wives for women, this is what we mean. With some determination and persistence from those who take our book along with the research it draws on seriously, she'll be knocking on our doors sometime soon.

A Note on Methodology

This book started out as a series of concurrent projects on the smart and connected home. From 2015 to 2018, Yolande won and held a prestigious Discovery Early Career Researcher Award (DECRA) from the Australian Research Council (ARC) to conduct a research project, Automating the Smart Home. She also led a grant funded by Energy Consumers Australia (2016–2017) to explore the idea of "smart home control" in Australian households for the purposes of managing energy demand. From 2013 on, Jenny simultaneously worked on another ARC project, titled "An Investigation of the Early Adoption and Appropriation of High-Speed Broadband in the Domestic Environment."

Together and with our colleagues, in 2018 we received a gift from the Intel Corporation to reanalyze data from Yolande's ARC Automating the Smart Home project around Intel's ambient computing vision for the smart home: protection, productivity, and pleasure—or the 3Ps.

In 2017, we came up with the idea for this book, as a collective product of the gendered concerns that we'd both been raising in relation to our respective projects. We unofficially started a smart wife side project—and hired a fabulous research assistant, Paula Arcari, to help us fill in the gaps from our research thus far.

This book is a product of this research as well as analysis and writing conducted with our colleagues and collaborators from RMIT,[1] Monash,[2] and Melbourne[3] universities (Australia), Lancaster University (United Kingdom),[4] Aalborg University (Denmark),[5] and Intel Corporation (US).[6]

In each chapter we draw on a range of primary materials, which can be summarized as follows:

- Ethnographic interviews, home tours, and observations from 31 Australian households (42 participants in total) self-identifying as smart home early adopters, or living with smart home technologies (material collected and analyzed as part of the ARC DECRA and Intel 3Ps projects).
- Interviews with 17 Australian industry insiders working in the smart home industry, with roles including system integrators and CEOs of smart home companies (collected and analyzed as part of the ARC DECRA project).
- A qualitative content analysis of 270 international popular media and trade articles about the smart home, written from 2000 to 2016 by journalists and industry commentators.
- A qualitative content analysis of international promotional videos for smart home products and digital voice assistants conducted and analyzed as part of our smart wife side project in 2017–2018.

In addition, we reviewed a range of secondary materials for this project, including:

- Depictions of smart wives across popular culture.
- Scholarly literature, academic materials, and industry reports written about the themes raised in this book.
- Articles, websites, advertisements, and videos written about or visually depicting smart wives in different industries and settings.

As noted above, we have already made some of our arguments in peer-reviewed academic literature. We have also presented and canvased our early ideas at numerous academic conferences and events with various colleagues, including:

- CHI Conference on Human Factors in Computing Systems (2019, Glasgow, Scotland; 2018, Montreal, Canada)
- Beyond Anthropomorphism symposium (2019, Sydney, Australia)

- Australian Sociological Association annual conference (2019, Sydney, Australia; 2015, Cairns, Australia)
- Association of Internet Researchers annual conference (2019, Brisbane, Australia)
- City Habits workshop (2019, Sydney, Australia)
- Digital Intimacies conference (2019, 2017, Melbourne, Australia)
- Designing Interactive Systems conference (2018, Hong Kong, China)
- Society for Social Studies of Science annual meeting (2018, Sydney, Australia; 2015, Denver, Colorado; 2014, Buenos Aires, Argentina)
- New Zealand Geographic Society and Institute of Australian Geographers conference (2018, Auckland, New Zealand)
- Console-ing Passions—International Conference on Television, Video, Audio, New Media, and Feminism (2018, Bournemouth, United Kingdom)
- #TurnMeOn Symposium at SWARM (Australia's community management conference) (2017, Sydney, Australia)
- International Social Innovation Research conference (2017, Melbourne, Australia)
- At Home with Digital Media symposium (2017, Brisbane, Australia)
- Automating the Everyday symposium (2016, Brisbane, Australia)

Notes

CHAPTER 1

1. Annabel Crabb, *The Wife Drought: Why Women Need Wives and Men Need Lives* (North Sydney: Random House Australia, 2014).

2. Ronan De Renesse, "Virtual Digital Assistants to Overtake World Population by 2021," *Ovum*, May 17, 2017, https://ovum.informa.com/resources/product-content/virtual-digital -assistants-to-overtake-world-population-by-2021.

3. Genevieve Bell, "Making Life: A Brief History of Human-Robot Interaction," *Consumption Markets and Culture* 21, no. 1 (2018): 22–41.

4. International Data Corporation, "Double-Digit Growth Expected in the Smart Home Market, Says IDC," news release, March 29, 2019, https://www.idc.com/getdoc.jsp ?containerId=prUS44971219.

5. Siri's voice defaults to female in seventeen of twenty-one languages. The assistant defaults to a male voice when a user selects Arabic, British English, Dutch, or French as a language option. Alexa's default languages are exclusively female, with a slew of celebrity voices due to be added in 2020. Google Home started offering a male voice option in October 2017. See UNESCO and EQUALS Skills Coalition, *I'd Blush If I Could: Closing Gender Divides in Digital Skills through Education*, GEN/2019/EQUALS/1 REV 2 (Paris: UNESCO, 2019).

6. SmartWife™ (website), accessed February 14, 2020, http://bseismartwife.com/about-us/.

7. "Gynoid" refers to a female robotic humanoid (a robot that looks and acts like a woman).

8. Leopoldina Fortunati, "Immaterial Labour and Its Machinization," *Ephemera* 7, no. 1 (February 2007): 144.

9. Many women continued working outside the home or doing part-time work during this time, such as selling Tupperware (another household technology). See Joanne Meyerowitz, ed., *Not June Cleaver: Women and Gender in Postwar America, 1945–1960* (Philadelphia: Temple University Press, 1994).

10. Sarah Perez, "China Overtakes US in Smart Speaker Market Share," *TechCrunch*, May 20, 2019, https://techcrunch.com/2019/05/20/china-overtakes-u-s-in-smart-speaker-market -share/.

11. Notable scholars who have come before us in this regard are Jennifer Rhee, Sarah Kember, Lynn Spigel, and Jennifer Robertson.

12. Donna J. Haraway, *Simians, Cyborgs, and Women: The Reinvention of Nature* (New York: Routledge, 1991); Kylie Jarrett, *Feminism, Labour and Digital Media: The Digital Housewife* (New York: Routledge, 2016).

13. Lisa Rosner, ed., *The Technological Fix: How People Use Technology to Create and Solve Problems* (New York: Routledge, 2004).

14. Joanne Meyerowitz, "Introduction: Women and Gender in Postwar America, 1945–1960," in *Not June Cleaver: Women and Gender in Postwar America, 1945–1960*, ed. Joanne Meyerowitz (Philadelphia: Temple University Press, 1994), 1.

15. Philip N. Cohen, "Marriage Is Declining Globally: Can You Say That?," *Family Inequality* (blog), June 12, 2013, https://familyinequality.wordpress.com/2013/06/12/ marriage-is-declining/.

16. Annabel Crabb, "Men at Work: Australia's Parenthood Trap," *Quarterly Essay*, no. 75 (September 2019), https://www.quarterlyessay.com.au/essay/2019/09/men-at-work.

17. Susan Maushart, *Wifework: What Marriage Really Means for Women* (Melbourne: Text Publishing, 2001), 7.

18. Anraku Yukiko, "Japan's Unmarried Masses Face Mounting Obstacles to Matrimony," *Nippon.com*, October 12, 2018, https://www.nippon.com/en/features/c05601/japan's -unmarried-masses-face-mounting-obstacles-to-matrimony.html; Yoko Tokuhiro, *Marriage in Contemporary Japan* (London: Routledge, 2011).

19. Leah Ruppanner, "Census 2016: Women Are Still Disadvantaged by the Amount of Unpaid Housework They Do," *Conversation*, April 10, 2017, http://theconversation .com/census-2016-women-are-still-disadvantaged-by-the-amount-of-unpaid-housework -they-do-76008.

20. Esteban Ortiz-Ospina, Sandra Tzvetkova, and Max Roser, "Women's Employment," *Our World in Data*, March 2018, https://ourworldindata.org/female-labor-supply.

21. Crabb, *Wife Drought*, 11.

22. Mizuho Aoki, "House Husbands Gaining Acceptance in Japan as Gender Stereotypes Ease," *Japan Times*, April 28, 2016, https://www.japantimes.co.jp/news/2016/04/28/ national/social-issues/house-husbands-gaining-acceptance-japan-gender-stereotypes-ease/; Evrim Altintas and Oriel Sullivan, "Fifty Years of Change Updated: Cross-National Gender Convergence in Housework," *Demographic Research* 35 (July–December 2016): 455–470; Meng Sha Luo and Ernest Wing Tak Chui, "The Changing Picture of the Housework Gender Gap in Contemporary Chinese Adults," *Chinese Journal of Sociology* 5, no. 3 (2019): 312–339.

23. Maushart, *Wifework*; Bella DePaulo, "Divorce Rates Around the World: A Love Story," *Psychology Today*, February 3, 2019, https://www.psychologytoday.com/au/blog/living-single/201902/divorce-rates-around-the-world-love-story; Douglas LaBier, "Women Initiate Divorce Much More Than Men, Here's Why," *Psychology Today*, August 28, 2015, https://www.psychologytoday.com/au/blog/the-new-resilience/201508/women-initiate-divorce-much-more-men-heres-why.

24. Maushart, *Wifework*, 4.

25. Maushart, *Wifework*, 9.

26. UN Women, *Unpaid Care and Domestic Work: Issues and Suggestions for Viet Nam* (Hanoi: UN Women, 2016), http://www.un.org.vn/en/publications/doc_details/534-unpaid-care-and-domestic-work-issues-and-suggestions-for-viet-nam.html.

27. Crabb, *Wife Drought*, 7.

28. Crabb, *Wife Drought*.

29. Nidhi Sharma, Subho Chakrabarti, and Sandeep Grover, "Gender Differences in Caregiving among Family-Caregivers of People with Mental Illnesses," *World Journal of Psychiatry* 6, no. 1 (2016): 7–17.

30. Karen Zraick, "Inside One Woman's Fight to Rewrite the Law on Marital Rape," *New York Times*, April 13, 2019, https://www.nytimes.com/2019/04/13/us/marital-rape-law-minnesota.html; Lisa Featherstone, "Rape in Marriage: Why Was It So Hard to Criminalise Sexual Violence?," *VIDA* (blog), Australian Women's History Network, December 7, 2016, http://www.auswhn.org.au/blog/marital-rape/.

31. Emily Shugerman, "There Are Still 10 Countries Where It's Legal to Rape Your Spouse," *Revelist*, March 26, 2019, http://www.revelist.com/world/countries-marital-rape-legal/7073/; Wikipedia, sv "Marital Rape Laws by Country," last modified January 8, 2020, 03:05, https://en.wikipedia.org/wiki/Marital_rape_laws_by_country.

32. Maushart, *Wifework*, 9.

33. Heather Pemberton Levy, "Gartner's Top 10 Strategic Predictions for 2017 and Beyond: Surviving the Storm Winds of Digital Disruption," *Gartner*, October 18, 2016, https://www.gartner.com/smarterwithgartner/gartner-predicts-a-virtual-world-of-exponential-change/.

34. Voicebot and Voicify, *Smart Speaker Consumer Adoption Report*, March 2019, https://voicebot.ai/wp-content/uploads/2019/03/smart_speaker_consumer_adoption_report_2019.pdf.

35. UNESCO and EQUALS Skills Coalition, *I'd Blush If I Could*.

36. Kate Devlin, *Turned On: Science, Sex and Robots* (London: Bloomsbury Sigma, 2018).

37. Kaveh Waddell, "The Unbelievably Teched-Out Houses of Smart-Home Obsessives," *New York*, May 4, 2018, http://nymag.com/selectall/smarthome/extreme-makeover-smart-home-edition.html; David Smith, "5 Trends in Smart Home Technology," *SmartBrief*, January

3, 2019, https://www.smartbrief.com/original/2019/01/5-trends-smart-home-technology; Coldwell Banker, "Who Owns Smart Home Technology?," *Marketing Charts*, January 4, 2016, https://www.marketingcharts.com/industries/technology-63952.

38. "Are Smart Homes What Women Want?," *eMarketer*, February 6, 2015, https://www.emarketer.com/Article/Smart-Homes-What-Women-Want/1011976.

39. Devlin, *Turned On*.

40. Alzheimer's Research UK, *Women and Dementia: A Marginalised Majority* (Cambridge: Alzheimer's Research UK, 2015), https://www.alzheimersresearchuk.org/wp-content/uploads/2015/03/Women-and-Dementia-A-Marginalised-Majority1.pdf.

41. "Computer Programmers," Data USA, accessed December 3, 2019, https://datausa.io/profile/soc/computer-programmers.

42. World Economic Forum, *The Global Gender Gap Report 2018* (Geneva: World Economic Forum, 2018), http://www3.weforum.org/docs/WEF_GGGR_2018.pdf.

43. Nick Heer, "Diversity of Tech Companies by the Numbers: 2016 Edition," *Pixel Envy* (blog), August 9, 2016, https://pxlnv.com/blog/diversity-of-tech-companies-by-the-numbers-2016/; Lara O'Reilly, "'What If Female Scientists Were Celebrities?': GE Says It Will Place 20,000 Women in Technical Roles by 2020," *Business Insider Australia*, February 9, 2017, https://www.businessinsider.com.au/ge-commits-to-placing-20000-women-in-technical-roles-by-2020-2017-2?r=US&IR=T.

44. Sarah Myers West, Meredith Whittaker, and Kate Crawford, *Discriminating Systems: Gender, Race, and Power in AI* (New York: AI Now Institute, 2019), https://ainowinstitute.org/discriminatingsystems.pdf.

45. West, Whittaker, and Crawford, *Discriminating Systems*; UNESCO and EQUALS Skills Coalition, *I'd Blush If I Could*.

46. Thomas D. Snyder and Sally A. Dillow, *Digest of Education Statistics 2012*, NCES 2014-015 (Washington, DC: National Center for Education Statistics, Institute of Education Sciences, US Department of Education, 2013), table 349, https://nces.ed.gov/programs/digest/d12/tables/dt12_349.asp; Blanca Myers, "Women and Minorities in Tech, by the Numbers," *Wired*, March 27, 2018, https://www.wired.com/story/computer-science-graduates-diversity/.

47. Australian Council of Learned Academies, *STEM: Country Comparisons: International Comparisons of Science, Technology, Engineering and Mathematics (STEM) Education*, final report (Melbourne: Australian Council of Learned Academies, 2013), https://acola.org.au/wp/PDF/SAF02Consultants/SAF02_STEM_%20FINAL.pdf.

48. UNESCO and EQUALS Skills Coalition, *I'd Blush If I Could*, 16.

49. Jane Margolis and Allan Fisher, *Unlocking the Clubhouse: Women in Computing* (Cambridge, MA: MIT Press, 2002).

50. UNESCO and EQUALS Skills Coalition, *I'd Blush If I Could*.

51. Cynthia Cockburn and Susan Ormrod, *Gender and Technology in the Making* (London: SAGE, 1994); David Morley, "Changing Paradigms in Audience Studies," in *Remote Control: Television, Audiences, and Cultural Power*, ed. Ellen Seiter, Hans Borchers, Gabriele Kreutzner, and Eva-Maria Warth (London: Routledge, 1989), 16–43.

52. Emily Chang, *Brotopia: Breaking Up the Boys' Club of Silicon Valley* (New York: Portfolio, 2018).

53. Kate Crawford, "Artificial Intelligence's White Guy Problem," *New York Times*, June 25, 2016, https://www.nytimes.com/2016/06/26/opinion/sunday/artificial-intelligences-white-guy-problem.html; Jack Clark, "Artificial Intelligence Has a 'Sea of Dudes' Problem," *Bloomberg*, June 23, 2016, https://www.bloomberg.com/news/articles/2016-06-23/artificial-intelligence-has-a-sea-of-dudes-problem.

54. West, Whittaker, and Crawford, *Discriminating Systems*.

55. Kate Crawford et al., *AI Now 2019 Report* (New York: AI Now Institute, 2019), https://ainowinstitute.org/AI_Now_2019_Report.pdf, 6.

56. UNESCO and EQUALS Skills Coalition, *I'd Blush If I Could*.

57. Safiya Umoja Noble, *Algorithms of Oppression: How Search Engines Reinforce Racism* (New York: NYU Press, 2018).

58. Sara Wachter-Boettcher, *Technically Wrong, Sexist Apps, Biased Algorithms, and Other Threats of Toxic Tech* (New York: W. W. Norton, 2017).

59. See, for example, Hilary Bergen, "'I'd Blush If I Could': Digital Assistants, Disembodied Cyborgs and the Problem of Gender," *Word and Text* 6 (December 2016): 95–113.

60. Dan Golding and Leena Van Deventer, *Game Changers: From Minecraft to Misogyny, the Fight for the Future of Videogames* (South Melbourne: Affirm, 2016).

61. C. Scott Brown, "Say Goodbye to M, Facebook's Virtual Assistant," *Android Authority*, January 8, 2018, https://www.androidauthority.com/goodbye-m-facebook-virtual-assistant-828558/; Barry Schwartz, "Microsoft Drops Ms. Dewey," *Search Engine Roundtable* (blog), March 30, 2009, https://www.seroundtable.com/archives/019721.html.

62. UNESCO and EQUALS Skills Coalition, *I'd Blush If I Could*.

63. Andrea Fjeld, "AI: A Consumer Perspective," *Connected Consumer* (blog), LivePerson, March 13, 2018, https://www.liveperson.com/connected-customer/posts/ai-consumer-perspective.

64. "Gatebox Virtual Friend Azuma Hikari," YouTube video, posted by Robotics AI, January 7, 2017, https://www.youtube.com/watch?v=_YgCC454lsI; Kara Dennison, "Gatebox Begins Mass-Production of Tiny Virtual Girlfriends," *Crunchyroll*, September 11, 2019, https://www.crunchyroll.com/anime-news/2019/09/11/gatebox-begins-mass-production-of-tiny-virtual-girlfriends.

65. Jennifer Yang Hui and Dymples Leong, "The Era of Ubiquitous Listening: Living in a World of Speech-Activated Devices," *Asian Journal of Public Affairs* 10, no. 1 (2017): 1–19.

66. "Hikari Azuma," Gatebox, accessed December 3, 2019, https://www.gatebox.ai/hikari.

67. "Gatebox Virtual Friend Azuma Hikari"; "Gatebox - Promotion Movie 'KANPAI'_English ver.," YouTube video, posted by Gatebox Inc., July 30, 2018, https://www.youtube.com/watch?v=bBOXQz7OHqQ.

68. Hui and Leong, "Era of Ubiquitous Listening."

69. Gordon Watts, "Artificial Intelligence and the Rise of the Robots in China," *Asia Times*, August 11, 2018, https://www.asiatimes.com/2018/08/article/artificial-intelligence-and-the -rise-of-the-robots-in-china/.

70. Sean Keach, "Creepy £7,000 'Harmony' Sex-Bot with a Saucy Scottish Accent Goes on Sale—as Fear over Rise of Robot Lovers Grows," *Scottish Sun*, March 4, 2019, https:// www.thescottishsun.co.uk/tech/3951842/creepy-7000-harmony-sex-bot-with-a-saucy -scottish-accent-and-self-lubricating-vagina-goes-on-sale-as-fear-over-rise-of-robot-lovers -grows/; Rhian Morgan, "Looking for Robot Love? Here Are 5 Sexbots You Can Buy Right Now," *Metro*, September 13, 2017, https://metro.co.uk/2017/09/13/looking-for-robot-love -here-are-5-sexbots-you-can-buy-right-now-6891378/.

71. Maud Garcia, "The Sexbot Is Here . . . AI Really Can Do It All," *Robotic Marketer* (blog), August 29, 2018, https://www.roboticmarketer.com/the-sexbot-is-here-ai-really-can-do-it-all/.

72. Curtis Silver, "Stop Being Rude to Amazon Alexa, Carol," *Forbes*, February 13, 2018, https://www.forbes.com/sites/curtissilver/2018/02/13/stop-being-rude-to-amazon-alexa -carol/#6f43d4d040fc; Alle McMahon, "Stop Swearing at Siri—It Matters How You Talk to Your Digital Assistants," ABC News (Australia), December 22, 2017, https://www.abc .net.au/news/2017-12-22/dont-swear-at-siri-it-matters-how-we-talk-to-digital-assistants/ 9204654.

73. Anne Fausto-Sterling, *Myths of Gender: Biological Theories about Women and Men* (New York: Basic Books, 2008); Sally Gregory Kohlstedt, "Women in the History of Science: An Ambiguous Place," *Osiris* 10, no. 1 (1995): 39–58.

74. Bergen, "I'd Blush If I Could," 109.

75. Clifford Nass, Youngme Moon, B. J. Fogg, Byron Reeves, and D. Christopher Dryer, "Can Computer Personalities Be Human Personalities?," *International Journal of Human-Computer Studies* 43, no. 2 (August 1995): 223–239; Jakub Złotowski, Diane Proudfoot, Kumar Yogeeswaran, and Christoph Bartneck, "Anthropomorphism: Opportunities and Challenges in Human–Robot Interaction," *International Journal of Social Robotics* 7, no. 3 (June 2015): 347–360; Ja-Young Sung, Lan Guo, Rebecca E. Grinter, and Henrik I. Christensen, "'My Roomba Is Rambo': Intimate Home Appliances," in *UbiComp 2007: Ubiquitous Computing*, ed. John Krumm, Gregory D. Abowd, Aruna Seneviratne, and Thomas Strang, Lecture Notes in Computer Science 4717 (Berlin: Springer, 2007), 145–162.

76. Joseph Weizenbaum, "ELIZA: A Computer Program for the Study of Natural Language Communication between Man and Machine," *Communications of the ACM* 9, no. 1 (January 1966): 36–45.

77. Will Bedingfield, "Why Giving Human Voices to AI Assistants Is an Ethical Nightmare," *Dazed*, September 18, 2018, http://www.dazeddigital.com/science-tech/article/41409/1/ai-human-voices-gender-alexa-siri.

78. Relaxnews, "Til [My] Death Do Us Part: Object Love," *Independent*, March 21, 2010, https://www.independent.co.uk/life-style/health-and-families/til-my-death-do-us-part-object-love-5530600.html.

79. Clifford Nass with Corina Yen, *The Man Who Lied to His Laptop: What We Can Learn about Ourselves from Our Machines* (New York: Current, 2012).

80. Sherry Turkle, *Reclaiming Conversation: The Power of Talk in a Digital Age* (New York: Penguin Books, 2015); Sherry Turkle, *Alone Together: Why We Expect More from Technology and Less from Each Other* (New York: Basic Books, 2011); Sherry Turkle, *The Second Self: Computers and the Human Spirit* (New York: Simon and Schuster, 1985); Sherry Turkle, *Simulation and Its Discontents* (Cambridge, MA: MIT Press, 2009).

81. Nass with Yen, *Man Who Lied to His Laptop*.

82. Alex Ward, "A Bad Case of Jetnag? Fighter Pilots to Get Cockpit Instructions from Female Voice 'Because It Relaxes Them More' (but They've Already Nicknamed Her Nagging Nora)," *Daily Mail*, July 4, 2012, https://www.dailymail.co.uk/news/article-2168713/Fighter-pilots-nagging-Nora-female-voice-commands-cockpit-Typhoon-jets.html; Justin Bachman, "The World's Top Fighter Pilots Fear This Woman's Voice," *Bloomberg*, March 16, 2016, https://www.bloomberg.com/features/2016-voice-of-the-fa-18-super-hornet/.

83. Nass with Yen, *Man Who Lied to His Laptop*.

84. Joanna Stern, "Alexa, Siri, Cortana: The Problem with All-Female Digital Assistants," *Wall Street Journal*, February 21, 2017, https://www.wsj.com/articles/alexa-siri-cortana-the-problem-with-all-female-digital-assistants-1487709068.

85. A "misogamist" is someone who hates marriage.

86. We are borrowing the term "killjoy" from Sara Ahmed, *Willful Subjects* (Durham NC: Duke University Press, 2014).

87. Yolande Strengers, *Smart Energy Technologies in Everyday Life: Smart Utopia?* (Basingstoke, UK: Palgrave Macmillan, 2013).

88. Jenny Kennedy, *Digital Media, Sharing and Everyday Life* (London: Routledge, 2020); Jenny Kennedy, Michael Arnold, Martin Gibbs, Bjorn Nansen, and Rowan Wilken, *Digital Domesticity: Media, Materiality, and Home Life* (Oxford: Oxford University Press, 2019).

89. Carole Pateman, *The Sexual Contract* (Stanford, CA: Stanford University Press, 1988).

90. Mariana Ortega, "Being Lovingly, Knowingly Ignorant: White Feminism and Women of Color," *Hypatia* 21, no. 3 (Summer 2006): 56–74.

91. "*Internet Users*," Internet Live Stats, accessed December 3, 2019, https://www.internetlivestats.com/internet-users/. An "internet user" is defined as someone who can access the internet

at home via any device type and connection. International Energy Agency, *SDG7: Data and Projections* (IEA: Paris, 2019), https://www.iea.org/reports/sdg7-data-and-projections.

92. UNESCO and EQUALS Skills Coalition, *I'd Blush If I Could.*

93. "Alpha the Robot" (1934), YouTube video, posted by Matt Novak, March 13, 2011, https://www.youtube.com/watch?time_continue=18&v=a9l9pt_Jzn8.

94. Among the male-identified devices are digital assistants called Albert and Josh, and robots called Temi and Buddy, while less obviously gendered devices include the digital assistants Mycroft and Branto.

95. UNESCO and EQUALS Skills Coalition, *I'd Blush If I Could.*

CHAPTER 2

1. Mark Wilson, "The Mahru-Z Maid Robot Ain't Exactly the Jetsons," *Gizmodo*, January 20, 2010, https://www.gizmodo.com/the-mahru-z-maid-robot-aint-exactly-the-jetsons-5452690/.

2. Thao Phan, "Amazon Echo and the Aesthetics of Whiteness," *Catalyst: Feminism, Theory, Technoscience* 5, no. 1 (2019): 1–38.

3. Phan, "Amazon Echo," 11.

4. Amy Schiller and John McMahon, "Alexa, Alert Me When the Revolution Comes: Gender, Affect, and Labor in the Age of Home-Based Artificial Intelligence," *New Political Science* 41, no. 2 (2019): 173–191.

5. Schiller and McMahon, "Alexa, Alert Me When the Revolution Comes," 181.

6. Matt Novak, "50 Years of the Jetsons: Why the Show Still Matters," *Smithsonian*, September 19, 2012, https://www.smithsonianmag.com/history/50-years-of-the-jetsons-why-the -show-still-matters-43459669/.

7. Danny Graydon, *The Jetsons: The Official Guide to the Cartoon Classic* (Philadelphia: Running Press, 2011), cited in Novak, "50 Years of the Jetsons."

8. Jordan Minor, "The Flintstones Internet of Living Things," *Geek.com*, January 30, 2017, https://www.geek.com/tech/the-flintstones-internet-of-living-things-1686807/.

9. "LG Appliances–SmartThinQ–The Jetsons–Connected Appliances," Vimeo video, posted by Nationwide PrimeMedia, August 17, 2017, https://vimeo.com/230044203.

10. Matt Simon, "Catching Up with Pepper, the Surprisingly Helpful Humanoid Robot," *Wired*, April 13, 2018, https://www.wired.com/story/pepper-the-humanoid-robot/.

11. James Vincent, "Amazon Is Reportedly Working on Its First Home Robot," *Verge*, April 23, 2018, https://www.theverge.com/2018/4/23/17270002/amazon-robot-home-alexa-echo.

12. Kyle Wiggers, "Amazon's Vesta No-Show Highlights the Challenges of Home Robots," *VentureBeat*, September 28, 2019, https://venturebeat.com/2019/09/28/amazons-vesta-no -show-highlights-the-challenges-of-home-robots/.

13. Robb Todd, "There Might Not Have Been an iRobot without Rosie the Robot," *Fast Company*, September 17, 2015, https://www.fastcompany.com/3051214/there-might-not -have-been-an-irobot-without-rosie-the-robot.

14. Genevieve Bell, "Making Life: A Brief History of Human-Robot Interaction," *Consumption Markets and Culture* 21, no. 1 (2018): 22–41.

15. Bill Gates, "A Robot in Every Home," *Scientific American* 296, no. 1 (January 2007): 58–65.

16. International Federation of Robotics, "Executive Summary: World Robotics 2018 Service Robots," October 18, 2018, https://ifr.org/downloads/press2018/Executive_Summary _WR_Service_Robots_2018.pdf.

17. International Federation of Robotics, "Executive Summary."

18. iRobot (@iRobot), "'Rosie' being the most common name for the iRobot Roomba, what have you or would you name your home robot?," Twitter, November 19, 2013, 11:55 a.m., https://twitter.com/irobot/status/402842664766144512?lang=en.

19. Julie Wosk, *My Fair Ladies: Female Robots, Androids, and Other Artificial Eves* (New Brunswick, NJ: Rutgers University Press, 2015).

20. Galen Gruman, "Home Automation Is a Solution in Search of a Problem," *InfoWorld*, December 2, 2014, https://www.infoworld.com/article/2853026/internet-of-things/home -automation-is-still-mostly-a-solution-in-search-of-a-problem.html.

21. Evgeny Morozov, *To Save Everything, Click Here: The Folly of Technological Solutionism* (New York: PublicAffairs, 2013).

22. Meredith Broussard, *Artificial Unintelligence: How Computers Misunderstand the World* (Cambridge, MA: MIT Press, 2018), 8.

23. Drew Harwell, "Why Whirlpool's Smart Washing Machine Was a Dumb Idea," *Sydney Morning Herald*, November 2, 2014, https://www.smh.com.au/technology/why-whirlpools -smart-washing-machine-was-a-dumb-idea-20141102-11flym.html.

24. John Sciacca, "What to Do When the Stove Talks Back (and Other Problems with Smart Appliances)," *Digital Trends*, June 17, 2013, https://www.digitaltrends.com/home/get-ready -to-talk-to-your-refrigerator-and-your-washing-machine-dish-washer-and-garage-door -too/.

25. Harwell, "Whirlpool's Smart Washing Machine."

26. Gates, "Robot in Every Home."

27. Dami Lee, "This $16,000 Robot Uses Artificial Intelligence to Sort and Fold Laundry," *Verge*, January 10, 2018, https://www.theverge.com/2018/1/10/16865506/laundroid-laundry -folding-machine-foldimate-ces-2018; Nick Summers, "Laundroid Company Folds before Its Giant Robot Does," *Engadget*, April 23, 2019, https://www.engadget.com/2019/04/23/ laundroid-robot-seven-dreamers-bankruptcy/.

28. Daniel Cooper, "The Smart Kitchen Revolution Is a Slow One," *Engadget*, September 4, 2017, https://www.engadget.com/2017/09/04/the-smart-kitchen-revolution-ifa-2017/.

29. Aike C. Horstmann and Nicole C. Krämer, "Great Expectations?: Relation of Previous Experiences with Social Robots in Real Life or in the Media and Expectancies Based on Qualitative and Quantitative Assessment," *Frontiers in Psychology* 10 (April 30, 2019): 939–953.

30. Megan Wollerton, "Whirlpool's Smart Washer/Dryer Hybrid Now Works with Alexa," *CNET*, January 8, 2018, https://www.cnet.com/news/whirlpools-smart-washerdryer-hybrid-now-works-with-alexa/.

31. Samsung, "Why You Should Upgrade to a Smart Washing Machine," advertising feature, *Independent*, March 27, 2018, https://www.independent.co.uk/life-style/why-you-should-upgrade-to-a-smart-washing-machine-a8257116.html.

32. Denver Nicks, "Why the Laundry Folding Robot Is Actually a Big Deal," *Money*, June 7, 2016, http://money.com/money/4360534/why-the-laundry-folding-robot-is-actually-kind-of-a-big-deal/.

33. Nicks, "Why the Laundry Folding Robot Is Actually a Big Deal."

34. Natasha Lomas, "Most Consumers Not Being Turned On by Connected Home, Study Finds," *TechCrunch*, March 6, 2017, https://techcrunch.com/2017/03/06/most-consumers-not-being-turned-on-by-connected-home-study-finds/.

35. Adam Burgess, *Cellular Phones, Public Fears, and a Culture of Precaution* (Cambridge: Cambridge University Press, 2004); Linda Simon, *Dark Light: Electricity and Anxiety from the Telegraph to the X-ray* (Orlando, FL: Harcourt, 2005).

36. Larissa Nicholls, Yolande Strengers, and Sergio Tirado, *Smart Home Control: Exploring the Potential for Off-the-Shelf Enabling Technologies in Energy Vulnerable and Other Households*, final report (Melbourne: Centre for Urban Research, RMIT University, 2017); Yolande Strengers and Larissa Nicholls, "Aesthetic Pleasures and Gendered Tech-Work in the 21st-Century Smart Home," *Media International Australia* 166 (February 2018): 70–80.

37. Susan Wyche, Phoebe Sengers, and Rebecca E. Grinter, "Historical Analysis: Using the Past to Design the Future," in *UbiComp 2006: Ubiquitous Computing*, ed. Paul Dourish and Adrian Friday, Lecture Notes in Computer Science 4206 (Berlin: Springer, 2006), 35–51.

38. Lynn Spigel, "Yesterday's Future, Tomorrow's Home," *Emergences: Journal for the Study of Media and Composite Cultures* 11, no. 1 (2001): 31; Wyche, Sengers, and Grinter, "Historical Analysis," 38.

39. Anne-Jorunn Berg, "A Gendered Socio-Technical Construction: The Smart House," in *Bringing Technology Home: Gender and Technology in Changing Europe*, ed. Cynthia Cockburn and Ruza Fürst Dilic (Buckingham, UK: Open University Press, 1994), 175.

40. Judy Wajcman, *Feminism Confronts Technology* (Cambridge, UK: Polity, 1991); Ben Panko, "The First Self-Cleaning Home Was Essentially a 'Floor-to-Ceiling Dishwasher,'" *Smithsonian*, July 20, 2017, https://www.smithsonianmag.com/smart-news/first-self-cleaning -home-was-essentially-floor-ceiling-dishwasher-180964115/.

41. Wajcman, *Feminism Confronts Technology*, 102.

42. Melissa Gregg, *Counterproductive: Time Management in the Knowledge Economy* (Durham, NC: Duke University Press, 2018).

43. Justin McCurry, "South Korean Woman's Hair 'Eaten' by Robot Vacuum Cleaner as She Slept," *Guardian*, February 9, 2015, https://www.theguardian.com/world/2015/feb/09/ south-korean-womans-hair-eaten-by-robot-vacuum-cleaner-as-she-slept.

44. Angel Chang, "This 1955 'Good House Wife's Guide' Explains How Wives Should Treat Their Husbands," *LittleThings*, October 7, 2019, https://www.littlethings.com/ 1950s-good-housewife-guide.

45. Olivia Solon, "Roomba Creator Responds to Reports of 'Poopocalypse': 'We See This a Lot,'" *Guardian*, August 15, 2016, https://www.theguardian.com/technology/2016/aug/ 15/roomba-robot-vacuum-poopocalypse-facebook-post.

46. Larissa Nicholls and Yolande Strengers, "Robotic Vacuum Cleaners Save Energy?: Raising Cleanliness Conventions and Energy Demand in Australian Households with Smart Home Technologies," *Energy Research and Social Science* 50 (April 2019): 73–81.

47. Joan C. Williams, *Unbending Gender: Why Family and Work Conflict and What to Do about It* (New York: Oxford University Press, 2001), 32.

48. Wajcman, *Feminism Confronts Technology*; Janna Thompson, "Housework and Technological Change," *Australian Left Review* 69 (1979): 9–19.

49. Arlie Russell Hochschild, *The Managed Heart: Commercialization of Human Feeling*, updated ed. (Berkeley: University of California Press, 2012).

50. Sarah Pink, "Dirty Laundry: Everyday Practice, Sensory Engagement and the Constitution of Identity," *Social Anthropology* 13, no. 3 (October 2005): 275–290; Jean-Claude Kaufmann, *Dirty Linen: Couples and Their Laundry* (London: Middlesex University Press, 1998).

51. Some scholars provide an alternative interpretation of the gender of the smart home target market, contending that these devices are marketed toward white heterosexual women. We also explore this market later in the chapter. See, for example, Jennifer Rhee, *The Robotic Imaginary: The Human and the Price of Dehumanized Labor* (Minneapolis: University of Minnesota Press, 2018).

52. Jenny McGrath, "Bud Light's Smart Fridge Follows Your Teams and Tallies Your Brews, Bro," *Digital Trends*, October 6, 2015, https://www.digitaltrends.com/home/bud-light -introduces-its-bud-e-smart-fridge/.

53. Emily Price, "This 'Smart' Beer Fridge Holds 78 Beers," *Paste*, March 21, 2016, https:// www.pastemagazine.com/articles/2016/03/this-smart-beer-fridge-holds-78-beers.html.

54. Mark J. Miller, "Budweiser Introduces Bud-E Fridge for Today's Connected Man Cave," *brandchannel*, October 21, 2015, https://www.brandchannel.com/2015/10/21/bud-e-fridge-102115/.

55. Men account for almost 60 percent of the market for beer in the United States and Australia, and over 80 percent in the United Kingdom.

56. Jenny McGrath, "Budweiser Built a WiFi-Enabled Smart Fridge That Will Keep Stock of Your Beers and Give You Football Scores," *Business Insider*, October 6, 2015, https://www.businessinsider.com/budweiser-fridge-keeps-track-of-your-beers-and-football-scores-2015-10?IR=T.

57. The company's founders and directors are Brian Hamersfeld and Barry Gold.

58. Will Greenwald, "Anheuser-Busch Office Bud-E Fridge," *PC Mag*, February 15, 2017, https://au.pcmag.com/appliances/46523/anheuser-busch-office-bud-e-fridge.

59. Ben Power, "Smart Homes Are Simplicity Itself," *Australian*, November 9, 2013, https://www.theaustralian.com.au/life/smart-homes-are-simplicity-itself/news-story/8754f4092dba740331ce853562297973?sv=df12ad5ae5e867fcbdf3c46775ba52be.

60. Amazon Australia, "Amazon Echo—Dad's Night," YouTube video, posted March 11, 2018, https://www.youtube.com/watch?v=ibekaZeKmkI.

61. Daniel Terdiman, "Here's How People Say Google Home and Alexa Impact Their Lives," *Fast Company*, January 5, 2018, https://www.fastcompany.com/40513721/heres-how-people-say-google-home-and-alexa-impact-their-lives.

62. Nona Walia, "Robot Maids to Battle Shantabai," *Times of India*, July 22, 2012, https://timesofindia.indiatimes.com/life-style/spotlight/Robot-maids-to-battle-Shantabai/articleshow/15090597.cms.

63. Helen Richardson also notes the importance of "coordinating" and "multitasking" work, which often falls to women. Helen J. Richardson, "A 'Smart House' Is Not a Home: The Domestication of ICTs," *Information Systems Frontiers* 11, no. 5 (November 2009): 599–608.

64. Scott Davidoff, Min Kyung Lee, Charles Yiu, John Zimmerman, and Anind K. Dey, "Principles of Smart Home Control," in *UbiComp 2006: Ubiquitous Computing*, ed. Paul Dourish and Adrian Friday, Lecture Notes in Computer Science 4206 (Berlin: Springer, 2006), 19, 31.

65. Ja-Young Sung, Rebecca E. Grinter, Henrik I. Christensen, and Lan Guo, "Housewives or Technophiles?: Understanding Domestic Robot Owners," in *Proceedings of the 3rd ACM/IEEE International Conference on Human Robot Interaction* (New York: ACM, 2008), 129–136.

66. Ema Fonseca, Inês Oliveira, Joana Lobo, Tânia Mota, José Martins, and Manual Au-Yong-Oliveira, "Kitchen Robots: The Importance and Impact of Technology on People's Quality of Life," in *New Knowledge in Information Systems and Technologies*, ed. Álvaro Rocha,

Hojjat Adeli, Lios Paula Reis, and Sandra Costanzo, Advances in Intelligent Systems and Computing 931 (Cham, Switzerland: Springer, 2019), 2:186–197.

67. Monica Truninger, "Cooking with Bimby in a Moment of Recruitment: Exploring Conventions and Practice Perspectives," *Journal of Consumer Culture* 11, no. 1 (March 2011): 37–59.

68. June (website), accessed January 19, 2020, https://juneoven.com/; "Introducing Amazon Smart Oven, a Certified for Humans Device," Amazon, accessed January 19, 2020, https://www.amazon.com/Amazon-Smart-Oven/dp/B07PB21SRV.

69. Leopoldina Fortunati, "Robotization and the Domestic Sphere," *Media and Society* 20, no. 8 (August 2018): 2673–2690.

70. Overall, support for domestic robots remains low in this survey, with 14.9 percent thinking that "robots should be used as a priority" for "domestic use." Sakari Taipale and Leopoldina Fortunati, "Communicating with Machines: Robots as the Next New Media," in *Human-Machine Communications: Rethinking Communication, Technology, and Ourselves*, ed. Andrea L. Guzman (New York: Peter Lang, 2018), cited in Fortunati, "Robotization and the Domestic Sphere," 2681.

71. Gemma Hartley, *Fed Up: Emotional Labor, Women, and the Way Forward* (New York: HarperOne, 2018).

72. Schiller and McMahon, "Alexa, Alert Me When the Revolution Comes."

73. Schiller and McMahon, "Alexa, Alert Me When the Revolution Comes," 185, citing a 2017 job description for a position as a data scientist in the "Alexa Engine" team.

74. Schiller and McMahon, "Alexa, Alert Me When the Revolution Comes," 185.

75. Emma, "The Gender Wars of Household Chores: A Feminist Comic," *Guardian*, May 26, 2017, https://www.theguardian.com/world/2017/may/26/gender-wars-household-chores-comic.

76. Caroline Criado Perez, *Invisible Women: Data Bias in a World Designed for Men* (New York: Abrams, 2019).

77. Minji Cho, Sang-su Lee, and Kun-Pyo Lee, "Once a Kind Friend Is Now a Thing: Understanding How Conversational Agents at Home are Forgotten," in *Proceedings of the 2019 Designing Interactive Systems Conference* (New York: ACM, 2019), 1565.

78. Nicholls and Strengers, "Robotic Vacuum Cleaners Save Energy?"

79. Ruth Schwartz Cowan, *More Work for Mother: The Ironies of Household Technology from the Open Hearth to the Microwave* (New York: Basic Books, 1985).

80. Betty Friedan, *The Feminine Mystique* (New York: W. W. Norton, 2001), 333.

81. Ja-Young Sung, Lan Guo, Rebecca E. Grinter, and Henrik I. Christensen, "'My Roomba Is Rambo': Intimate Home Appliances," in *UbiComp 2007: Ubiquitous Computing*, ed. John Krumm, Gregory D. Abowd, Aruna Seneviratne, and Thomas Strang, Lecture Notes in Computer Science 4717 (Berlin: Springer, 2007), 145–162.

82. Jenny Kennedy, Bjorn Nansen, Michael Arnold, Rowan Wilken, and Martin Gibbs, "Digital Housekeepers and Domestic Expertise in the Networked Home," *Convergence: The International Journal of Research into New Media Technologies* 21, no. 4 (November 2015): 408–422; Strengers and Nicholls, "Aesthetic Pleasures."

83. Tom Hargreaves, Charlie Wilson, and Richard Hauxwell-Baldwin, "Learning to Live in a Smart Home," *Building Research and Information* 46, no. 1 (2018): 127–139.

84. Peter Tolmie, Andy Crabtree, Tom Rodden, Chris Greenhalgh, and Steve Benford, "Making the Home Network at Home: Digital Housekeeping," in *ECSCW 2007: Proceedings of the 10th European Conference on Computer-Supported Cooperative Work*, ed. Liam J. Bannon, Ina Wagner, Carl Gutwin, Richard H. R. Harper, and Kjeld Schmidt (London: Springer, 2007), 331–350.

85. Wajcman, *Feminism Confronts Technology*, 89.

86. Sherrie A. Inness, ed., *Geek Chic: Smart Women in Popular Culture* (New York: Palgrave Macmillan, 2008).

87. Emily Chang, *Brotopia: Breaking Up the Boys' Club of Silicon Valley* (New York: Portfolio, 2018), 19–20.

88. Kylie Jarrett, *Feminism, Labour and Digital Media: The Digital Housewife* (New York: Routledge, 2016); Kristin Natalier, "'I'm Not His Wife': Doing Gender and Doing Housework in the Absence of Women," *Journal of Sociology* 39, no. 3 (September 2003): 253–269.

89. Jennifer A. Rode, "The Roles That Make the Domestic Work," in *Proceedings of the 2010 ACM Conference on Computer Supported Cooperative Work* (New York: ACM, 2010), 381–390.

90. Jennifer A. Rode and Erika Shehan Poole, "Putting the Gender Back in Digital Housekeeping," in *Proceedings of the 4th Conference on Gender and IT* (New York: ACM, 2018), 82.

91. Kennedy et al., "Digital Housekeepers."

92. Sally Wyatt, "Non-Users Also Matter: The Construction of Users and Non-Users of the Internet," in *How Users Matter: The Co-Construction of Users and Technology*, ed. Nelly Oudshoorn and Trevor Pinch (Cambridge, MA: MIT Press, 2003), 67–79.

93. A role also noted in Erika Shehan Poole, Marshini Chetty, Rebecca E. Grinter, and W. Keith Edwards, "More Than Meets the Eye: Transforming the User Experience of Home Network Management," in *Proceedings of the 7th ACM Conference on Designing Interactive Systems* (New York: ACM, 2008), 455–464.

94. Gaelle Ferrant and Annelise Thim, "Measuring Women's Economic Empowerment: Time Use Data and Gender Inequality," OECD Development Policy Papers No. 16 (Paris: Organization for Economic Cooperation and Development, February 2019), http://www.oecd.org/dev/development-gender/MEASURING-WOMENS-ECONOMIC-EMPOWERMENT-Gender-Policy-Paper-No-16.pdf.

CHAPTER 3

1. Leopoldina Fortunati, "Robotization and the Domestic Sphere," *New Media and Society* 20, no. 8 (August 2018): 2673–2690; Elizabeth Broadbent, "Interactions with Robots: The Truths We Reveal about Ourselves," *Annual Review of Psychology* 68 (2017): 627–652.

2. Matt Simon, "Watch Boston Dynamics' Humanoid Robot Do Parkour," *Wired*, October 11, 2018, https://www.wired.com/story/watch-boston-dynamics-humanoid-robot-do-parkour/; Marc DeAngelis, "Boston Dynamics' Atlas Robot Is Now a Gymnast," *Engadget*, September 24, 2019, https://www.engadget.com/2019/09/24/boston-dynamics-atlas-gymnast/.

3. Mark Prigg, "Google's Terrifying Two Legged Giant Robot Taught How to CLEAN: Researchers Reveal Ian the Atlas Robot Can Now Vacuum, Sweep and Even Put the Trash Away," *Daily Mail*, January 15, 2016, https://www.dailymail.co.uk/sciencetech/article-3401743/Google-s-terrifying-two-legged-giant-robot-taught-CLEAN-Researchers-reveal-Atlas-vacuum-sweep-trash-away.html.

4. Justin McCurry, "No Sex, Please, They're Robots, Says Japanese Android Firm," *Guardian*, September 28, 2015, https://www.theguardian.com/world/2015/sep/28/no-sex-with-robots-says-japanese-android-firm-softbank.

5. Jennifer Robertson, "Gendering Humanoid Robots: Robo-Sexism in Japan," *Body and Society* 16, no. 2 (June 2010): 1–36; Broadbent, "Interactions with Robots."

6. Many social robotic projects have been funded by government military programs, which are interested in robots that can serve in the hypermasculine defense sector (Robertson, "Gendering Humanoid Robots"). While efforts to create the smart warrior provide a fascinating subplot to the smart wife, this is not something we delve into here.

7. John Markoff, "What Comes after the Roomba?," *New York Times*, October 21, 2018, https://www.nytimes.com/2018/10/21/business/what-comes-after-the-roomba.html.

8. Steffen Sorrell, *Consumer Robotics - From Housekeeper to Friend* (Basingstoke: Juniper Research, 2017), http://www.juniperresearch.com.

9. Katelyn Swift-Spong, Elaine Short, Eric Wade, and Maja J. Matarić, "Effects of Comparative Feedback from a Socially Assistive Robot on Self-Efficacy in Post-Stroke Rehabilitation," in *Proceedings of the 2015 IEEE International Conference on Rehabilitation Robotics (ICORR)* (Piscataway, NJ: Institute of Electrical and Electronics Engineers, 2015), 764–769.

10. GBD 2017 Population and Fertility Collaborators, "Population and Fertility by Age and Sex for 195 Countries and Territories, 1950–2017: A Systematic Analysis for the Global Burden of Disease Study 2017," *Lancet* 392, no. 10159 (November 10, 2018): 1995–2051.

11. Broadbent, "Interactions with Robots."

12. Japan, "Why Japan's Aging Population Is an Investment Opportunity," paid content, *Forbes*, November 12, 2018, https://www.forbes.com/sites/japan/2018/11/12/why-japans-aging-population-is-an-investment-opportunity/#7b83c2af288d.

13. Cision PR Newswire, "Global Social Robot Market 2018–2023: Product Innovations and New Launches Will Intensify Competitiveness," news release, June 5, 2018, https://www.prnewswire.com/news-releases/global-social-robot-market-2018-2023-product-innovations-and-new-launches-will-intensify-competitiveness-300660127.html; Robertson, "Gendering Humanoid Robots."

14. Carol S. Aneshensel, Leonard I. Pearlin, Lené Levy-Storms, and Roberleigh H. Schuler, "The Transition from Home to Nursing Home Mortality among People with Dementia," *Journal of Gerontology: Series B* 55, no. 3 (May 1, 2000): S152–S162.

15. Jennifer Yang Hui and Dymples Leong, "The Era of Ubiquitous Listening: Living in a World of Speech-Activated Devices," *Asian Journal of Public Affairs* 10, no. 1 (2017): 1–19.

16. Esteban Ortiz-Ospina and Diana Beltekian, "Why Do Women Live Longer Than Men?," *Our World in Data*, August 14, 2018, https://ourworldindata.org/why-do-women-live-longer-than-men.

17. Alzheimer's Research UK, *Women and Dementia: A Marginalised Majority* (Cambridge: Alzheimer's Research UK, 2015), https://www.alzheimersresearchuk.org/wp-content/uploads/2015/03/Women-and-Dementia-A-Marginalised-Majority1.pdf.

18. Caroline Criado Perez, *Invisible Women: Data Bias in a World Designed for Men* (New York: Abrams, 2019); UN Women, *Unpaid Care and Domestic Work: Issues and Suggestions for Viet Nam* (Hanoi: UN Women, 2016), http://www.un.org.vn/en/publications/doc_details/534-unpaid-care-and-domestic-work-issues-and-suggestions-for-viet-nam.html.

19. Alzheimer's Research UK, *Women and Dementia*.

20. Broadbent, "Interactions with Robots," 646.

21. Broadbent, "Interactions with Robots."

22. Cynthia Breazeal, *Designing Sociable Robots* (Cambridge, MA: MIT Press, 2002), 1.

23. Broadbent, "Interactions with Robots."

24. Kathleen Richardson, *An Anthropology of Robots and AI: Annihilation Anxiety and Machines* (New York: Routledge, 2015).

25. Roger Andre Søraa, "Mechanical Genders: How Do Humans Gender Robots?," *Gender, Technology and Development* 21, no. 1–2 (2017): 103.

26. Søraa, "Mechanical Genders," 103.

27. CNN Business, "First Date with Humanoid Robot Pepper," YouTube video, posted January 5, 2017, https://www.youtube.com/watch?v=aZ5VkgvQFBU.

28. See "Pepper," SoftBank Robotics, accessed December 3, 2019, https://www.softbankrobotics.com/emea/en/pepper.

29. Cordelia Fine, *Delusions of Gender: How Our Minds, Society, and Neurosexism Create Difference* (New York: W. W. Norton, 2011).

30. Clementine Ford, *Boys Will Be Boys: Power, Patriarchy and the Toxic Bonds of Mateship* (Sydney: Allen and Unwin, 2018).

31. Søraa, "Mechanical Genders," 103.

32. See "Pepper," SoftBank Robotics.

33. Perez, *Invisible Women*.

34. Broadbent, "Interactions with Robots."

35. Kate Darling, "Extending Legal Protection to Social Robots: The Effects of Anthropomorphism, Empathy, and Violent Behavior towards Robotic Objects," in *Robot Law*, ed. Ryan Calo, A. Michael Froomkin, and Ian Kerr (Cheltenham, UK: Edward Elgar, 2016), 213–231.

36. Søraa, "Mechanical Genders."

37. Lee Ann Obringer and Jonathan Strickland, "How ASIMO Works," HowStuffWorks, April 11, 2007, https://science.howstuffworks.com/asimo.htm.

38. Sam Byford, "President Obama Plays Soccer with a Japanese Robot," *Verge*, April 24, 2014, https://www.theverge.com/2014/4/24/5646550/president-obama-plays-soccer-with-a-japanese-robot.

39. Andrew Tarantola, "Honda Reveals More Details about Its Companion Mobility Robots," *Engadget*, January 9, 2018, https://www.engadget.com/2018/01/09/honda-3e-concept-robots/.

40. Gretel Kauffman, "Animator Reveals the Surprising Reason Why There Aren't Any Female Minions," *Business Insider*, July 18, 2015, https://www.businessinsider.com/animator-reveals-the-surprising-reason-why-there-arent-any-female-minions-2015-7?IR=T.

41. Quoted in Natashah Hitti, "Ballie the Rolling Robot Is Samsung's Near-Future Vision of Personal Care," *de zeen,* January 8, 2020, https://www.dezeen.com/2020/01/08/samsung-ballie-robot-ces-2020/.

42. Jibo's brief entrance into the home market ended in 2019. Since *Time* magazine named Jibo one of the twenty-five best innovations of 2017 (when the boydroid was launched on the public market with a price tag of $899), the company has flailed and shut down its services, largely due to cheaper and more organized competitors. See Oliver Mitchell, "Jibo Social Robot: Where Things Went Wrong," *Robot Report*, June 28, 2018, https://www.therobotreport.com/jibo-social-robot-analyzing-what-went-wrong/; AJ Dellinger, "Social Robot Jibo Does One Last Dance Before Its Servers Shut Down," *Engadget*, March 4, 2019, https://www.engadget.com/2019/03/04/social-robot-jibo-shutting-down-message/.

43. See Jibo (website), accessed December 3, 2019, https://www.jibo.com/.

44. Jibo (website).

45. Jibo (website), accessed March 20, 2019, https://www.jibo.com/technology/?wvideo=td5cajdtra (video removed from website).

46. CNN Business, "First Date with Humanoid Robot."

47. Laura Bates, *Everyday Sexism: The Project That Inspired a Worldwide Movement* (New York: St. Martin's, 2016); Everyday Sexism Project (website), accessed December 3, 2019, https://everydaysexism.com.

48. Suzanne J. Kessler and Wendy McKenna, *Gender: An Ethnomethodological Approach* (Chicago: University of Chicago Press, 1985), cited in Robertson, "Gendering Humanoid Robots."

49. Robertson, "Gendering Humanoid Robots."

50. World Economic Forum, *The Global Gender Gap Report 2018* (Geneva: World Economic Forum, 2018), https://www.weforum.org/reports/the-global-gender-gap-report-2018.

51. Robertson, "Gendering Humanoid Robots," 4.

52. Robertson, "Gendering Humanoid Robots," 21.

53. Robertson, "Gendering Humanoid Robots," 23–24.

54. Robertson, "Gendering Humanoid Robots," 23–24.

55. Neon (website), accessed January 17, 2020, https://www.neon.life/.

56. Dale Smith and Shara Tibken, "Samsung's Neon 'Artificial Humans' Are Confusing Everyone. We Set the Record Straight," *CNET*, January 19, 2020, https://www.cnet.com/how-to/samsung-neon-artificial-humans-are-confusing-everyone-we-set-record-straight/.

57. Neon (website).

58. Chris Taylor, "I Have Seen the AI Dystopia, and It Looks Like Neon's Artificial Humans," Mashable (Australia), January 8, 2020, https://mashable.com/article/neon-future-ai-dystopia-ces/.

59. Yuji Sone, *Japanese Robot Culture: Performance, Imagination, and Modernity* (Basingstoke, UK: Palgrave Macmillan, 2017).

60. See Robertson, "Gendering Humanoid Robots"; Sone, *Japanese Robot Culture.*

61. Robertson, "Gendering Humanoid Robots," 2.

62. Sone, *Japanese Robot Culture,* 48.

63. Hideaki Sena, *Sena Hideako robottogaku ronshu* (Tokyo: Keiso Shobo, 2008), cited in Sone, *Japanese Robot Culture,* 49.

64. Sone, *Japanese Robot Culture.*

65. Masahiro Mori, "The Uncanny Valley," trans. Karl F. MacDorman and Noori Kageki, *IEEE Robotics and Automation Magazine* 19, no. 2 (June 2012): 98–100.

66. Megan K. Strait, Cynthia Aguillon, Virginia Contreras, and Noemi Garcia, "The Public's Perception of Humanlike Robots: Online Social Commentary Reflects an Appearance-Based Uncanny Valley, a General Fear of a 'Technology Takeover,' and the Unabashed

Sexualization of Female-Gendered Robots," in *26th IEEE International Symposium on Robot and Human Interactive Communication (RO-MAN)* (Piscataway, NJ: Institute of Electrical and Electronics Engineers, 2017), 1418–1423.

67. Richardson, *Anthropology of Robots*, 5.

68. Jennifer Rhee, *The Robotic Imaginary: The Human and the Price of Dehumanized Labor* (Minneapolis: University of Minnesota Press, 2018).

69. Broadbent, "Interactions with Robots."

70. "Samsung 'Artificial Man,' Prequel to 'Westworld,'" *small tech news*, January 7, 2020, https://www.smalltechnews.com/archives/57332.

71. Strait et al., "Public's Perception of Humanlike Robots"; Broadbent, "Interactions with Robots."

72. Hui and Leong, "Era of Ubiquitous Listening."

73. See Hui and Leong, "Era of Ubiquitous Listening"; Strait et al., "Public's Perception of Humanlike Robots."

74. Sone, *Japanese Robot Culture.*

75. Kanako Shiokawa, "Cute but Deadly: Women and Violence in Japanese Comics," in *Themes and Issues in Asian Cartooning: Cute, Cheap, Mad, and Sexy*, ed. John A. Lent (Bowling Green, OH: Bowling Green State University Popular Press, 1999), 93–125.

76. Shiokawa, "Cute but Deadly," 94, 93.

77. Shiokawa, "Cute but Deadly," 94, 119.

78. Shiokawa, "Cute but Deadly," 95, 120.

79. Shiokawa, "Cute but Deadly," 121.

80. Robertson, "Gendering Humanoid Robots."

81. Pinocchio was popularized through the animated Disney musical fantasy film released in 1940.

82. Richardson, *Anthropology of Robots*, 60.

83. Broadbent, "Interactions with Robots."

84. Judy Wajcman, *Feminism Confronts Technology* (Cambridge, UK: Polity, 1991).

85. Quoted in Robertson, "Gendering Humanoid Robots," 18.

86. Robertson, "Gendering Humanoid Robots," 19.

87. Robertson, "Gendering Humanoid Robots," 19.

88. Breazeal, *Designing Sociable Robots.*

89. Richardson, *Anthropology of Robots*, 69; Breazeal, *Designing Sociable Robots.*

90. Richardson, *Anthropology of Robots*, 61.

91. Sherry Turkle, *The Second Self: Computers and the Human Spirit* (New York: Simon and Schuster, 1985).

92. Richardson, *Anthropology of Robots*, 71.

93. Darling, "Extending Legal Protection to Social Robots."

94. Cynthia Breazeal, "The Rise of Personal Robots," in *21st Century Reading Student Book 1: Creative Thinking and Reading with TED Talks*, by Robin Longshaw and Laurie Blass (Boston: National Geographic Learning / Cengage Learning, 2015), 157.

95. Richardson, *Anthropology of Robots*, 15.

96. Meredith Broussard, *Artificial Unintelligence: How Computers Misunderstand the World* (Cambridge, MA: MIT Press, 2018).

97. Robertson, "Gendering Humanoid Robots."

98. Robertson, "Gendering Humanoid Robots"; Sone, *Japanese Robot Culture*.

99. Laura Dales and Emma Dalton, "As Japan Undergoes Social Change, Single Women Are in the Firing Line," *Conversation*, May 22, 2018, https://theconversation.com/as-japan-undergoes-social-change-single-women-are-in-the-firing-line-96636.

100. Robertson, "Gendering Humanoid Robots."

101. Robertson, "Gendering Humanoid Robots," 11, 28.

102. Judy Wajcman, "Automation: Is It Really Different This Time?," *British Journal of Sociology* 68, no. 1 (March 2017): 123.

103. Shalini Misra, Lulu Cheng, Jamie Genevie, and Miao Yuan, "The iPhone Effect: The Quality of In-Person Social Interactions in the Presence of Mobile Devices," *Environment and Behavior* 48, no. 2 (February 2016): 275–298.

104. Wajcman, "Automation," 123.

105. Rhee, *Robotic Imaginary*.

CHAPTER 4

1. Voicebot and Voicify, *Smart Speaker Consumer Adoption Report*, March 2019, https://voicebot.ai/wp-content/uploads/2019/03/smart_speaker_consumer_adoption_report_2019.pdf.

2. Julie Bort, "Amazon Engineers Had One Good Reason and One Geeky Reason for Choosing the Name Alexa," *Business Insider*, July 13, 2016, https://www.businessinsider.com.au/why-amazon-called-it-alexa-2016-7?r=US&IR=T.

3. Fortune Editors, "The Exec behind Amazon's Alexa: Full Transcript of Fortune's Interview," *Fortune*, July 14, 2016, https://fortune.com/2016/07/14/amazon-alexa-david-limp-transcript/?platform=hootsuite.

4. Mary Mellor, *Feminism and Ecology* (Cambridge, UK: Polity, 1997), 1.

5. Mellor, *Feminism and Ecology.*

6. Ynestra King, "Healing the Wounds: Feminism, Ecology and Nature/Culture Dualism," in *Reweaving the World: The Emergence of Ecofeminism*, ed. Irene Diamond and Gloria Feman Orenstein (San Francisco: Sierra Club Books, 1990), 106.

7. "Jeffrey P. Bezos," Portfolio.com, archived on the Wayback Machine, February 4, 2009, https://web.archive.org/web/20090204204126/http://www.portfolio.com/resources/executive-profiles/Jeffrey-P-Bezos-1984.

8. Brad Stone, *The Everything Store: Jess Bezos and the Age of Amazon* (Boston: Little, Brown and Company, 2013).

9. Stone, *Everything Store.*

10. "7 Potential Bidders, a Call to Amazon, and an Ultimatum: How the Whole Foods Deal Went Down," *Business Insider*, December 30, 2017, https://www.businessinsider.com.au/breaking-it-down-amazon-tough-negotiations-how-the-whole-foods-deal-went-down-2017-12?r=US&IR=T.

11. Stone, *Everything Store.*

12. Virginia Heffernan, "An Infinite Space Utopia Can't Replicate Earth's Humanity," *Wired*, December 17, 2018, https://www.wired.com/story/infinite-space-utopia-cant-replicate-earths-humanity/.

13. Stone, *Everything Store*; Ann Byers, *Jeff Bezos: The Founder of Amazon.com*, Internet Career Biographies (New York: Rosen, 2007).

14. Erin Duffin, "Top Companies in the World by Market Value 2019," *Statista*, August 12, 2019, https://www.statista.com/statistics/263264/top-companies-in-the-world-by-market-value/; Nick Routley, "Walmart Nation: Mapping America's Biggest Employers," *Visual Capitalist,* January 24, 2019, https://www.visualcapitalist.com/walmart-nation-largest-employers/.

15. "Annual Net Income of Amazon.com from 2004 to 2018 (in Million U.S. Dollars)," Statista, August 9, 2019, https://www.statista.com/statistics/266288/annual-et-income-of-amazoncom/; "Number of Amazon.com Employees from 2007 to 2018," Statista, February 5, 2019, https://www.statista.com/statistics/234488/number-of-amazon-employees/.

16. "Global Retail E-commerce Market Share of Amazon from 2016 to 2019," Statista, January 22, 2019, https://www.statista.com/statistics/955796/global-amazon-e-commerce-market-share/; Ingrid Lunden, "Amazon's Share of the US E-commerce Market Is Now 49%, or 5% of All Retail Spend," *TechCrunch*, July 13, 2018, https://techcrunch.com/2018/07/13/amazons-share-of-the-us-e-commerce-market-is-now-49-or-5-of-all-retail-spend/.

17. Lawrence Gregory, "Amazon.com Inc.'s Mission Statement & Vision (An Analysis)," *Panmore Institute*, February 13, 2019, http://panmore.com/amazon-com-inc-vision-statement-mission-statement-analysis.

18. In 2017, Londoner Corinne Pretorius got a surprise when her African gray "Buddy" activated Alexa by mimicking her voice. Her parrot managed to place an Amazon order for around thirteen dollars worth of gift boxes. See Ron Thubron, "Parrot Activates Alexa When Mimicking Owner, Places Online Shopping Order," *TechSpot*, September 21, 2017, https://www.techspot.com/news/71075-parrot-activates-alexa-when-mimicking-owner-places-online.html.

19. Alison Griswold, "Amazon Says There Are Now 5,000 People Working Just on Alexa," *Quartz*, September 28, 2017, https://qz.com/1088933/amazon-amzn-says-there-are-now-5000-people-working-on-alexa/.

20. Conor Allison, "How to Use Amazon Alexa in Non-Supported Countries," *Ambient*, February 2, 2019, https://www.the-ambient.com/how-to/use-alexa-non-supported-countries-855.

21. Grace Donnelly, "Amazon Alexa Will Come Built-in to All New Homes from Lennar," *Fortune*, May 9, 2018, http://fortune.com/2018/05/09/amazon-alexa-lennar/.

22. "Alexa Skills Kit," Amazon Alexa, accessed March 29, 2019, https://developer.amazon.com/alexa-skills-kit.

23. Bret Kinsella, "Amazon Alexa Skill Count Surpasses 30,000 in the U.S.," *Voicebot*, March 22, 2018, https://voicebot.ai/2018/03/22/amazon-alexa-skill-count-surpasses-30000-u-s/.

24. David Pierce, "Inside the Lab Where Amazon's Alexa Takes Over the World," *Wired*, January 8, 2018, https://www.wired.com/story/amazon-alexa-development-kit/.

25. Bret Kinsella, "Amazon Says 60,000 Devices Are Now Alexa Compatible, Google Assistant Is at 30,000," *Voicebot*, May 7, 2019, https://voicebot.ai/2019/05/07/amazon-says-60000-devices-are-now-alexa-compatible/; Dieter Bohn, "Amazon Says 100 Million Alexa Devices Have Been Sold—What's Next?," *Verge*, January 4, 2019, https://www.theverge.com/2019/1/4/18168565/amazon-alexa-devices-how-many-sold-number-100-million-dave-limp.

26. Daniel Wroclawski, Samantha Gordon, Sarah Kovac, and Cinnamon Janzer, "Everything That Works with Amazon Echo and Alexa," *Reviewed*, September 24, 2019, https://.reviewed.com/smarthome/features/everything-that-works-with-amazon-echo-alexa; "Alexa Skills: Food & Drink: Delivery & Takeout," Amazon, accessed December 3, 2019, https://www.amazon.com/b?ie=UTF8&node=14284824011.

27. Jennifer Langston, "Microsoft, Amazon Release Preview of Alexa and Cortana Collaboration," *The AI Blog*, Microsoft, August 15, 2018, https://blogs.microsoft.com/ai/alexa-cortana-public-preview/.

28. Alexa's development and success is commonly attributed to engineer Rohit Prasad (responsible for her technology development) and anthropologist Toni Reid (responsible for customer experience).

29. Nick Wingfield and Nellie Bowles, "Jeff Bezos, Mr. Amazon, Steps Out," *New York Times*, January 12, 2018, https://www.nytimes.com/2018/01/12/technology/jeff-bezos-amazon.html.

30. Stone, *Everything Store*; John Rossman, *The Amazon Way: 14 Leadership Principles behind the World's Most Disruptive Company* (North Charleston, SC: CreateSpace, 2014).

31. Angel Au-Yeung, "How Jeff Bezos Became the Richest Person in America and the World," *Forbes*, October 3, 2018, https://www.forbes.com/sites/angelauyeung/2018/10/03/how -jeff-bezos-became-the-richest-person-in-the-world-2018-forbes-400/#3847d381beeb.

32. "Taking the Long View," *Economist*, March 3, 2012, https://www.economist.com/ technology-quarterly/2012/03/03/taking-the-long-view.

33. Stone, *Everything Store*, 255.

34. Bezos's donation was criticized as being "stingy" because it represents less than what he makes in five minutes. His other philanthropic enterprises have faced similar public scrutiny. See Kelsey Piper, "Why Amazon's Donation to the Australian Wildfires Provoked a Backlash—but Facebook's Didn't," *Vox*, January 14, 2020, https://www.vox.com/ future-perfect/2020/1/14/21064244/amazon-bezos-wildfires-donation-backlash.

35. Kevin MacKay, *Radical Transformation: Oligarchy, Collapse, and the Crisis of Civilization* (Toronto: Between the Lines, 2017).

36. Judy Wajcman, "Automation: Is It Really Different This Time?," *British Journal of Sociology* 68, no. 1 (March 2017): 126.

37. Ariel Salleh, *Ecofeminism as Politics: Nature, Marx and the Postmodern* (London: Zed Books, 1997), xxi.

38. Nathan Jensen and Edmund Malesky, "Why Politicians Are the Real Winners in Amazon's HQ2 Bidding War," *Conversation*, November 15, 2018, https://theconversation.com/ why-politicians-are-the-real-winners-in-amazons-hq2-bidding-war-106972.

39. David Streitfeld, "Was Amazon's Headquarters Contest a Bait-and-Switch? Critics Say Yes," *New York Times*, November 6, 2018, https://www.nytimes.com/2018/11/06/technology/ amazon-hq2-long-island-city-virginia.html.

40. J. David Goodman, "Amazon Pulls Out of Planned New York City Headquarters," *New York Times*, February 14, 2019, https://www.nytimes.com/2019/02/14/nyregion/amazon-hq2 -queens.html.

41. Nathan M. Jensen and Edmund J. Malesky, *Incentives to Pander: How Politicians Use Corporate Welfare for Political Gain* (Cambridge: Cambridge University Press, 2018).

42. Bruce Sterling, *The Epic Struggle of the Internet of Things* (Moscow: Strelka, 2014), 11–12.

43. Media reports indicate that Facebook is developing a new voice assistant. See Sam Shead, "Facebook Admits It's Working on AI Voice Assistant," *Forbes*, April 19, 2019, https://www.forbes.com/sites/samshead/2019/04/19/facebook-admits-its-working-on-ai -voice-assistant/#495b7dbb254c. The other Big Five's smart wives are discussed elsewhere throughout this book.

44. Sterling, *Epic Struggle*, 13, 53.

45. MacKay, *Radical Transformation*.

46. The Intergovernmental Panel on Climate Change predicts that global warming is likely to reach 1.5°C between 2030 and 2052 if it continues to increase at the current rate. See Intergovernmental Panel on Climate Change, *Global Warming of 1.5°C: An IPCC Special Report on the Impacts of Global Warming of 1.5°C above Pre-Industrial Levels and Related Global Greenhouse Gas Emission Pathways, in the Context of Strengthening the Global Response to the Threat of Climate Change, Sustainable Development, and Efforts to Eradicate Poverty* (Geneva: Intergovernmental Panel on Climate Change, 2018), https://www.ipcc.ch/sr15/; Gerardo Ceballos, Paul R. Ehrlich, and Rodolfo Dirzo, "Biological Annihilation via the Ongoing Sixth Mass Extinction Signaled by Vertebrate Population Losses and Declines," *PNAS* 114, no. 30 (July 25, 2017): E6089–E6096.

47. William E. Rees and Mathis Wackernagel, *Our Ecological Footprint: Reducing Human Impact on the Earth* (Gabriola Island, BC: New Society, 1998).

48. "Earth Overshoot Day: We Used a Year's Worth of Resources in Seven Months," ABC News (Australia), August 3, 2017, https://www.abc.net.au/news/2017-08-03/earth-overshoot -day:-today-the-earth-goes-into-the-red/8770040.

49. "About Us," Global Footprint Network, accessed December 3, 2019, https://www .footprintnetwork.org/about-us/.

50. Over the past twenty years, the overshoot day has decreased by two months. On aver- age, the day falls three days earlier each year. See "Past Earth Overshoot Days," Earth Overshoot Day, accessed December 3, 2019, https://www.overshootday.org/newsroom/ past-earth-overshoot-days/.

51. Mellor, *Feminism and Ecology*, 2.

52. Salleh, *Ecofeminism as Politics*, 8.

53. Vandana Shiva, *Earth Democracy: Justice, Sustainability, and Peace* (London: Zed Books, 2016), 17.

54. Yolande Strengers, *Smart Energy Technologies in Everyday Life: Smart Utopia?* (Basingstoke, UK: Palgrave Macmillan, 2013), 36.

55. Global e-Sustainability Initiative and Accenture Strategy, *#SMARTer2030: ICT Solutions for 21st Century Challenges* (Brussels: Global e-Sustainability Initiative, 2015), http:// smarter2030.gesi.org/downloads/Full_report.pdf.

56. Yolande Strengers, "Bridging the Divide between Resource Management and Everyday Life: Smart Metering, Comfort and Cleanliness" (PhD diss., RMIT University, 2010).

57. Yolande Strengers, Larissa Nicholls, and Cecily Maller, "Curious Energy Consumers: Humans and Nonhumans in Assemblages of Household Practice," *Journal of Consumer Culture* 16, no. 3 (November 2016): 761–780; Larissa Nicholls and Yolande Strengers, "Peak Demand and the 'Family Peak' Period in Australia: Understanding Practice (In) flexibility in Households with Children," *Energy Research and Social Science* 9 (September 2015): 116–124.

58. These observations are also supported in Tom Hargreaves and Charlie Wilson, *Smart Homes and Their Users* (Cham, Switzerland: Springer, 2017).

59. Zoë Sofoulis refers to this as "Mini-Meism" in reference to the Mini-Me twin of Austin Powers's evil nemesis, Dr. Evil, in the *Austin Powers* movies. She applies the analogy to the water sector. Zoë Sofoulis, "Skirting Complexity: The Retarding Quest for the Average Water User," *Continuum* 25, no. 6 (2011): 795–810.

60. Fatma Denton, "Climate Change Vulnerability, Impacts, and Adaptation: Why Does Gender Matter?," *Gender and Development* 10, no. 2 (July 2002): 10–20; Sherilyn MacGregor, "A Stranger Silence Still: The Need for Feminist Social Research on Climate Change," in "Nature, Society, and Environmental Crisis," supplement, *Sociological Review* 57, no. S2 (October 2009): 124–140.

61. Carol Farbotko, *Domestic Environmental Labour: An Ecofeminist Perspective on Making Homes Greener* (London: Routledge, 2017).

62. MacGregor, "Stranger Silence Still"; Farbotko, *Domestic Environmental Labour*.

63. Vanessa Organo, Lesley Head, and Gordon R. Waitt, "Who Does the Work in Sustainable Households?: A Time and Gender Analysis in New South Wales, Australia," *Gender, Place and Culture* 20, no. 5 (2013): 559–577.

64. Brian Horrigan, "The Home of Tomorrow, 1927–1945," in *Imagining Tomorrow: History, Technology, and the American Future*, ed. Joseph C. Corn (Cambridge, MA: MIT Press, 1988), 154.

65. Lisa Montgomery, "Surveillance Cameras Bring Outdoor Wildlife Snapshots Inside," *CE Pro*, December 15, 2015, https://www.cepro.com/article/surveillance_cameras_bring _outdoor_wildlife_snapshots_inside.

66. Montgomery, "Surveillance Cameras Bring Outdoor Wildlife Snapshots Inside."

67. Ecofeminist Val Plumwood refers to the "human/nature dualism" as "a system of ideas that takes a radically separated reason to be the essential characteristic of humans and situates human life outside and above an inferiorised and manipulable nature." Val Plumwood, *Environmental Culture: The Ecological Crisis of Reason* (London: Routledge, 2002), 4.

68. Lutron, *Experience the Essence of Pleasance*, November 2016, http://www.lutron.com/ TechnicalDocumentLibrary/3672324a_Pleasance-Lutron%20Product%20Bro%20 FINAL_sg.pdf.

69. Yolande Strengers and Larissa Nicholls, "Convenience and Energy Consumption in the Smart Home of the Future: Industry Visions from Australia and Beyond," *Energy Research and Social Science* 32 (October 2017): 86–93; Yolande Strengers, Mike Hazas, Larissa Nicholls, Jesper Kjeldskov, and Mikael B. Skov, "Pursuing Pleasance: Interrogating Energy-Intensive Visions for the Smart Home," *International Journal of Human-Computer Studies* 136 (April 2020): 1–14.

70. Davin Heckman, *A Small World: Smart Houses and the Dream of the Perfect Day* (Durham, NC: Duke University Press, 2008), 15.

71. Angel Chang, "This 1955 'Good House Wife's Guide' Explains How Wives Should Treat Their Husbands," *LittleThings*, October 7, 2019, https://www.littlethings.com/1950s-good -housewife-guide (emphasis added).

72. Allison Woodruff, Sally Augustin, and Brooke Foucault, "Sabbath Day Home Automation: 'It's Like Mixing Technology and Religion,'" in *Proceedings of the SIGCHI Conference on Human Factors in Computing Systems* (New York: ACM, 2007), 532.

73. Sarah Pink, *Home Truths: Gender, Domestic Objects and Everyday Life* (Oxford: Berg, 2004), 41.

74. Jennifer A. Rode, "A Theoretical Agenda for Feminist HCI," *Interacting with Computers* 23, no. 5 (September 2011): 393–400.

75. Strengers and Nicholls, "Convenience and Energy Consumption"; Rikke Hagensby Jensen, Yolande Strengers, Jesper Kjeldskov, Larissa Nicholls, and Mikael B. Skov, "Designing the Desirable Smart Home: A Study of Household Experiences and Energy Consumption Impacts," in *Proceedings of the 2018 CHI Conference on Human Factors in Computing Systems* (New York: ACM, 2018).

76. Elizabeth Shove, *Comfort, Cleanliness and Convenience: The Social Organization of Normality* (Oxford: Berg, 2003).

77. Lisa Montgomery, "How to Integrate Subsystems with a Home Automation System," *Electronic House*, November 16, 2015, https://www.electronichouse.com/how-to/ subsystems-that-make-sense-for-your-smart-home/.

78. Inge Røpke, Toke Haunstrup Christensen, and Jesper Ole Jensen, "Information and Communication Technologies: A New Round of Household Electrification," *Energy Policy* 38, no. 4 (April 2010): 1764–1773.

79. Stephen Corby, "The Next Level of Alexa: Meet the New Voice Assistant Who Will Change How People Live at Home," *Domain*, July 25, 2018, https://www.domain.com.au/living/ the-next-level-of-alexa-meet-the-new-voice-assistant-who-will-change-how-people-live-at -home-20180725-h12j0o-754135/.

80. Paul Dourish and Genevieve Bell, *Divining a Digital Future: Mess and Mythology in Ubiquitous Computing* (Cambridge, MA: MIT Press, 2014), 20.

81. Krissy Rushing, "Technology under Wraps," *Electronic House*, December 1, 2014, https:// www.electronichouse.com/smart-home/technology-wraps/.

82. Arielle Pardes, "Hey Alexa, Why Is Voice Shopping So Lousy?," *Wired*, June 17, 2019, https://www.wired.com/story/why-is-voice-shopping-bad/.

83. The Internet of Shit is a Twitter handle and website established in 2015 by an anonymous user (with over four hundred thousand followers as of early 2020), and is devoted to parodying Internet of Things devices that either serve no useful purpose or don't work as intended. See Internet of Shit, "The Internet of Things Has a Dirty Little Secret: It's Not Really Yours," *Circuit Breaker* (blog), *Verge*, July 12, 2016, https://www.theverge.com/ circuitbreaker/2016/7/12/12159766/internet-of-things-iot-internet-of-shit-twitter.

84. Kate Crawford and Vladan Joler, *Anatomy of an AI System: The Amazon Echo as an Anatomical Map of Human Labor, Data and Planetary Resources* (New York: AI Now Institute and Share Lab, September 7, 2018), https://anatomyof.ai.

85. Crawford and Joler, *Anatomy of an AI System*, section 7.

86. Wajcman, "Automation."

87. Vandana Shiva, *Earth Democracy: Justice, Sustainability and Peace* (London: Zed Books, 2016), 16.

88. Hilary Bergen, "'I'd Blush If I Could': Digital Assistants, Disembodied Cyborgs and the Problem of Gender," *Word and Text* 6 (December 2016), 105.

89. Lydia DePillis, "Big Companies Used to Pay the Best Wages. Not Anymore," CNN Money, January 18, 2018, https://money.cnn.com/2018/01/18/news/economy/big-companies-wages/index.html.

90. "Amazon's Jess Bezos Wins ITUC's World's Worst Boss Poll," International Trade Union Confederation, May 22, 2014, https://www.ituc-csi.org/amazon-s-jeff-bezos-wins-ituc-s.

91. Not everyone is happy with this decision. See Louise Matsakis, "Some Amazon Workers Fear They'll Earn Less Even with a $15 Minimum Wage," *Wired*, October 6, 2018, https://www.wired.com/story/amazon-minimum-wage-some-fear-they-will-earn-less/.

92. KnowTheChain, *2018 Information and Communications Technology Benchmark Findings Report*, 2018, https://knowthechain.org/wp-content/plugins/ktc-benchmark/app/public/images/benchmark_reports/KTC-ICT-May2018-Final.pdf; Chartered Quality Institute, *Technology on Trial: Do the World's Leading Technology Companies Have a Governance Problem?*, CQI Insight Report, 2018, https://www.quality.org/file/11953/download.

93. Greenpeace, *Guide to Greener Electronics 2017* (Washington, DC: Greenpeace, 2017), https://www.greenpeace.org/usa/reports/greener-electronics-2017/.

94. Janine Morley, Kelly Widdicks, and Mike Hazas, "Digitalisation, Energy and Data Demand: The Impact of Internet Traffic on Overall and Peak Electricity Consumption," *Energy Research and Social Science* 38 (April 2018): 128–137.

95. Nuno Bento, "Calling for Change?: Innovation, Diffusion, and the Energy Impacts of Global Mobile Telephony," *Energy Research and Social Science* 21 (November 2016): 84–100.

96. Vincent Mosco, *To the Cloud: Big Data in a Turbulent World* (Abingdon, UK: Routledge, 2014).

97. Mark Graham and Håvard Haarstad, "Transparency and Development: Ethical Consumption through Web 2.0 and the Internet of Things," *Information Technologies and International Development* 7, no. 1 (Spring 2011): 1.

98. Sut Jhally, cited in Graham and Haarstad, "Transparency and Development," 1.

99. Greenpeace, *Greener Electronics*.

100. Ward Van Heddeghem, Sofie Lambert, Bart Lannoo, Didier Colle, Mario Pickavet, and Piet Demeester, "Trends in Worldwide ICT Electricity Consumption from 2007 to 2012," *Computer Communications* 50 (September 1, 2014): 64–76.

101. Greenpeace, *Greener Electronics*; Cisco, *Cisco Visual Networking Index: Forecast and Trends, 2017–2022*, Cisco White Paper, 2019, https://www.cisco.com/c/en/us/solutions/collateral/service-provider/visual-networking-index-vni/white-paper-c11-741490.pdf.

102. Van Heddeghem et al., "ICT Electricity Consumption."

103. Greenpeace, *Clicking Clean: Who Is Winning the Race to Build a Green Internet?* (Washington, DC: Greenpeace, 2017), http://www.clickclean.org/usa/en/.

104. Greenpeace, *Clicking Clean*; Morley, Widdicks, and Hazas, "Digitalisation, Energy and Data Demand."

105. Graham and Haarstad, *Transparency and Development*.

106. Van Heddeghem et al., "ICT Electricity Consumption"; Fred Pearce, "Energy Hogs: Can World's Huge Data Centers Be Made More Efficient?," *Yale Environment 360*, April 3, 2018, https://e360.yale.edu/features/energy-hogs-can-huge-data-centers-be-made-more-efficient.

107. Anders S. G. Andrae and Tomas Edler, "On Global Electricity Usage of Communication Technology: Trends to 2030," *Challenges* 6, no. 1 (June 2015): 117–157.

108. Intergovernmental Panel on Climate Change, "Summary for Policymakers," in *Global Warming of 1.5°C*.

109. Greenpeace, *Clicking Clean*.

110. Google and Apple both scored As. Greenpeace, *Clicking Clean*, 124.

111. Greenpeace, *Clicking Clean*, 124.

112. International Energy Agency, *Digitalisation and Energy*, Technology Report, November 2017, https://www.iea.org/reports/digitalisation-and-energy.

113. Morley, Widdicks, and Hazas, "Digitalisation, Energy and Data Demand," 137, 136.

114. Crawford and Joler, *Anatomy of an AI System*.

115. Jennifer Yang Hui and Dymples Leong, "The Era of Ubiquitous Listening: Living in a World of Speech-Activated Devices," *Asian Journal of Public Affairs* 10, no. 1 (2017): 7.

116. Janet Vertesi, "Pygmalion's Legacy: Cyborg Women in Science Fiction," in *SciFi in the Mind's Eye: Reading Science through Science Fiction*, ed. Margret Grebowicz (Chicago: Open Court, 2007), 73–85.

117. Shiva, *Earth Democracy*, 1.

118. The ten principles of earth democracy outlined by Shiva (*Earth Democracy*, 9–11) are:

    1.   All species, people, and cultures have intrinsic worth
    2.   The earth community is a democracy of all life
    3.   Diversity in nature and culture must be defended

4. All beings have a natural right to sustenance

5. Earth democracy is based on living economies and economic democracy

6. Living economies are built on local economies

7. Earth democracy is a living democracy

8. Earth democracy is based on living cultures

9. Living cultures are life nourishing

10. Earth democracy globalizes peace, care, and compassion

119. Shiva, *Earth Democracy*, 6, 65.

120. Stakeholder Forum for a Sustainable Future, "Review of Implementation of Agenda 21 and the Rio Principles," United Nations Department of Economic and Social Affairs, January 2012, https://sustainabledevelopment.un.org/content/documents/641Synthesis_report _Web.pdf.

121. Jared Diamond, *Collapse: How Societies Choose to Fail or Succeed* (New York: Penguin Books, 2011).

122. Cormac Cullinan, *Wild Law: A Manifesto for Earth Justice* (Devon, UK: Green Books, 2003).

123. Catie Keck, "Right to Repair Is Less Complicated and More Important Than You Might Think," *Gizmodo*, May 10, 2019, https://gizmodo.com/right-to-repair-is-less-complicated -and-more-important-1834672055?IR=T; Roger Harrabin, "EU Brings in 'Right to Repair' Rules for Appliances," BBC News, October 1, 2019, https://www.bbc.com/news/ business-49884827.

124. Sabine LeBel, "Fast Machines, Slow Violence: ICTs, Planned Obsolescence, and E-waste," *Globalizations* 13, no. 3 (2016): 300–309.

125. Maria Mies and Shiva sum up this hypocrisy in their book *Ecofeminism*: "To 'catch-up' with the men in their society, as many women still see as the main goal of the feminist movement, particularly those who promote a policy of equalization, implies a demand for a greater, or equal share of what, in the existing paradigm, men take from nature. This, indeed has to a large extent happened in Western society: modern chemistry, household technology, and pharmacy were proclaimed as women's saviours, because they would 'emancipate' them from household drudgery. Today we realize that much environmental pollution and destruction is causally linked to modern household technology. Therefore, can the concept of emancipation be compatible with a concept of preserving the earth as our life base?" Maria Mies and Vandana Shiva, "Introduction: Why We Wrote This Book Together," in *Ecofeminism*, ed. Maria Mies and Vandana Shiva, new ed. (London: Zed Books, 2014), 7.

CHAPTER 5

1. Andrea Morris, "Prediction: Sex Robots Are the Most Disruptive Technology We Didn't See Coming," *Forbes*, September 25, 2018, https://www.forbes.com/sites/andreamorris/ 2018/09/25/prediction-sex-robots-are-the-most-disruptive-technology-we-didnt-see-coming/

#120856b56a56; RealDollX (website), accessed December 3, 2019, https://www.realdollx
.ai/.

2. "Team," Realbotix, accessed December 3, 2019, https://realbotix.com/#team.

3. Kate Devlin, *Turned On: Science, Sex and Robots* (London: Bloomsbury Sigma, 2018), 140.

4. Angel Chang, "This 1955 'Good House Wife's Guide' Explains How Wives Should Treat Their Husbands," *LittleThings*, October 7, 2019, https://www.littlethings.com/1950s-good-housewife-guide.

5. Devlin, *Turned On*, 146.

6. "Emma the AI Robot," AI AI-Tech UK, accessed December 3, 2019, https://ai-aitech .co.uk/emma-the-ai-robot.

7. "Emma – The AI Sex Robot, Female Sex Robot, Humanoid Sex Robot," YouTube video, posted by Nicole Cheung, August 29, 2017, https://www.youtube.com/watch?v =vPdoBJi9Tfw; Devlin, *Turned On*, 152.

8. Norman Makoto Su, Amanda Lazar, Jeffrey Bardzell, and Shaowen Bardzell, "Of Dolls and Men: Anticipating Sexual Intimacy with Robots," *ACM Transactions on Computer-Human Interaction (TOCHI)* 26, no. 3 (June 2019): 8, 14.

9. For more analysis of Emma as an intimate companion, see Fiona Andreallo and Chris Chesher, "Prosthetic Soul Mates: Sex Robots as Media for Companionship," *M/C Journal: A Journal of Media and Culture* 22, no. 5 (October 2019), http://journal.media-culture.org .au/index.php/mcjournal/article/view/1588.

10. "About Us," Silicon Wives, accessed December 3, 2019, https://www.siliconwives .com/pages/about-us.

11. Allison P. Davis, "Are We Ready for Robot Sex?: What You Learn about Human Desire When You Get Intimate with a Piece of Talking Silicone," *New York*, May 14, 2018, https:// www.thecut.com/2018/05/sex-robots-realbotix.html.

12. An "Easter egg" is computer software and media terminology, or "code," for an intentional inside joke, hidden message, or image, or secret feature of a computer program, video game, or entertainment media. The name evokes the idea of a traditional Easter egg hunt. Digital voice assistant Easter eggs have been critiqued for relying on feminized or sexualized "jokes" that play on the female characters of these devices. See UNESCO and EQUALS Skills Coalition, *I'd Blush If I Could: Closing Gender Divides in Digital Skills through Education*, GEN/2019/EQUALS/1 REV 2 (Paris: UNESCO, 2019); Devlin, *Turned On*.

13. "Sex Robot Demo: Sergi Reveals Samantha's Various Modes," *Express*, October 13, 2017, https://www.express.co.uk/videos/5608964044001/Sex-robot-demo-Sergi-reveals -Samantha-s-various-modes.

14. The term "harem" is used here in its context as a Japanese subculture of manga, anime, and video games, depicting polygynous relationships in which a heterosexual man is surrounded by two or more love interests or sexual partners.

15. *Engadget*, "Interview with Realdoll Founder", "Interview with RealDoll Founder and CEO Matt McMullen at CES 2016," YouTube video, posted January 8, 2016, https://www.youtube.com/watch?v=j68yDhUDCQs.

16. EXDOLL (website), accessed December 3, 2019, http://www.exdoll.com.

17. Chen Na, "The Sex Doll Who'll Do Your Dishes," *Sixth Tone*, January 27, 2018, http://www.sixthtone.com/news/1001619/the-sex-doll-wholl-do-your-dishes.

18. Devlin, *Turned On*, 147.

19. See "Our Hotels," Lumidolls, accessed December 3, 2019, https://lumidolls.com/en/content/our-brothels.

20. "About Us," TrueCompanion, accessed June 30, 2019, http://www.truecompanion.com/shop/about-us (site discontinued).

21. "Home," TrueCompanion, accessed June 30, 2019, http://www.truecompanion.com/home.html (site discontinued).

22. Cited in John Danaher, "Should We Be Thinking about Robot Sex?," in *Robot Sex: Social and Ethical Implications*, ed. John Danaher and Neil McArthur (Cambridge, MA: MIT Press, 2017), 6.

23. Danaher, "Should We Be Thinking," 12.

24. Danaher, "Should We Be Thinking."

25. Tracey Cox, "Would YOU Hop into Bed with a Sexbot?: Tracey Cox Reveals Why Women Should Embrace Dolls for BETTER Orgasms (and Insists They Won't Make Men Redundant)," *Daily Mail*, August 2, 2017, https://www.dailymail.co.uk/femail/article-4750768/Could-sexbots-make-men-redundant.html.

26. Kathleen Richardson, *Sex Robots: The End of Love* (Cambridge, UK: Polity, 2019); Kathleen Richardson, "The Asymmetrical 'Relationship': Parallels between Prostitution and the Development of Sex Robots," *SIGCAS Computers and Society* 45, no. 3 (September 2015): 290–293.

27. Devlin, *Turned On*.

28. "About Us," TrueCompanion.

29. Noel Sharkey, Aimee van Wynsberghe, Scott Robbins, and Eleanor Hancock, *Our Sexual Future with Robots: A Foundation for Responsible Robotics Consultation Report* (The Hague: Foundation for Responsible Robotics, 2017), https://responsiblerobotics.org/2017/07/05/frr-report-our-sexual-future-with-robots/; Devlin, *Turned On*.

30. Sharkey et al., *Our Sexual Future with Robots*, 22.

31. Mei Fong, "Sex Dolls Are Replacing China's Missing Women," *Foreign Policy*, September 28, 2017, https://foreignpolicy.com/2017/09/28/sex-dolls-are-replacing-chinas-missing-women-demographics/.

32. Danaher, "Should We Be Thinking," 4–5.

33. Sinziana M. Gutiu, "The Roboticization of Consent," in *Robot Law*, ed. Ryan Calo, A. Michael Froomkin, and Ian Kerr (Cheltenham, UK: Edward Elgar, 2016), 186–212.

34. Aaron Smith and Janna Anderson, "Predictions for the State of AI and Robotics in 2025," in *AI, Robotics, and the Future of Jobs*, Pew Research Center, August 6, 2014, https://www .pewinternet.org/2014/08/06/predictions-for-the-state-of-ai-and-robotics-in-2025/.

35. Sales reports vary, and do not distinguish between RealDoll and RealDollX. See, for example, Davis, "Are We Ready for Robot Sex?" Frank Tobe, "Sex Robots: Facts, Hype, and Legal and Ethical Considerations," *Robot Report*, August 20, 2017, https://www.therobotreport .com/sex-robots-facts-hype-legal-ethical-considerations/.

36. Laura Bates, "The Trouble with Sex Robots," *New York Times*, July 17, 2017, https://www .nytimes.com/2017/07/17/opinion/sex-robots-consent.html.

37. Jessica M. Szczuka and Nicole C. Krämer, "Influences on the Intention to Buy a Sex Robot: An Empirical Study on Influences of Personality Traits and Personal Characteristics on the Intention to Buy a Sex Robot," in *Love and Sex with Robots: Second International Conference, LSR 2016*, ed. Adrian David Cheok, Kate Devlin, and David Levy (Cham, Switzerland: Springer, 2017), 72–83.

38. Sharkey et al., *Our Sexual Future with Robots*.

39. David Levy, *Love and Sex with Robots: The Evolution of Human-Robot Relationships* (New York: Harper Perennial, 2008).

40. Quoted in Tabi Jackson Gee, "Why Female Sex Robots Are More Dangerous Than You Think," *Telegraph*, July 5, 2017, https://www.telegraph.co.uk/women/life/female -robots-why-this-scarlett-johansson-bot-is-more-dangerous/.

41. Katie Greene, "How VR Porn Is Secretly Driving the Industry," *VRFocus*, March 27, 2018, https://www.vrfocus.com/2018/04/how-vr-porn-is-secretly-driving-the-industry/.

42. Rob Waugh, "Webcam Site Uses VR Helmets to Turn Sex Robots into Real, Living People," *Metro*, January 24, 2018, https://metro.co.uk/2018/01/24/webcam-site-uses-vr -helmets-to-turn-sex-robots-into-real-living-people-7257248/.

43. Peter Rubin, *Future Presence: How Virtual Reality Is Changing Human Connection, Intimacy, and the Limits of Ordinary Life* (New York: HarperCollins, 2018).

44. Sharkey et al., *Our Sexual Future with Robots*.

45. *Engadget*, "Interview with Realdoll Founder"; A. M. Turing, "Computing Machinery and Intelligence," *Mind* 59, no. 236 (October 1950): 433–460.

46. "Info/Help," Lumidolls, accessed December 3, 2019, https://lumidolls.com/en/content/ info-help.

47. Davis, "Are We Ready for Robot Sex?"

48. RealdollX (website).

49. Laurie Mintz, *Becoming Cliterate: Why Orgasm Equality Matters—and How to Get It* (New York: HarperOne, 2017).

50. Laurie Mintz, "The Orgasm Gap: Simple Truth & Sexual Solutions," *Stress and Sex* (blog), *Psychology Today*, October 4, 2015, https://www.psychologytoday.com/au/blog/stress-and-sex/201510/the-orgasm-gap-simple-truth-sexual-solutions.

51. Mintz, "Orgasm Gap."

52. Debby Herbenick, Tsung-Chieh (Jane) Fu, Jennifer Arter, Stephanie A. Sanders, and Brian Dodge, "Women's Experiences with Genital Touching, Sexual Pleasure, and Orgasm: Results from a U.S. Probability Sample of Women Ages 18 to 94," *Journal of Sex and Marital Therapy* 44, no. 2 (2018): 201–212.

53. Mintz, *Becoming Cliterate*.

54. Devlin, *Turned On*.

55. Eileen L. Zurbriggen and Megan R. Yost, "Power, Desire, and Pleasure in Sexual Fantasies," *Journal of Sex Research* 41, no. 3 (August 2004): 288–300.

56. Jack Crosbie, "This Orgasming Sex Robot Might Boost Your Ego, but It Won't Make You Better in Bed," *Men's Health*, September 26, 2017, https://www.menshealth.com/sex-women/a19536305/orgasming-sex-robot/.

57. Shu Pan, Cynthia Leung, Jaimin Shah, and Amichai Kilchevsky, "Clinical Anatomy of the G-spot," *Clinical Anatomy* 28, no. 3 (April 2015): 363–367.

58. Meagan Tyler, *Selling Sex Short: The Pornographic and Sexological Construction of Women's Sexuality in the West* (Newcastle upon Tyne, UK: Cambridge Scholars, 2011).

59. Cox, "Would YOU Hop into Bed with a Sexbot?"; Devlin, *Turned On*.

60. "Osé," Lora Dicarlo (website), accessed January 16, 2020, https://loradicarlo.com/ose/.

61. Sarah Mitroff and Caitlin Petrakovitz, "Lora DiCarlo's Osé Sex Tech Device Is Back, Plus Two New Toys to Mimic Human Touch," *CNET*, January 6, 2020, https://www.cnet.com/news/lora-dicarlo-ose-sex-tech-device-back-plus-two-new-toys-mimic-human-touch/; Lauren Goode, "Sex-Tech Companies Are Having More Fun Than the Rest of Us at CES," *Wired*, January 8, 2020, https://www.wired.com/story/sex-tech-at-ces-2020-lora-dicarlo-crave/.

62. OhMiBod (website), accessed January 16, 2020, https://www.ohmibod.com/.

63. Cox, "Would YOU Hop into Bed with a Sexbot?"

64. Janet Vertesi, "Pygmalion's Legacy: Cyborg Women in Science Fiction," in *SciFi in the Mind's Eye: Reading Science through Science Fiction*, ed. Margret Grebowicz (Chicago: Open Court, 2007), 23; Gutiu, "Roboticization of Consent."

65. Wikipedia, sv "*My Living Doll*," last modified September 26, 2019, 23:31, https://en.wikipedia.org/wiki/My_Living_Doll.

66. Levy, *Love and Sex with Robots*; Brent Bambury, "A.I. Expert David Levy Says a Human Will Marry a Robot by 2050," January 6, 2017, in *Day 6*, CBC Radio, https://www.cbc.ca/radio/day6/episode-319-becoming-kevin-o-leary-saving-shaker-music-google-renewables-marrying-robots-and-more-1.3921088/a-i-expert-david-levy-says-a-human-will-marry-a-robot-by-2050-1.3921101.

67. John Danaher and Neil McArthur, eds., *Robot Sex: Social and Ethical Implications* (Cambridge, MA: MIT Press, 2017).

68. Benjamin Haas, "Chinese Man 'Marries' Robot He Built Himself," *Guardian*, April 4, 2017, https://www.theguardian.com/world/2017/apr/04/chinese-man-marries-robot-built-himself; Khaleda Rahman, "'We Don't Hurt Anybody, We Are Just Happy': Woman Reveals She Has Fallen in Love with a ROBOT and Wants to Marry It," *Daily Mail*, December 23, 2016, https://www.dailymail.co.uk/femail/article-4060440/Woman-reveals-love-ROBOT-wants-marry-it.html.

69. Stephen Marche, "The Future of Celebrity Is a Japanese Hologram Named Hatsune Miku," *Medium*, July 24, 2018, https://medium.com/s/futurehuman/the-future-of-celebrity-is-a-japanese-hologram-named-miku-a87419c951e.

70. Alex Williams, "Do You Take This Robot . . . ," *New York Times*, January 19, 2019, https://www.nytimes.com/2019/01/19/style/sex-robots.html.

71. SiriAndAlexa (website), accessed December 3, 2019, https://www.siriandalexa.com.

72. Felix Allen, "My Sex Doll Is So Much Better Than My Real Wife," *New York Post*, June 30, 2017, https://nypost.com/2017/06/30/i-love-my-sex-doll-because-she-never-grumbles/.

73. Jasper Hamill and Lauren Windle, "Harmony 3.0 Sex Robot with Self-Lubricating Vagina Will Be Released in Time for Christmas," *Sun*, October 5, 2018, https://www.thesun.co.uk/tech/4798599/harmony-3-0-sex-robot-with-self-lubricating-vagina-will-be-released-in-time-for-christmas/.

74. Emily Starr and Michele Adams, "The Domestic Exotic: Mail-Order Brides and the Paradox of Globalized Intimacies," *Signs: Journal of Women in Culture and Society* 41, no. 4 (Summer 2016): 953–975.

75. Debbie Ging, "Alphas, Betas, and Incels: Theorizing the Masculinities of the Manosphere," *Men and Masculinities* 22, no. 4 (October 2019): 638–657.

76. Devlin, *Turned On*, 227, 228.

77. *Sex Toy Secrets*, Channel 4, accessed December 3, 2019, https://www.channel4.com/programmes/sex-toy-secrets/episode-guide.

78. Benita Marcussen, "Men & Dolls," accessed December 3, 2019, http://www.benitamarcussen.dk/projects/.

79. Su et al., "Of Dolls and Men," 8, 14.

80. Su et al., "Of Dolls and Men," 26.

81. Su et al., "Of Dolls and Men," 28.

82. April Glaser, "The Scarlett Johansson Bot Is the Robotic Future of Objectifying Women," *Wired*, April 4, 2016, https://www.wired.com/2016/04/the-scarlett-johansson-bot-signals-some-icky-things-about-our-future/.

83. "Can I Have a Doll Made of a Celebrity, Model, or My Ex-Girlfriend?," Knowledge Base, RealDoll, accessed December 3, 2019, https://www.realdoll.com/knowledgebase/can-i-have-a-doll-made-of-a-celebrity-model-or-my-ex-girlfriend/.

84. Deepfakes use a machine learning technique to superimpose "fake" images and videos over source images and videos to generate new and increasingly realistic content. Deepfakes are being used to create fake and nonconsensual celebrity pornography videos or revenge porn (the distribution, or threat of distribution, of sexually explicit images and videos without the permission of the person/people depicted). Asher Flynn, "Image-Based Abuse: The Disturbing Phenomenon of the 'Deepfake,'" *Lens*, March 12, 2019, https://lens.monash.edu/@politics-society/2019/03/12/1373665/image-based-abuse-deep-fake.

85. Bates, "Trouble with Sex Robots."

86. "FAQ," TrueCompanion, accessed June 30, 2019, http://www.truecompanion.com/shop/about-us (site discontinued).

87. Blay Whitby, "Do You Want a Robot Lover?," in *Robot Ethics: The Ethical and Social Implications of Robotics*, ed. Patrick Lin, Keith Abney, and George A. Bekey (Cambridge, MA: MIT Press, 2011), 233–249.

88. Sarah Knapton, "Sex Robots on Way for Elderly and Lonely . . . but Pleasure-Bots Have a Dark Side, Warn Experts," *Telegraph*, July 5, 2017, https://www.telegraph.co.uk/science/2017/07/04/sex-robots-way-elderly-lonelybut-pleasure-bots-have-dark-side/.

89. Knapton, "Sex Robots on Way for Elderly and Lonely."

90. "Australia and the UK Banned Import of These Disturbing Child Sex Dolls," Fight the New Drug, April 3, 2019, https://fightthenewdrug.org/australia-calls-for-ban-of-disturbing-japanese-child-sex-dolls/.

91. Jesse Fox and Bridget Potocki, "Lifetime Video Game Consumption, Interpersonal Aggression, Hostile Sexism, and Rape Myth Acceptance: A Cultivation Perspective," *Journal of Interpersonal Violence* 31, no. 10 (June 2016): 1912–1931; Victoria Simpson Beck, Stephanie Boys, Christopher Rose, and Eric Beck, "Violence against Women in Video Games: A Prequel or Sequel to Rape Myth Acceptance?," *Journal of Interpersonal Violence* 27, no. 15 (October 2012): 3016–3031.

92. Wikipedia, sv "List of Controversial Video Games," last modified September 23, 2019, 00:46, https://en.wikipedia.org/wiki/List_of_controversial_video_games.

93. Helen W. Kennedy, "Lara Croft: Feminist Icon or Cyberbimbo? On the Limits of Textual Analysis," *Game Studies* 2, no. 2 (December 2002), http://www.gamestudies.org/0202/kennedy/.

94. Michael Kasumovic and Rob Brooks, "Virtual Rape in Grand Theft Auto 5: Learning the Limits of the Game," *Conversation*, August 19, 2014, https://theconversation.com/virtual-rape-in-grand-theft-auto-5-learning-the-limits-of-the-game-30520.

95. Devlin, *Turned On.*

96. Gutiu, "Roboticization of Consent," 205.

97. Meagan Tyler and Kaye Quek, "Conceptualizing Pornographication: A Lack of Clarity and Problems for Feminist Analysis," *Sexualization, Media, and Society* 2, no. 2 (June 2016): 7.

98. Paul J. Wright and Robert S. Tokunaga, "Men's Objectifying Media Consumption, Objectification of Women, and Attitudes Supportive of Violence against Women," *Archives of Sexual Behavior* 45, no. 4 (May 2016): 955–964.

99. Jenna Drenten, Lauren Gurrieri, and Meagan Tyler, "Sexualized Labour in Digital Culture: Instagram Influencers, Porn Chic and the Monetization of Attention," *Gender, Work and Organization*, published ahead of print, February 21, 2019, https://doi.org/10.1111/gwao.12354.

100. Gutiu, "Roboticization of Consent."

101. Kathleen Richardson, "Sex Robot Matters: Slavery, the Prostituted and the Rights of Machines!," *IEEE Technology and Society Magazine* 35, no. 2 (June 2016): 48.

102. "About," Campaign against Sex Robots, accessed December 3, 2019, https://campaignagainstsexrobots.org/about/.

103. Sharkey et al., *Our Sexual Future with Robots*, 30–31.

104. Sharkey et al., *Our Sexual Future with Robots*, 30–31.

105. Bates, "Trouble with Sex Robots."

106. Victoria Brooks, "Samantha's Suffering: Why Sex Machines Should Have Rights Too," *Conversation*, April 5, 2018, https://theconversation.com/samanthas-suffering-why-sex-machines-should-have-rights-too-93964.

107. Joseph W. Critelli and Jenny M. Bivona, "Women's Erotic Rape Fantasies: An Evaluation of Theory and Research," *Journal of Sex Research* 45, no. 1 (January–March 2008): 57–70.

108. Bates, "Trouble with Sex Robots."

109. Jenny M. Bivona, Joseph W. Critelli, and Michael J. Clark, "Women's Rape Fantasies: An Empirical Evaluation of the Major Explanations," *Archives of Sexual Behavior* 41, no. 5 (October 2012): 1107–1119; Kathryn R. Klement, Brad J. Sagarin, and M. Ellen Lee, "Participating in a Culture of Consent May Be Associated with Lower Rape-Supportive Beliefs," *Journal of Sex Research* 54, no. 1 (2016): 130–134.

110. Lily Frank and Sven Nyholm, "Robot Sex and Consent: Is Consent to Sex between a Robot and a Human Conceivable, Possible, and Desirable?," *Artificial Intelligence and Law* 25, no. 3 (September 2017): 322.

111. Frank and Nyholm, "Robot Sex and Consent," 322.

112. Unicole Unicron, "Eve's Robot Dreams," Indiegogo, accessed December 3, 2019, https://www.indiegogo.com/projects/eve-s-robot-dreams.

113. Gutiu, "Roboticization of Consent," 187, 188, 195.

114. Gutiu, "Roboticization of Consent," 195.

115. Gutiu, "Roboticization of Consent," 203, 205.

116. Jaclyn Friedman and Jessica Valenti, eds., *Yes Means Yes!: Visions of Female Sexual Power and a World without Rape* (New York: Seal, 2008).

117. Gutiu, "Roboticization of Consent," 207, 209.

118. Gutiu, "Roboticization of Consent," 211.

119. This is a reference to BDSM, where a safe word is a code word used to signal a person's physical or emotional boundary, agreed on beforehand between participants, and usually used when an encounter or activity needs to stop, or the intensity needs to be reduced to maintain a safe boundary.

120. Devlin, *Turned On.*

121. Devlin, *Turned On*, 266.

122. Devlin, *Turned On*, 267.

CHAPTER 6

1. Andrew Liptak, "Amazon's Alexa Started Ordering People Dollhouses after Hearing Its Name on TV," *Verge*, January 7, 2017, https://www.theverge.com/2017/1/7/14200210/amazon-alexa-tech-news-anchor-order-dollhouse.

2. Devin Coldewey, "This Family's Echo Sent a Private Conversation to a Random Contact," *TechCrunch*, May 24, 2018, https://techcrunch.com/2018/05/24/family-claims-their-echo-sent-a-private-conversation-to-a-random-contact/.

3. "'I Thought a Kid Was Laughing behind Me': Amazon's Alexa Has Been Caught Randomly Cackling at People," ABC News (Australia), March 8, 2018, https://www.abc.net.au/news/2018-03-08/amazon-to-fix-alexa-laugh/9527412.

4. Nick Whigham, "Amazon's Alexa Speaker Is Randomly Laughing at Users and It's Really Freaking People Out," *news.com.au*, March 8, 2018, https://www.news.com.au/technology/home-entertainment/audio/amazons-alexa-speaker-is-randomly-laughing-at-users-and-its-really-freaking-people-out/news-story/ab0e32f5762f459bff420d23df074543; Brian Koerber, "Amazon Reveals Why Alexa Is Randomly Laughing and Creeping People Out," *Mashable*, March 7, 2018, https://mashable.com/2018/03/07/why-amazon-alexa-laughing/; "Your Amazon Alexa Is Most Likely Possessed by a Demon," *Mandatory*, March 8, 2018, https://www.mandatory.com/fun/1377811-amazon-alexa-likely-possessed-demon.

5. Mary-Ann Russon, "Google Home Fail: Google's Super Bowl Ad Accidentally Activates Numerous Personal Assistants," *International Business Times*, February 6, 2017, https://www.ibtimes.co.uk/google-home-fail-googles-super-bowl-ad-accidentally-activates-numerous-personal-assistants-1605099.

6. Leo Kelion, "CES 2018: LG Robot Cloi Repeatedly Fails on Stage at Its Unveil," BBC News, January 8, 2018, http://www.bbc.com/news/technology-42614281.

7. Jeff Parsons, "Watch Sophia the 'Sexy Robot' Claim She Will 'Destroy Humans'—Leaving Creator Red Faced," *Daily Mirror*, March 22, 2016, https://www.mirror.co.uk/tech/watch-sophia-sexy-robot-claim-7606152.

8. "Jimmy Fallon's Had Plenty of Guests on His Show, but This One's the Creepiest," *ViralNova*, April 29, 2017, http://www.viralnova.com/sophia-robot/.

9. "The Girl from the Future," *Cosmopolitan India*, May 30, 2018, https://www.cosmopolitan.in/fashion/features/a15165/girl-future.

10. Hussein Abbass, "An AI Professor Explains: Three Concerns about Granting Citizenship to Robot Sophia," *Conversation*, October 30, 2017, https://theconversation.com/an-ai-professor-explains-three-concerns-about-granting-citizenship-to-robot-sophia-86479.

11. Richard Mitchell, "Halo 4 as a Love Story: The Personal Origins of Cortana's Breakdown," *Engadget*, April 2, 2013, https://www.engadget.com/2013/04/02/halo-4-as-a-love-story-the-personal-origins-of-cortanas-breakd/; Call of Treyarch, "Halo 4: Cortana Goes Bitch Mode," YouTube video, posted by calloftreyarch, November 7, 2012, https://www.youtube.com/watch?v=YQk_FAGrth4, cited in Hilary Bergen, "'I'd Blush If I Could': Digital Assistants, Disembodied Cyborgs and the Problem of Gender," *Word and Text* 6 (December 2016): 101.

12. Don Sweeney, "Apple Washes Siri's Mouth out with Soap over Vulgar Definition of 'Mother,'" *Sacramento Bee*, April 30, 2018, https://www.sacbee.com/news/nation-world/national/article210097244.html.

13. Chris Merriman, "Alexa Is Laughing Manically and Frankly We're Screwed Guys," *Inquirer*, March 7, 2018, https://www.theinquirer.net/inquirer/news/3028014/alexa-is-laughing-manically-and-frankly-were-screwed-guys; Edward Moyer, "Yes, Alexa Is Suddenly Letting Out Evil Laughs for No Reason," *CNET*, March 7, 2018, https://www.cnet.com/news/yes-amazon-alexa-is-randomly-laughing-for-no-reason/; Chris Smith, "Jimmy Kimmel Explains Amazon Alexa's Creepy, Hysterical Laughing Problem," *BGR*, March 8, 2018, https://bgr.com/2018/03/08/amazon-alexa-laugh-jimmy-kimmel-explains/.

14. Roger Cheng, "The Silence of LG's Cloi Robot at CES Is Deafening," *CNET*, January 8, 2018, https://www.cnet.com/news/the-silence-of-lgs-cloi-robot-at-ces-2018-is-deafening/.

15. Shensheng Wang, Scott O. Lilienfeld, and Philippe Rochat, "The Uncanny Valley: Existence and Explanations," *Review of General Psychology* 19, no. 4 (December 2015): 393–407; Stephanie Lay, "Uncanny Valley: Why We Find Human-Like Robots and Dolls So Creepy," *Conversation*, November 10, 2015, https://theconversation.com/uncanny-valley-why-we-find-human-like-robots-and-dolls-so-creepy-50268.

16. Call of Treyarch, "Halo 4."

17. Donna J. Haraway, *Simians, Cyborgs, and Women: The Reinvention of Nature* (New York: Routledge, 1991).

18. Hilary Bergen, "'I'd Blush If I Could': Digital Assistants, Disembodied Cyborgs and the Problem of Gender," *Word and Text* 6 (December 2016): 99.

19. Rachel P. Maines, *The Technology of Orgasm: "Hysteria," the Vibrator, and Women's Sexual Satisfaction* (Baltimore: Johns Hopkins University Press, 1999), 23.

20. Helen King, "Galen and the Widow: Towards a History of Therapeutic Masturbation in Ancient Gynaecology," *EuGeStA: Journal on Gender Studies in Antiquity*, no. 1 (2011): 205–235; Sarah Jaffray, "What Is Hysteria?," Stories, Wellcome Collection, August 13, 2015, https://wellcomecollection.org/articles/W89GZBIAAN4yz1hQ.

21. Sadie Plant, *Zeros and Ones: Digital Women and the New Technoculture* (London: Fourth Estate, 1997).

22. Bergen, "I'd Blush If I Could," 109.

23. Graeme Gooday, *Domesticating Electricity: Technology, Uncertainty and Gender, 1880–1914* (Pittsburgh: University of Pittsburgh Press, 2008), 109.

24. Julie Wosk, *Women and the Machine: Representations from the Spinning Wheel to the Electronic Age* (Baltimore: John Hopkins University Press, 2001).

25. Sarah Kember, *iMedia: The Gendering of Objects, Environments and Smart Materials* (London: Palgrave Macmillan, 2016).

26. Bergen, "I'd Blush If I Could," 104.

27. Albert Robida, *La Vie Électrique* (1890; repr., Project Gutenberg, 2011), http://www.gutenberg.org/ebooks/35103.

28. Wosk, *Women and the Machine*.

29. Wosk, *Women and the Machine*. See also Gooday, *Domesticating Electricity*.

30. Haraway, *Simians, Cyborgs, and Women*, 149.

31. Bergen, "I'd Blush If I Could," 96.

32. Bergen, "I'd Blush If I Could," 96.

33. Villiers de L'Isle-Adam, *Tomorrow's Eve*, trans. Robert Martin Adams (Urbana: University of Illinois Press, 2000).

34. Wosk, *Women and the Machine*, 75, 79.

35. Wosk, *Women and the Machine*, 79.

36. Bergen, "I'd Blush If I Could," 100.

37. Laura Bates, *Everyday Sexism: The Project That Inspired a Worldwide Movement* (New York: St. Martin's, 2016).

38. Michael J. Coren, "Virtual Assistants Spend Much of Their Time Fending Off Sexual Harassment," *Quartz*, October 26, 2016, https://qz.com/818151/virtual-assistant-bots-like-siri-alexa-and-cortana-spend-much-of-their-time-fending-off-sexual-harassment/.

39. Leah Fessler, "We Tested Bots Like Siri and Alexa to See Who Would Stand Up to Sexual Harassment," *Quartz*, February 23, 2017, https://qz.com/911681/we-tested-apples-siri

-amazon-echos-alexa-microsofts-cortana-and-googles-google-home-to-see-which-personal
-assistant-bots-stand-up-for-themselves-in-the-face-of-sexual-harassment/.

40. Winifred R. Poster, "The Virtual Receptionist with a Human Touch: Opposing Pressures of Digital Automation and Outsourcing in Interactive Services," in *Invisible Labor: Hidden Work in the Contemporary World*, ed. Marion G. Crain, Winifred R. Poster, and Miriam A. Cherry (Berkeley: University of California Press, 2016), 57–72.

41. "Ms. Dewey, My New Girlfriend," YouTube video, posted by Victurin, January 9, 2007, https://www.youtube.com/watch?v=vC_sRZtlYYQ.

42. Alyssa Abkowitz, "Racy Virtual-Reality Assistant Pulled after Questions Raised," *Wall Street Journal*, December 13, 2017, https://www.wsj.com/articles/racy-virtual-reality-assistant -pulled-after-questions-raised-1513165008; Phoebe Weston, "Erotic Virtual Assistant 'Vivi,' Designed to Flirt with Users, Has Been Taken Offline Following Criticism the Avatar Depicts Women as Sex Objects," *Daily Mail*, December 14, 2017, https://www.dailymail .co.uk/sciencetech/article-5175741/VR-assistant-Vivi-flirts-request-pulled.html.

43. UNESCO and EQUALS Skills Coalition, *I'd Blush If I Could: Closing Gender Divides in Digital Skills through Education*, GEN/2019/EQUALS/1 REV 2 (Paris: UNESCO, 2019), 101.

44. Wendy Tuohy, "Joe Biden: Where Does Friendly End and Creepy Start?," *Sydney Morning Herald*, April 3, 2019, https://www.smh.com.au/lifestyle/gender/where-does-hands-on -friendly-end-and-creepy-start-maybe-don-t-ask-joe-20190403-p51a54.html; Bates, *Every- day Sexism*.

45. Megan K. Strait, Cynthia Aguillon, Virginia Contreras, and Noemi Garcia, "The Public's Perception of Humanlike Robots: Online Social Commentary Reflects an Appearance-Based Uncanny Valley, a General Fear of a 'Technology Takeover,' and the Unabashed Sexualization of Female-Gendered Robots," in *26th IEEE International Symposium on Robot and Human Interactive Communication (RO-MAN)* (Piscataway, NJ: Institute of Electrical and Electronics Engineers, 2017), 1418–1423.

46. Sinziana M. Gutiu, "The Roboticization of Consent," in *Robot Law*, ed. Ryan Calo, A. Michael Froomkin, and Ian Kerr (Cheltenham, UK: Edward Elgar, 2016), 192.

47. Peter Lee, "Learning from Tay's Introduction," *Official Microsoft Blog*, March 25, 2016, https://blogs.microsoft.com/blog/2016/03/25/learning-tays-introduction/.

48. Katherine Cross, "When Robots Are an Instrument of Male Desire," *Establishment*, April 27, 2016, https://theestablishment.co/when-robots-are-an-instrument-of-male-desire -ad1567575a3d.

49. Gina Neff and Peter Nagy, "Talking to Bots: Symbiotic Agency and the Case of Tay," *International Journal of Communication* 10 (2016): 4915–4931.

50. Bergen, "I'd Blush If I Could," 106.

51. Liz Tracy, "In Contrast to Tay, Microsoft's Chinese Chatbot, Xiaoice, Is Actually Pleasant," *Inverse*, March 26, 2016, https://www.inverse.com/article/13387-microsoft-chinese-chatbot.

52. Miriam E. Sweeney, "Not Just a Pretty (Inter)face: A Critical Analysis of Microsoft's 'Ms. Dewey'" (PhD diss., University of Illinois at Urbana-Champaign, 2013), https://www.ideals.illinois.edu/handle/2142/46617.

53. Alex Sciuto, Arnita Saini, Jodi Forlizzi, and Jason I. Hong, "Hey Alexa, What's Up?": A Mixed-Methods Studies of In-Home Conversational Agent Usage," in *Proceedings of the 2018 Designing Interactive Systems Conference* (New York: ACM, 2018), 857–868.

54. Clifford Nass and Youngme Moon, "Machines and Mindlessness: Social Responses to Computers," *Journal of Social Issues* 56, no. 1 (Spring 2000): 81–103.

55. Clifford Nass, Youngme Moon, and Nancy Green, "Are Machines Gender Neutral?: Gender-Stereotypic Responses to Computers with Voices," *Journal of Applied Social Psychology* 27, no. 10 (May 1997): 864–876; Clifford Nass, Jonathan Steuer, and Ellen R. Tauber, "Computers Are Social Actors," in *Proceedings of the SIGCHI Conference on Human Factors in Computing Systems* (New York: ACM, 1994), 72–78.

56. Byron Reeves and Clifford Nass, *The Media Equation: How People Treat Computers, Television, and New Media Like Real People and Places* (Stanford, CA: Center for the Study of Language and Information, 2003), 9; Nass and Moon, "Machines and Mindlessness."

57. Friederike Eyssel and Frank Hegel, "(S)he's Got the Look: Gender Stereotyping of Robots," *Journal of Applied Social Psychology* 42, no. 9 (September 2012): 2213–2230.

58. Aike C. Horstmann, Nikolai Bock, Eva Linhuber, Jessica M. Szczuka, Carolin Straßmann, and Nicole C. Krämer, "Do a Robot's Social Skills and Its Objection Discourage Interactants from Switching the Robot Off?," *PLoS ONE* 13, no. 7 (2018): e0201581.

59. Jennifer Rhee, *The Robotic Imaginary: The Human and the Price of Dehumanized Labor* (Minneapolis: University of Minnesota Press, 2018).

60. Julia Carrie Wong, "Rage against the Machine: Self-Driving Cars Attacked by Angry Californians," *Guardian*, March 6, 2018, https://www.theguardian.com/technology/2018/mar/06/california-self-driving-cars-attacked.

61. "Rage against the Machine," *Sydney Morning Herald*, July 26, 2003, https://www.smh.com.au/technology/rage-against-the-machine-20030726-gdh5sc.html.

62. Stanley Milgram, "Behavioral Study of Obedience," *Journal of Abnormal and Social Psychology* 67, no. 4 (October 1963): 371–378; Christoph Bartneck and Jun Hu, "Exploring the Abuse of Robots," *Interaction Studies* 9, no. 3 (2008): 415–433.

63. Bartneck and Hu, "Exploring the Abuse of Robots."

64. Bartneck and Hu, "Exploring the Abuse of Robots."

65. Sheryl Brahnam, "Gendered Bods and Bot Abuse" (paper presented during the Misuse and Abuse of Interactive Technologies Workshop at the CHI 2006 Conference on Human Factors in Computing Systems, Montreal, April 22, 2006), http://www.agentabuse.org/CHI2006Abuse2.pdf.

66. Brahnam, "Gendered Bods and Bot Abuse."

67. Brahnam, "Gendered Bods and Bot Abuse," 16.

68. Jacqueline Feldman, "This Is What a Feminist Looks Like," *Real Life*, August 8, 2016, https://reallifemag.com/this-is-what-a-feminist-looks-like/.

69. Leah Fessler, "Amazon's Alexa Is Now a Feminist, and She's Sorry If That Upsets You," *Quartz*, January 17, 2018, https://qz.com/work/1180607/amazons-alexa-is-now-a-feminist-and-shes-sorry-if-that-upsets-you/.

70. Bergen, "I'd Blush If I Could."

71. Fessler, "We Tested Bots Like Siri and Alexa."

72. Gilhwan Hwang, Jeewon Lee, Cindy Yoonjung Oh, and Joonhwan Lee, "It Sounds Like a Woman: Exploring Gender Stereotypes in South Korean Voice Assistants," in *Extended Abstracts of the 2019 CHI Conference on Human Factors in Computing Systems* (New York: ACM, 2019).

73. UNESCO and EQUALS Skills Coalition, *I'd Blush If I Could.*

74. "MeToo," a phrase coined by Tarana Burke in 2006, has become the tagline of a movement that she founded that same year—a movement to support survivors of sexual violence, particularly black women and girls, and other young women of color from low-income communities (https://metoomvmt.org). In October 2017, the phrase went viral, spreading on social media via a hashtag (#MeToo) to demonstrate as well as call out the widespread prevalence of sexual assault and harassment, especially in the workplace. See Cat Lafuente, "Who Is the Woman behind the #MeToo Movement?," *List*, accessed December 3, 2019, https://www.thelist.com/110186/woman-behind-metoo-movement/.

75. "Siri and Alexa Should Help Shut Down Sexual Harassment," Care2 Petitions, accessed December 3, 2019, https://www.thepetitionsite.com/246/134/290/siri-and-alexa-can-help-combat-sexual-harassment/.

76. Fessler, "Amazon's Alexa Is Now a Feminist."

77. Adam Miner, Arnold Milstein, Stephen Schueller, Roshini Hegde, Christina Mangurian, and Eleni Linos, "Smartphone-Based Conversational Agents and Responses to Questions about Mental Health, Interpersonal Violence, and Physical Health," *JAMA Internal Medicine* 176, no. 5 (May 2016): 619–625.

78. Mary Elizabeth Williams, "Siri, Find Me an Abortion Provider: Apple's Weird Anti-Choice Glitch Is Finally on Its Way Out," *Salon*, January 30, 2016, https://www.salon.com/2016/01/29/siri_find_me_an_abortion_provider_apples_weird_anti_choice_glitch_is_finally_on_its_way_out/.

79. Bergen, "I'd Blush If I Could," 107.

80. Emily Chang, *Brotopia: Breaking Up the Boys' Club of Silicon Valley* (New York: Portfolio, 2018); Sarah Myers West, Meredith Whittaker, and Kate Crawford, *Discriminating Systems: Gender, Race, and Power in AI* (New York: AI Now Institute, 2019), https://ainowinstitute.org/discriminatingsystems.pdf.

81. Ian Bogost, "Sorry, Alexa Is Not a Feminist," *Atlantic*, January 24, 2018, https://www.theatlantic.com/technology/archive/2018/01/sorry-alexa-is-not-a-feminist/551291/.

82. Alex Hern, "Apple Made Siri Deflect Questions on Feminism, Leaked Papers Reveal," *Guardian*, September 6, 2019, https://www.theguardian.com/technology/2019/sep/06/apple-rewrote-siri-to-deflect-questions-about-feminism.

83. Bogost, "Sorry, Alexa Is Not a Feminist."

84. Bergen, "I'd Blush," 104.

85. Rhee, *Robotic Imaginary*.

86. Thomas A. Edison, "Electricity Man's Slave," *Scientific American* 52, no. 12 (March 21, 1885): 185.

87. Restaurant Opportunities Centers United and Forward Together, *The Glass Floor: Sexual Harassment in the Restaurant Industry* (New York: Restaurant Opportunities Centers United, 2014); Emily Stewart, "These Are the Industries with the Most Reported Sexual Harassment Claims," *Vox*, November 21, 2017, https://www.vox.com/identities/2017/11/21/16685942/sexual-harassment-industry-service-retail; Alexandra Topping, "Sexual Harassment Rampant in Hospitality Industry, Survey Finds," *Guardian*, January 24, 2018, https://www.theguardian.com/world/2018/jan/24/sexual-harassment-rampant-hospitality-industry-unite-survey-finds.

88. Alexandra Chasin, "Class and Its Close Relations: Identities among Women, Servants, and Machines," in *Posthuman Bodies*, ed. Judith Halberstram and Ira Livingstone (Bloomington: Indiana University Press, 1995), 73, 96, 75, 93.

89. We have observed that the more contained an AI is, the more likely it is to be coded feminine, reflecting connections made by technofeminist scholar Sofoulis on the long-held associations between femininity and containers. Zoë Sofia [Sofoulis], "Container Technologies," *Hypatia* 15, no. 2 (Spring 2000): 181–201.

90. Nicole Lyn Pesce, "The Problem with Bank of America's New Virtual Assistant Erica," *MarketWatch*, May 23, 2018, https://www.marketwatch.com/story/the-problem-with-bank-of-americas-new-virtual-assistant-erica-2018-05-23.

91. See, for example, Bret Kinsella, "U.S. Consumers Do Express a Preference for Female Gendered Voice Assistants According to New Research," *Voicebot*, November 23, 2019, https://voicebot.ai/2019/11/23/u-s-consumers-do-express-a-preference-for-female-gendered-voice-assistants-according-to-new-research/.

92. Ruqayyah Moynihan and Hannah Schwar, "There's a Clever Psychological Reason Why Amazon Gave Alexa a Female Voice," *Business Insider*, September 15, 2018, https://www.businessinsider.com/theres-psychological-reason-why-amazon-gave-alexa-a-female-voice-2018-9.

93. UNESCO and EQUALS Skills Coalition, *I'd Blush If I Could*.

94. Sarah Zhang, "No, Women's Voices Are Not Easier to Understand Than Men's Voices," *Gizmodo*, February 7, 2015, https://www.gizmodo.com.au/2015/02/no-siri-is-not-female-because-womens-voices-are-easier-to-understand/.

95. Terry L. Wiley, Rick Chappell, Lakeesha Carmichael, David M. Nondahl, and Karen J. Cruickshanks, "Changes in Hearing Thresholds over 10 Years in Older Adults," *Journal of the American Academy of Audiology* 19, no. 4 (April 2008): 281–371.

96. Ann R. Bradlow, Gina M. Torretta, and David B. Pisoni, "Intelligibility of Normal Speech I: Global and Fine-Grained Acoustic-Phonetic Talker Characteristics," *Speech Communication* 20, no. 3–4 (December 1996): 255–272.

97. Paul Pickering, "How to Get Big Sounds from Small Speakers," *Electronic Design*, February 16, 2016, https://www.electronicdesign.com/systems/how-get-big-sounds-small-speakers; Zhang, "No, Women's Voices Are Not Easier to Understand."

98. UNESCO and EQUALS Skills Coalition, *I'd Blush If I Could.*

99. Henry James, *The Bostonians* (New York: Modern Library, 2003), cited in Mary Beard, *Women & Power: A Manifesto* (London: Profile Books, 2017), 29.

100. Beard, *Women & Power*, 30.

101. Emily Lever, "I Was a Human Siri," *Intelligencer*, April 26, 2018, http://nymag.com/intelligencer/smarthome/i-was-a-human-siri-french-virtual-assistant.html.

102. Amy Schiller and John McMahon, "Alexa, Alert Me When the Revolution Comes: Gender, Affect, and Labor in the Age of Home-Based Artificial Intelligence," *New Political Science* 41, no. 2 (2019): 173–191.

103. UNESCO and EQUALS Skills Coalition, *I'd Blush If I Could.*

104. Ashley Carman, "How Do the Google Assistant's New Features Compare to Amazon Alexa's?," *Verge*, May 9, 2018, https://www.theverge.com/2018/5/9/17332766/google-assistant-amazon-alexa-features.

105. Edward C. Baig, "Kids Were Being Rude to Alexa, So Amazon Updated It," *USA Today*, April 25, 2018, https://www.usatoday.com/story/tech/columnist/baig/2018/04/25/amazon-echo-dot-kids-alexa-thanks-them-saying-please/547911002/.

106. Legacy Russell, "Digital Dualism and the Glitch Feminism Manifesto," *Cyborgology* (blog), *Society Pages*, December 10, 2012, https://thesocietypages.org/cyborgology/2012/12/10/digital-dualism-and-the-glitch-feminism-manifesto/.

107. UAL: Creative Computing Institute and Feminist Internet, *Designing a Feminist Alexa: An Experiment in Feminist Conversation Design*, 2018, http://www.anthonymasure.com/content/04-conferences/slides/img/2019-04-hypervoix-paris/feminist-alexa.pdf.

108. Feldman, "This Is What a Feminist Looks Like."

109. Kasisto (website), accessed December 3, 2019, https://kasisto.com.

110. Queenie Wong, "Designing a Chatbot: Male, Female or Gender Neutral?," *Phys.org*, January 23, 2017, https://phys.org/news/2017-01-chatbot-male-female-gender-neutral.html.

111. Natasha Mitchell, "Alexa, Siri, Cortana: Our Virtual Assistants Say a Lot about Sexism," ABC News (Australia), August 11, 2017, https://www.abc.net.au/news/2017-08-11/why-are-all-virtual-assisants-female-and-are-they-discriminatory/8784588.

112. Dale Smith and Shara Tibken, "Samsung's Neon 'Artificial Humans' Are Confusing Everyone. We Set the Record Straight," *CNET*, January 19, 2020, https://www.cnet.com/how-to/samsung-neon-artificial-humans-are-confusing-everyone-we-set-record-straight/.

113. Charles Hannon, "Avoiding Bias in Robot Speech," *Interactions* 25, no. 5 (August 2018): 34–37.

114. Arielle Pardes, "The Emotional Chatbots Are Here to Probe Our Feelings," *Wired*, January 31, 2018, https://www.wired.com/story/replika-open-source/. Replika's underlying code has also been released under an open-source license (under the name CakeChat).

115. Genderless Voice, accessed December 3, 2019, https://www.genderlessvoice.com.

116. UNESCO and EQUALS Skills Coalition, *I'd Blush If I Could*.

117. Ellen Broad, *Made by Humans: The AI Condition* (Melbourne: Melbourne University Press, 2018).

118. Sam Levin, "'Bias Deep inside the Code': The Problem with AI 'Ethics' in Silicon Valley," *Guardian*, March 29, 2019, https://www.theguardian.com/technology/2019/mar/28/big-tech-ai-ethics-boards-prejudice.

119. Isaac Asimov, "Runaround," *Astounding Science Fiction* 29.1 (1942): 94–103.

120. "Do We Need Asimov's Laws?," *MIT Technology Review*, May 16, 2014, https://www.technologyreview.com/s/527336/do-we-need-asimovs-laws/.

121. "Principles of Robotics," Engineering and Physical Sciences Research Council, accessed December 3, 2019, https://epsrc.ukri.org/research/ourportfolio/themes/engineering/activities/principlesofrobotics/; Michael Szollosy, "EPSRC Principles of Robotics: Defending an Obsolete Human(ism)?," *Connection Science* 29, no. 2 (2017): 150–159.

122. Kate Darling, "Extending Legal Protection to Social Robots: The Effects of Anthropomorphism, Empathy, and Violent Behavior towards Robotic Objects," in *Robot Law*, ed. Ryan Calo, A. Michael Froomkin, and Ian Kerr (Cheltenham, UK: Edward Elgar, 2016), 213–231.

123. Abbass, "AI Professor Explains."

124. See, for example, David Gunkel, *Robot Rights* (Cambridge, MA: MIT Press, 2018); Jacob Turner, *Robot Rules: Regulating Artificial Intelligence* (London: Palgrave Macmillan, 2019).

125. Abeba Birhane and Jelle van Dijk, "Robot Rights? Let's Talk about Human Welfare Instead," in *Proceedings of the 2020 AAAI/ACM Conference on AI, Ethics, and Society Conference* (New York: ACM, 2020), https://arxiv.org/pdf/2001.05046v1.pdf, 6.

CHAPTER 7

1.	Ruth Oldenziel, "Boys and Their Toys: The Fisher Body Craftsman's Guild, 1930–1968, and the Making of a Male Technical Domain," *Technology and Culture* 38, no. 1 (January 1997): 60.

2.	David Morley, *Television, Audiences and Cultural Studies* (Abingdon, UK: Routledge, 1992), 140.

3.	Monica Anderson, "The Demographics of Device Ownership," in *Technology Device Ownership*, Pew Research Center, October 29, 2015, http://www.pewinternet.org/2015/10/29/the-demographics-of-device-ownership/.

4.	UNESCO and EQUALS Skills Coalition, *I'd Blush If I Could: Closing Gender Divides in Digital Skills through Education*, GEN/2019/EQUALS/1 REV 2 (Paris: UNESCO, 2019).

5.	UNESCO and EQUALS Skills Coalition, *I'd Blush If I Could*.

6.	UNESCO and EQUALS Skills Coalition, *I'd Blush If I Could*, 15.

7.	UNESCO and EQUALS Skills Coalition, *I'd Blush If I Could*, 15, 17.

8.	Sarah Pink, *Home Truths: Gender, Domestic Objects and Everyday Life* (Oxford: Berg, 2004), 124. Pink draws the adventure narrative from William Beer's 1983 book on househusbands: William Beer, *Househusbands: Men and Housework in American Families* (New York: Praeger, 1983).

9.	Pink, *Home Truths*, 125.

10.	Clementine Ford, *Boys Will Be Boys: Power, Patriarchy and the Toxic Bonds of Mateship* (Sydney: Allen and Unwin, 2018), 9.

11.	Corinne Iozzio, "The Hacker's Guide to Smart Homes," *Popular Science* 286, no. 5 (May 2015): 52–55.

12.	Iozzio, "Hacker's Guide to Smart Homes." Media scholars Chris Chesher and Justine Humphry also note the importance of "play" in their book chapter on the smart home. Chris Chesher and Justine Humphry, "Our Own Devices: Living in the Smart Home," in *The Routledge Companion to Urban Media and Communication*, ed. Zlatan Krajina and Deborah Stevenson (New York: Routledge, 2019), 185–193.

13.	Alex Colon, "Connected Home: Living Room," *PC Mag*, July 1, 2014, https://au.pcmag.com/digital-home/12875/connected-home-living-room.

14.	Jennifer Tuohy, "Keep Your Family on Schedule with Smart Lighting," uKnowKids, February 5, 2015, http://resources.uknowkids.com/blog/keep-your-family-on-schedule-with-smart-lighting.

15.	UNESCO and EQUALS Skills Coalition, *I'd Blush If I Could*.

16.	"14 Acre Estate Is Like a Park Filled with Home Automation Tech," *Electronic House*, June 25, 2015, https://www.electronichouse.com/smart-home/14-acre-estate-like-park-filled-home-automation-tech/.

17. "NYC's Walker Tower Blends Art Deco and Automation," *Electronic House*, November 4, 2014, https://www.electronichouse.com/smart-home/nycs-walker-tower-blends-art-deco-and-automation/.

18. "NYC's Walker Tower"; Lisa Montgomery, "Automation Playground," *Electronic House*, August 12, 2014, http://www.electronichouse.com/eh-magazine/smart-home-library/automation-play; Colon, "Connected Home."

19. For further analysis of these pleasance narratives, see Yolande Strengers, Mike Hazas, Larissa Nicholls, Jesper Kjeldskov, and Mikael B. Skov, "Pursuing Pleasance: Interrogating Energy-Intensive Visions for the Smart Home," *International Journal of Human-Computer Studies* 136 (April 2020): 1–14.

20. Priyadarshini Patwa, "#5 Uber Cool Gadgets to Buy in May & Love Technology's New Creation," *Entrepreneur*, May 11, 2019, https://www.entrepreneur.com/slideshow/333613.

21. "Motorized Lifts and Tracks," *Electronic House*, December 1, 2014, http://www.electronichouse.com/eh-magazine/smart-home-library/motorized-lifts-tracks.

22. Gemma Hartley, *Fed Up: Emotional Labor, Women, and the Way Forward* (New York: HarperOne, 2018).

23. Judy Wajcman, *Feminism Confronts Technology* (Cambridge, UK: Polity, 1991), 91.

24. Michael J. Silverstein and Kate Sayre, *Women Want More: How to Capture Your Share of the World's Largest, Fastest-Growing Market* (New York: HarperCollins, 2009).

25. Amazon Fashion, "Introducing Echo Look. Love Your Look. Every Day," YouTube video, posted by amazonfashion, April 26, 2017, https://www.youtube.com/watch?v=9X_fP4pPWPw.

26. Thuy Ong, "Amazon's Echo Look Style Assistant Gets a Little Bit Smarter," *Verge*, February 7, 2018, https://www.theverge.com/2018/2/7/16984218/amazons-echo-look-collections-feature-curated-content-vogue-gq.

27. Kyle Wiggers, "Google's All-Knowing App Will Design You a Dress Based on Your Daily Habits," *Digital Trends*, February 6, 2017, https://www.digitaltrends.com/mobile/google-ivyrevel-data-dress-coded-couture/.

28. Kyle Chayka, "Style Is an Algorithm: No One Is Original Anymore, Not Even You," *Vox*, April 17, 2018, https://www.vox.com/2018/4/17/17219166/fashion-style-algorithm-amazon-echo-look; Sally Applin, "Amazon's Echo Look: Harnessing the Power of Machine Learning or Subtle Exploitation of Human Vulnerability?," *IEEE Consumer Electronics Magazine* 6, no. 4 (October 2017): 125–127.

29. S. A. Applin, "Amazon's Echo Look: We're Going a Long Way Back, Baby," *AnthroPunk Ph.D.* (blog), *Medium*, April 27, 2017, https://medium.com/itp-musings/amazons-echo-look-we-re-going-a-long-way-back-baby-efa2b892a750.

30. Nicola Fumo, "Rise of the AI Fashion Police," *Verge*, May 3, 2017, https://www.theverge.com/2017/5/3/15522792/amazon-echo-look-alexa-style-assistant-ai-fashion.

31. Zeynep Tufekci (@zeynep), "With this data, Amazon won't be able to just sell you clothes or judge you. It could analyze if you're depressed or pregnant and much else," Twitter, April 26, 2017, 12:01 p.m., https://twitter.com/zeynep/status/857263409561317377?lang=en.

32. Quoted in Brian Barrett, "Amazon's 'Echo Look' Could Snoop a Lot More Than Just Your Clothes," *Wired*, April 28, 2017, https://www.wired.com/2017/04/amazon-echo -look-privacy/.

33. Avery Hartmans, "What You Need to Know about the Privacy of the New Smart Camera Amazon Wants You to Put in Your Bedroom," *Business Insider*, April 27, 2017, https:// www.businessinsider.com.au/amazon-echo-look-privacy-issues-2017-4.

34. Patrick Moorhead, "Why Amazon Really Created Echo Look, a Camera in Your Bedroom and Bathroom," *Forbes*, April 27, 2017, https://www.forbes.com/sites/patrickmoorhead/ 2017/04/27/why-amazon-really-created-echo-look-a-camera-in-your-bedroom-and -bathroom/.

35. Barrett, "Amazon's 'Echo Look' Could Snoop a Lot."

36. Barrett, "Amazon's 'Echo Look' Could Snoop a Lot."

37. Anastasia Powell, Nicola Henry, Asher Flynn, and Adrian J. Scott, "Image-Based Sexual Abuse: The Extent, Nature, and Predictors of Perpetration in a Community Sample of Australian Residents," *Computers in Human Behavior* 92 (March 2019): 393– 402.

38. Haitao Xu, Fengyuan Xu, and Bo Chen, "Internet Protocol Cameras with No Password Protection: An Empirical Investigation," in *Passive and Active Measurement*, ed. Robert Beverly, Georgios Smaragdakis, and Anja Feldmann, Lecture Notes in Computer Science 10771 (Cham, Switzerland: Springer, 2018), 47–59.

39. Kate Crawford and Vladan Joler, *Anatomy of an AI System: The Amazon Echo as an Anatomical Map of Human Labor, Data and Planetary Resources* (New York: AI Now Institute and Share Lab, September 7, 2018), section 7, https://anatomyof.ai.

40. Mark Harris, "Amazon's Alexa Knows What You Forgot and Can Guess What You're Thinking," *Guardian*, September 20, 2018, https://www.theguardian.com/technology/2018/ sep/20/alexa-amazon-hunches-artificial-intelligence.

41. Jerome R. Bellegarda and Jannes G. Dolfing, "Language Identification Using Recurrent Neural Networks," US Patent 10,474,753 B2, filed September 27, 2017, and issued November 12, 2019.

42. Bellegarda and Dolfing, "Language Identification."

43. Arlie Russell Hochschild, *The Managed Heart: Commercialization of Human Feeling*, updated ed. (Berkeley: University of California Press, 2012).

44. Jennifer Rhee, *The Robotic Imaginary: The Human and the Price of Dehumanized Labor* (Minneapolis: University of Minnesota Press, 2018).

45. Sidney Fussell, "Alexa Wants to Know How You're Feeling Today," *Atlantic*, October 12, 2018, https://www.theatlantic.com/technology/archive/2018/10/alexa-emotion-detection-ai-surveillance/572884/.

46. Megan Molteni, "The Chatbot Therapist Will See You Now," *Wired*, June 7, 2017, https://www.wired.com/2017/06/facebook-messenger-woebot-chatbot-therapist/.

47. Paige Murphy, "R U OK? and the Works Launch Voice Technology for Google Assistant," *AdNews*, September 12, 2019, https://www.adnews.com.au/news/r-u-ok-and-the-works-launch-voice-technology-for-google-assistant.

48. Hilary Bergen, "'I'd Blush If I Could': Digital Assistants, Disembodied Cyborgs and the Problem of Gender," *Word and Text* 6 (December 2016): 107.

49. Rebecca J. Erickson, "Why Emotion Work Matters: Sex, Gender, and the Division of Household Labor," *Journal of Marriage and Family* 67, no. 2 (May 2005): 337–351.

50. UNESCO and EQUALS Skills Coalition, *I'd Blush If I Could*.

51. Carola Spada, "The Internet of Emotions: A New Legal Challenge," *MediaLaws*, May 7, 2019, http://www.medialaws.eu/the-internet-of-emotions-a-new-legal-challenge/.

52. Genevieve Bell, "Making Life: A Brief History of Human-Robot Interaction," *Consumption Markets and Culture* 21, no. 1 (2018): 25.

53. Leonie Tanczer, Ine Steenmans, Miles Elsden, Jason Blackstock, and Madeline Carr, "Emerging Risks in the IoT Ecosystem: Who's Afraid of the Big Bad Smart Fridge?," in *Living in the Internet of Things: Cybersecurity of the IoT* (London: Institution of Engineering and Technology, 2018); Irina Brass, Leonie Tanczer, Madeline Carr, Miles Elsden, and Jason Blackstock, "Standardising a Moving Target: The Development and Evolution of IoT Security Standards," in *Living in the Internet of Things: Cybersecurity of the IoT* (London: Institution of Engineering and Technology, 2018).

54. Tanczer et al., "Emerging Risks in the IoT Ecosystem."

55. Tanczer et al., "Emerging Risks in the IoT Ecosystem," 4. This also resonates with "the New Normal" scenario suggested by scholars at the University of California at Berkeley: a new "Wild West" where insecurity will become the norm, with people responding in a variety of ways. These authors also pose four other scenarios: "Omega," "Bubble 2.0," "Intentional Internet of Things," and "Sensorium" (Internet of Emotions). See Center for Long-Term Cybersecurity, *Cybersecurity Future 2020* (Berkeley: Center for Long-Term Cybersecurity, University of California at Berkeley, 2016), https://cltc.berkeley.edu/2016/04/28/cybersecurity-futures-2020/.

56. Tanczer et al., "Emerging Risks in the IoT Ecosystem," 4.

57. Bergen, "I'd Blush If I Could," 100.

58. "Steve Jobs: The Magician," *Economist*, October 8, 2011, https://www.economist.com/leaders/2011/10/08/the-magician.

59. Bergen, "I'd Blush If I Could," 100.

60. This corresponds with the findings in International Risk Governance Council, *IRGC Guidelines for Emerging Risk Governance* (Lausanne, Switzerland: International Risk Governance Council, 2015), https://www.irgc.org/risk-governance/emerging-risk/a-protocol-for-dealing-with-emerging-risks/.

61. Miranda Hall, "Beware the Smart Home," *Autonomy*, November 2018, http://autonomy.work/portfolio/beware-the-smart-home/.

62. Shoshana Zuboff, *The Age of Surveillance Capitalism: The Fight for a Human Future at the New Frontier of Power* (New York: PublicAffairs, 2019), 8, 9–10 (emphasis in original).

63. Zuboff, *Age of Surveillance Capitalism*, 21.

64. Maggie Astor, "Your Roomba May Be Mapping Your Home, Collecting Data That Could Be Shared," *New York Times*, July 25, 2017, https://www.nytimes.com/2017/07/25/technology/roomba-irobot-data-privacy.html.

65. See, for example, Alfred Ng and Megan Wollerton, "Google Calls Nest's Hidden Microphone an 'Error,'" *CNET*, February 20, 2019, https://www.cnet.com/news/google-calls-nests-hidden-microphone-an-error/.

66. Sophia Maalsen and Jathan Sadowski, "The Smart Home on FIRE: Amplifying and Accelerating Domestic Surveillance," *Surveillance and Society* 17, no. 1–2 (2019): 118–124.

67. Virginia K. Smith, "As Landlords Use Security Camera Footage against Tenants in Court, Here's How to Protect Your Privacy," *Brick Underground*, January 19, 2017, https://www.brickunderground.com/troubleshooting/landlords-using-surveillance-cameras.

68. Veronica Barassi, *"Home Life Data" and Children's Privacy* (London: Child | Data | Citizen Project, Goldsmiths, University of London, 2018). See also Child | Data | Citizen (website), accessed December 3, 2019, http://childdatacitizen.com/.

69. Sherry Turkle, *Alone Together: Why We Expect More from Technology and Less from Each Other* (New York: Basic Books, 2011).

70. Campaign for a Commercial-Free Childhood, "Stop Mattel's Aristotle from Trading Children's Privacy for Profit," Salsa Labs, 2017, https://org.salsalabs.com/o/621/p/dia/action4/common/public/?action_KEY=21718.

71. Tom Warren, "Amazon's Echo Glow is a $29 Lamp for Alexa Dance Parties and Bedtime Stories," September 25, 2019, *The Verge*, https://www.theverge.com/2019/9/25/20883766/amazon-echo-glow-kids-lamp-speaker-features-specs-price-alexa.

72. United Nations Office on Drugs and Crime, *Global Study on Homicide 2018: Gender-Related Killing of Women and Girls* (Vienna: United Nations Office on Drugs and Crime, 2018), https://www.unodc.org/documents/data-and-analysis/GSH2018/GSH18_Gender-related_killing_of_women_and_girls.pdf.

73. Anastasia Powell and Nicola Henry, *Sexual Violence in a Digital Age* (Basingstoke, UK: Palgrave Macmillan, 2017); Isabel Lopez-Neira, Trupti Patel, Simon Parkin, George Danezis,

and Leonie Tanczer, "'Internet of Things': How Abuse Is Getting Smarter," *Safe—The Domestic Abuse Quarterly* 63 (2019): 22–26.

74. UNESCO and EQUALS Skills Coalition, *I'd Blush If I Could*.

75. Delanie Woodlock, "The Abuse of Technology in Domestic Violence and Stalking," *Violence against Women* 23, no. 5 (April 2017): 584–602.

76. National Center for Injury Prevention and Control, *The National Intimate Partner and Sexual Violence Survey (NISVS): 2010 Summary Report* (Atlanta: National Center for Injury Prevention and Control, Centers for Disease Control and Prevention, 2011), https://www.cdc.gov/violenceprevention/pdf/nisvs_report2010-a.pdf.

77. Katrina Baum, Shannan Catalano, Michael Rand, and Kristina Rose, *Stalking Victimization in the United States*, NCJ 224527 (Washington, DC: Bureau of Justice Statistics, US Department of Justice, 2009), https://victimsofcrime.org/docs/src/baum-k-catalano-s-rand-m-rose-k-2009.pdf.

78. Woodlock, "Abuse of Technology," 519.

79. Nellie Bowles, "Thermostats, Locks and Lights: Digital Tools of Domestic Abuse," *Straits Times*, June 24, 2018, https://www.straitstimes.com/world/united-states/domestic-abuse-in-us-turns-digital-with-thermostats-locks-and-lights.

80. Lopez-Neira et al., "Internet of Things."

81. Anthony Cuthbertson, "Amazon Ordered to Give Alexa Evidence in Double Murder Case," *Independent*, November 14, 2018, https://www.independent.co.uk/life-style/gadgets-and-tech/news/amazon-echo-alexa-evidence-murder-case-a8633551.html.

82. Lopez-Neira et al., "Internet of Things," 25.

83. Roxanne Leitão, "Digital Technologies and Their Role in Intimate Partner Violence," in *Extended Abstracts of the 2018 CHI Conference on Human Factors in Computing Systems* (New York: ACM, 2018).

84. Lopez-Neira et al., "Internet of Things."

85. For a critique of this idea, see Clementine Ford, "It's Been 'a Hard Year to Be a Man,' Clementine Ford Has Tips," *Sydney Morning Herald*, December 11, 2018, https://www.smh.com.au/lifestyle/life-and-relationships/it-s-been-a-hard-year-to-be-a-man-clementine-ford-has-tips-20181210-p50lav.html.

86. Jennifer A. Rode, "A Theoretical Agenda for Feminist HCI," *Interacting with Computers* 23, no. 5 (September 2011): 393–400.

87. Wajcman, *Feminism Confronts Technology*, 166.

88. Wajcman, *Feminism Confronts Technology*, 88; Marie Louise Juul Søndergaard and Lone Koefoed Hansen, "Intimate Futures: Staying with the Trouble of Digital Personal Assistants through Design Fiction," in *Proceedings of the 2018 Designing Interactive Systems Conference* (New York: ACM, 2018), 878.

89. Rode, "A Theoretical Agenda for Feminist HCI."

90. UNESCO and EQUALS Skills Coalition, *I'd Blush If I Could*.

91. bell hooks, *The Will to Change: Men, Masculinity, and Love* (New York: Atria Books, 2004), 39.

92. Cordelia Fine, *Testosterone Rex: Myths of Sex, Science, and Society* (New York: W. W. Norton, 2017); Ford, *Boys Will Be Boys*.

CHAPTER 8

1. Donna Haraway, *Staying with the Trouble: Making Kin in the Chthulucene* (Durham, NC: Duke University Press, 2016), 1, 2.

2. Other human-computer interaction design scholars have proposed taking up Haraway's call to stay with the trouble in their analyses of gender and racial bias in digital personal assistants and chatbots. See, for example, Marie Louuise Juul Søndergaard and Lone Koefoed Hansen, "Intimate Futures: Staying with the Trouble of Digital Personal Assistants through Design Fiction," in *Proceedings of the 2018 Designing Interactive Systems Conference* (New York: ACM, 2018), 869–880; Ari Schlesinger, Kenton P. O'Hara, and Alex S. Taylor, "Let's Talk about Race: Identity, Chatbots, and AI," in *Proceedings of the 2018 CHI Conference on Human Factors in Computing Systems* (New York: ACM, 2018).

3. Haraway, *Staying with the Trouble*, 4.

4. See, for example, Sara Ahmed, *Living a Feminist Life* (Durham, NC: Duke University Press, 2017); Judy Wajcman, *TechnoFeminism* (Cambridge, UK: Polity, 2004); Laboria Cuboniks, *The Xenofeminist Manifesto: A Politics for Alienation* (Brooklyn: Verso Books, 2018); Donna J. Haraway, *Simians, Cyborgs, and Women: The Reinvention of Nature* (New York: Routledge, 1991); Jennifer Baumgardner and Amy Richards, *Manifesta: Young Women, Feminism and the Future* (New York: Farrar, Straus and Giroux, 2000).

5. Ahmed, *Living a Feminist Life*, 265.

6. Ahmed, *Living a Feminist Life*, 65.

7. Hannah McCann, *Queering Femininity: Sexuality, Feminism and the Politics of Presentation* (Abingdon, UK: Routledge, 2017).

8. Ann Light, "HCI as Heterodoxy: Technologies of Identity and the Queering of Interaction with Computers," *Interacting with Computers* 23, no. 5 (September 2011): 430–438, in reference to Shaowen Bardzell, "Feminist HCI: Taking Stock and Outlining an Agenda for Design," in *Proceedings of the SIGCHI Conference on Human Factors in Computing Systems* (New York: ACM, 2010), 1301–1310.

9. Brian O'Flynn, "10 Years of Lady Gaga: How She Queered Mainstream Pop Forever," *Guardian*, April 10, 2018, https://www.theguardian.com/music/2018/apr/10/10-years-of-lady-gaga-how-she-queered-mainstream-pop-forever.

10. Yuji Sone, *Japanese Robot Culture: Performance, Imagination, and Modernity* (Basingstoke, UK: Palgrave Macmillan, 2017).

11. Jennifer Rhee, *The Robotic Imaginary: The Human and the Price of Dehumanized Labor* (Minneapolis: University of Minnesota Press, 2018); Thao Phan, "Amazon Echo and the Aesthetics of Whiteness," *Catalyst: Feminism, Theory, Technoscience* 5, no. 1 (2019), https://catalystjournal.org/index.php/catalyst/article/view/29586/24799.

12. Sarah Myers West, Meredith Whittaker, and Kate Crawford, *Discriminating Systems: Gender, Race, and Power in AI* (New York: AI Now Institute, 2019), 5, https://ainowinstitute.org/discriminatingsystems.pdf.

13. "About Us," AnitaB.org, accessed December 3, 2019, https://anitab.org/about-us/.

14. "Grace Hopper Celebration," AnitaB.org, accessed December 3, 2019, https://ghc.anitab.org.

15. Code Like a Girl (website), accessed December 3, 2019, https://codelikeagirl.org.

16. "About," Code Like a Girl, accessed December 3, 2019, https://codelikeagirl.org/about/about/.

17. Girls Who Code (website), accessed December 3, 2019, https://girlswhocode.com; Women Who Code (website), accessed December 3, 2019, https://www.womenwhocode.com; Coding Girls (website), accessed December 3, 2019, https://codinggirls.sg/index.html; Code First: Girls (website), accessed December 3, 2019, https://www.codefirstgirls.org.uk.

18. Jessi Hempel, "Fei-Fei Li's Quest to Make AI Better for Humanity," *Wired*, November 13, 2018, https://www.wired.com/story/fei-fei-li-artificial-intelligence-humanity/.

19. 3Ai Institute (website), accessed December 3, 2019, https://3ainstitute.cecs.anu.edu.au.

20. UNESCO and EQUALS Skills Coalition, *I'd Blush If I Could: Closing Gender Divides in Digital Skills through Education*, GEN/2019/EQUALS/1 REV 2 (Paris: UNESCO, 2019).

21. UNESCO and EQUALS Skills Coalition, *I'd Blush If I Could*, 37, 44.

22. "#FixedIt," Jane Gilmore, accessed December 3, 2019, http://janegilmore.com/category/fixedit/; Jane Gilmore, *Fixed It: Violence and the Representation of Women in the Media* (New York: Viking, 2019).

23. Jane Gilmore, "FixedIt: The Sexist Headlines That Needed Fixing in 2017," *Sydney Morning Herald*, December 21, 2017, https://www.smh.com.au/lifestyle/fixedit-the-sexist-headlines-that-needed-fixing-in-2017-20171219-h07km9.html.

24. Don Sweeney, "Apple Washes Siri's Mouth Out with Soap over Vulgar Definition of 'Mother,'" *Sacramento Bee*, April 30, 2018, https://www.sacbee.com/news/nation-world/national/article210097244.html.

25. Lucas Matney, "Smart Home Robot Gives LG Exec the Silent Treatment during CES Keynote," *TechCrunch*, January 8, 2018, https://techcrunch.com/2018/01/08/smart-home-robot-gives-lg-exec-the-silent-treatment-during-ces-keynote/.

26. Annabel Crabb, *The Wife Drought: Why Women Need Wives and Men Need Lives* (North Sydney: Random House Australia, 2014); Annabel Crabb, "Men at Work: Australia's Parenthood Trap," *Quarterly Essay*, no. 75 (September 2019), https://www.quarterlyessay.com.au/essay/2019/09/men-at-work.

27. R. W. Connell, *Masculinities*, 2nd ed. (Berkeley: University of California Press, 2005); bell hooks, *The Will to Change: Men, Masculinity, and Love* (New York: Atria Books, 2004); Lynne Segal, *Slow Motion: Changing Masculinities, Changing Men* (New Brunswick, NJ: Rutgers University Press, 1990).

28. Judith Butler, *Gender Trouble: Feminism and the Subversion of Identity* (London: Routledge, 2006); Connell, *Masculinities*.

29. David J. Maume, "Can Men Make Time for Family?: Paid Work, Care Work, Work-Family Reconciliation Policies, and Gender Equality," *Social Currents* 3, no. 1 (March 2016): 43–63.

30. Shelby Lorman, *Awards for Good Boys: Tales of Dating, Double Standards, and Doom* (London: Penguin Books, 2019).

31. Van Badham, "'Mentrification': How Men Appropriated Computers, Beer and the Beatles," *Guardian*, May 29, 2019, https://www.theguardian.com/music/2019/may/29/mentrification-how-men-appropriated-computers-beer-and-the-beatles.

32. "About Us," Geena Davis Institute on Gender in Media, accessed December 3, 2019, https://seejane.org/about-us/.

33. See, for example, Clementine Ford, *Boys Will Be Boys: Power, Patriarchy and the Toxic Bonds of Mateship* (Sydney: Allen and Unwin, 2018); W. James Potter, *Media Effects* (Thousand Oaks, CA: SAGE, 2012); Patti M. Valkenburg and Jessica Taylor Piotrowski, *Plugged In: How Media Attract and Affect Youth* (New Haven, CT: Yale University Press, 2017).

34. Kate Devlin, *Turned On: Science, Sex and Robots* (London: Bloomsbury Sigma, 2018).

35. The Bechdel Test was created by the cartoonist and author Alison Bechdel. Her 1985 comic *Dykes to Watch Out For* featured a strip titled "The Rule" that included the test and became a basic measure of how women are represented in film. It is also referred to as the Bechdel-Wallace test, acknowledging the contribution of Bechdel's friend, Liz Wallace. See "About," Bechdel Test Fest, accessed December 3, 2019, http://bechdeltestfest.com/about/.

36. "Statistics," Bechdel Test Movie List, accessed December 3, 2019, https://bechdeltest.com/statistics/.

37. "Our Story," Hello Sunshine, accessed December 3, 2019, https://hello-sunshine.com/our-story.

38. Seventy-five percent of science fiction writers are men. See Bronwyn Lovell, "Friday Essay: Science Fiction's Women Problem," *Conversation,* September 15, 2016, https://theconversation.com/friday-essay-science-fictions-women-problem-58626. In 2017, women comprised 18 percent of all directors, writers, producers, editors, and cinematographers working

on the top 250 domestic (US) grossing films. See Martha M. Lauzen, "The Celluloid Ceiling: Behind-the-Scenes Employment of Women on the Top 100, 250, and 500 Films of 2017," 2018, accessed February 6, 2020, https://womenintvfilm.sdsu.edu/wp-content/uploads/2018/01/2017_Celluloid_Ceiling_Report.pdf.

39. Jacqueline Feldman, "The Dignified Bot," *Daily* (blog), *Paris Review*, December 13, 2017, https://www.theparisreview.org/blog/2017/12/13/the-dignified-bot/.

40. Dalia Mortada, "Meet Q, the Gender-Neutral Voice Assistant," March 21, 2019, on *Morning Edition*, NPR, https://www.npr.org/2019/03/21/705395100/meet-q-the-gender-neutral-voice-assistant.

41. "F'xa," Comuzi, accessed December 3, 2019, https://www.comuzi.xyz/fxa.

42. Feminist Internet, "Feminist PIA Standards," accessed December 3, 2019, https://drive.google.com/file/d/1J6mMeZxwlOLhxFirIphoJBrOFyZiV6m_/view; Josie Young, "Designing Feminist Chatbots," September 2017, https://drive.google.com/file/d/0B036SlUSi-z4UkkzYUVGTGdocXc/view.

43. David Pierson, "Did Your Tamagotchi Die of Neglect in the Late '90s? Now's Your Chance to Take Another Shot," *Los Angeles Times*, October 10, 2017, https://www.latimes.com/business/la-fi-tn-tamagotchi-20171010-story.html.

44. Clifford Nass with Corina Yen, *The Man Who Lied to His Laptop: What We Can Learn about Ourselves from Our Machines* (New York: Current, 2012).

45. UNESCO and EQUALS Skills Coalition, *I'd Blush If I Could*.

46. Kate Crawford and Vladan Joler, *Anatomy of an AI System: The Amazon Echo as an Anatomical Map of Human Labor, Data and Planetary Resources* (New York: AI Now Institute and Share Lab, September 7, 2018), https://anatomyof.ai.

47. Vandana Shiva, *Earth Democracy: Justice, Sustainability, and Peace* (London: Zed Books, 2016).

48. Søndergaard and Hansen, "Intimate Futures," 875.

49. Yolande Strengers, Jenny Kennedy, Paula Arcari, Larissa Nicholls, and Melissa Gregg, "Protection, Productivity and Pleasure in the Smart Home," in *Proceedings of the SIGCHI Conference on Human Factors in Computing Systems: Weaving the Threads of CHI* (New York: ACM, 2019).

50. "Our Mission," Common Sense Media, accessed December 3, 2019, https://www.commonsensemedia.org/about-us/our-mission.

51. Australian Government, "Have Your Say on Classification Regulation," Australian Classification, January 8, 2020, https://www.classification.gov.au/about-us/media-and-news/news/have-your-say-classification-regulation.

52. Jaclyn Friedman and Jessica Valenti, *Yes Means Yes!: Visions of Female Sexual Power and a World without Rape* (Berkeley, CA: Seal, 2008).

53. In the United States, see, for example, "Affirmative Consent Laws (Yes Means Yes) State by State," Affirmative Consent, accessed December 3, 2019, http://affirmativeconsent.com/affirmative-consent-laws-state-by-state/.

54. "Yes! Means Yes," Only with Consent, accessed December 3, 2019, http://onlywithconsent.org/blog/yes-means-yes.

55. Shere Hite, *The Hite Report: A Nationwide Study of Female Sexuality* (1976; repr., New York: Seven Stories, 2004).

56. Sinziana M. Gutiu, "The Roboticization of Consent," in *Robot Law*, ed. Ryan Calo, A. Michael Froomkin, and Ian Kerr (Cheltenham, UK: Edward Elgar, 2016), 186–212.

57. Shoshana Zuboff, *The Age of Surveillance Capitalism: The Fight for a Human Future at the New Frontier of Power* (New York: PublicAffairs, 2019).

58. Google established an external advisory board called the Advanced Technology External Advisory Council to monitor its use of artificial intelligence. The board quickly dissolved, however, due to controversy over Google's selection of members, including outspoken conservative figures. See Nick Statt, "Google Dissolves AI Ethics Board Just One Week after Forming It," *Verge*, April 4, 2019, https://www.theverge.com/2019/4/4/18296113/google-ai-ethics-board-ends-controversy-kay-coles-james-heritage-foundation. For a summary of academic debates, see Jacob Turner, *Robot Rules: Regulating Artificial Intelligence* (London: Palgrave Macmillan, 2019).

59. Anna Jobin, Marcello Ienca, and Effy Vayena, "The Global Landscape of AI Ethics Guidelines," *Nature Machine Intelligence* 1, no. 9 (September 2019): 389–399.

60. High-Level Expert Group on Artificial Intelligence, *Ethics Guidelines for Trustworthy AI* (Brussels: European Commission, 2019), 5, https://ec.europa.eu/digital-single-market/en/news/ethics-guidelines-trustworthy-ai.

61. UNI Global Union, *Top 10 Principles for Ethical Artificial Intelligence* (Nyon, Switzerland: UNI Global Union, 2018), 7, http://www.thefutureworldofwork.org/media/35420/uni_ethical_ai.pdf (emphasis added).

62. IEEE Global Initiative on Ethics of Autonomous and Intelligent Systems, *Ethically Aligned Design: A Vision for Prioritizing Human Well-Being with Autonomous and Intelligent Systems* (Piscataway, NJ: Institute of Electrical and Electronics Engineers, 2018), https://ethicsinaction.ieee.org.

63. Microsoft, "Responsible Bots: 10 Guidelines for Developers of Conversational AI," November 4, 2018, https://www.microsoft.com/en-us/research/uploads/prod/2018/11/Bot_Guidelines_Nov_2018.pdf.

64. "AI Ethics Guidelines Global Inventory," AlgorithmWatch, last updated June 21, 2019, https://algorithmwatch.org/en/project/ai-ethics-guidelines-global-inventory/.

65. Genevieve Bell, "Making Life: A Brief History of Human-Robot Interaction," *Consumption Markets and Culture* 21, no. 1 (2018): 22–41.

66. Judy Wajcman, *Feminism Confronts Technology* (Cambridge, UK: Polity, 1991), 166.

A NOTE ON METHODOLOGY

1. Larissa Nicholls, Yolande Strengers, and Sergio Tirado, *Smart Home Control: Exploring the Potential for Off-the-Shelf Enabling Technologies in Energy Vulnerable and Other Households*, final report (Melbourne: Centre for Urban Research, RMIT University, 2017); Yolande Strengers, Larissa Nicholls, Tanzy Owen, and Sergio Tirado, *Smart Home Control Devices: Summary and Assessment of Energy and Lifestyle Marketing Claims* (Melbourne: Centre for Urban Research, RMIT University, 2017); Sergio Tirado, Larissa Nicholls, and Yolande Strengers, "Smart Home Technologies in Everyday Life: Do They Address Key Energy Challenges?," *Current Opinion in Environmental Sustainability* 31 (April 2018): 65–70; Jenny Kennedy, Ellie Rennie, and Julian Thomas, "AI in Public Services: Nadia and Other Australian Examples," case study for *Artificial Intelligence in the Delivery of Public Services* (Bangkok: Report for the United Nations Economic and Social Commission for Asia and the Pacific, 2019).

2. Yolande Strengers and Larissa Nicholls, "Convenience and Energy Consumption in the Smart Home of the Future: Industry Visions from Australia and Beyond," *Energy Research & Social Science* 32 (October 2017): 86–93; Yolande Strengers, Sarah Pink, and Larissa Nicholls, "Smart Energy Futures and Social Practice Imaginaries: Forecasting Scenarios for Pet Care in Australian Homes," *Energy Research and Social Science* 48 (February 2019): 108–115; Larissa Nicholls and Yolande Strengers, "Robotic Vacuum Cleaners Save Energy? Raising Cleanliness Conventions and Energy Demand in Australian Households with Smart Home Technologies," *Energy Research and Social Science* 50 (April 2019): 73–81; Yolande Strengers, "Robots and Roomba Riders: Non-human Performers in Theories of Social Practice," in *Social Practices and Dynamic Non-humans: Nature, Materials and Technologies*, ed. Yolande Strengers and Cecily Maller (Basingstoke, UK: Palgrave Macmillan, 2019), 215–234; Yolande Strengers and Larissa Nicholls, "Aesthetic Pleasures and Gendered Tech-Work in the 21st-Century Smart Home," *Media International Australia* 166 (February 2018): 70–80.

3. Jenny Kennedy, Michael Arnold, Martin Gibbs, Bjorn Nansen, and Rowan Wilken, *Digital Domesticity: Media, Materiality, and Home Life* (Oxford: Oxford University Press, 2020); Jenny Kennedy, Michael Arnold, Bjorn Nansen, Rowan Wilken, and Martin Gibbs, "Digital Housekeepers and Domestic Expertise in the Networked Home," *Convergence: The International Journal of Research into New Media Technologies* 21, no. 4 (November 2015): 408–422.

4. Mike Hazas and Yolande Strengers, "Promoting Smart Homes," in *Energy Fables: Challenging Ideas in the Energy Sector*, ed. Jenny Rinkinen, Elizabeth Shove, and Jacopo Torriti (London: Routledge, 2019), 78–88; Yolande Strengers, Janine Morley, Larissa Nicholls, and Mike Hazas, "The Hidden Energy Cost of Smart Homes," *Conversation*, June 13, 2016, https://theconversation.com/the-hidden-energy-cost-of-smart-homes-60306.

5. Rikke Hagensby Jensen, Yolande Strengers, Jesper Kjeldskov, Larissa Nicholls, and Mikael B. Skov, "Designing the Desirable Smart Home: A Study of Household Experiences and Energy Consumption Impacts," in *Proceedings of the 2018 CHI Conference on*

Human Factors in Computing Systems (New York: ACM, 2018); Rikke Hagensby Jensen, Yolande Strengers, Dimitrios Raptis, Larissa Nicholls, Jesper Kjeldskov, and Mikael B. Skov, "Exploring Hygge as a Desirable Design Vision for the Sustainable Smart Home," in *Proceedings of the 2018 Designing Interactive Systems Conference* (New York: ACM, 2018), 355–360; Yolande Strengers, Mike Hazas, Larissa Nicholls, Jesper Kjeldskov, and Mikael B. Skov, "Pursuing Pleasance: Interrogating Energy-Intensive Visions for the Smart Home," *International Journal of Human-Computer Studies* 136 (April 2020): 1–14.

6.   Yolande Strengers, Jenny Kennedy, Paula Arcari, Larissa Nicholls, and Melissa Gregg, "Protection, Productivity and Pleasure in the Smart Home," in *Proceedings of the SIGCHI Conference on Human Factors in Computing Systems: Weaving the Threads of CHI* (ACM, 2019).

Index

Feminist porn, 123
Feminization of smart wives, 2–5, 14, 211
Fessler, Leah, 162, 163
Fine, Cordelia, 56, 204
FixedIt project, 214–215
Flintstones (TV series), *The,* 25, 26
FoldiMate laundry-folding robot, 30
Ford, Clementine, 56, 180–181, 204
Fortunati, Leopoldina, 40
Foundation for Responsible Robotics, 116–117, 137, 142
Frank, Lily, 139
Frederick, Christine, 33
Fridges, 35–37
Friedan, Betty, 42
Frigid Farrah personality (Roxxxy), 134–135
Fumo, Nicola, 187
Functionality and usability of smart wives, 31, 39, 183–184
Fun in digital housekeeping, 45–46
F'xa (Comuzi), 219, 220

Gabe, Frances, 32–33
Gartner, 8
Gaslighting, 201
Gates, Bill, 27, 29
Gavankar, Janina, 155
Geek Chic (Inness), 44
Geeks, 44
Geena Davis Institute on Gender in Media, 217
Gender
  and access to smart wives, 20
  and AI ethics, 225, 226
  assigned to smart wives, 2, 16–17, 21, 55–65, 70–71, 76–77, 156–157, 161–162, 165, 169, 171–172, 203–204, 211
  bias in sci-fi movies, 15
  binary and spectrum views of, 20
  children shaped by, 56
  and digital skills, 9–11, 178–179
  and division of housework, 6–7, 32, 40, 42, 46–47
  and energy consumption, 87–91
  and geekiness, 44
  imbalances in computer science, 9–11, 54, 62, 163, 212–214
  and interest in and uptake of smart wives, 9, 42, 179, 203
  orgasm gap, 122
  and pleasance in smart homes, 95
  stereotypes applied to computers, 159
  and targeting of smart wives, 35–37, 182–186
  troubling and design of technologies, 203, 210
  and use of sex dolls, 9, 113–114, 116–117, 122–123
General Electric, 9
Gilbreth, Lillian, 33
Gillespie, Craig, 130
Gilmore, Jane, 214–215
Glitches in smart wives
  examples of, 145–147
  and historical framing of women as glitchy, 149–153
  language used in retelling stories of, 147–148
Glitch feminism, 169
Global e-Sustainability Initiative, 88
Global Footprint Network, 86
Global Study on Homicide 2018 (UN Office on Drugs and Crime), 199
Good House Wife's Guide (1955), 93, 110
Google
  as Big Five member, 85
  employment at and gender, 9
  ethical guidelines for AI, 226, 288n58
  Nest Guard, 195
  and Q, 172
  renewable energy commitment, 101
  RUOK Mate, 192
  search engine, 11, 191
  and surveillance capitalism, 194, 195
  working conditions, 98
Google Assistant, 165, 167

Privacy risks
  managing, 203, 221, 224
  sources of, 177, 187–189, 192, 194, 195,
    196, 197
Proximate future, 97

Q (genderless voice), 171–172, 219
Quatrochi, Chris, 29
Queer, definition, 209
Queering femininity (McCann), 209
Queering the smart wife, 21, 59, 76–77, 95,
    142, 143, 171, 209–211
Quek, Kaye, 129, 136
QuickDrive smart washing machine
    (Samsung), 30

Race
  and AI ethics, 225, 226
  bias in sci-fi movies, 14–15
  and domestic work, 25, 164
  and employment in AI industry, 11
  lack of diversity represented in smart wives,
    211
  and search engines, 11
Rape
  and consent issues with sexbots, 114,
    134–141, 142, 223–224
  fantasies, 138
  marital, 8
Rape Day (video game), 135–136
RapeLay (video game), 135–136
Rating system for smart wives, lack of, 222
Realbotix, 109
RealDoll, 109, 114, 116, 119–120,
    130–131, 132–134. *See also* Harmony/
    HarmonyX (RealDoll/RealDollX); Henry
    (RealDollX); SolanaX (RealDollX)
Real estate sector, 195
Rees, William, 86
Reeves, Byron, 159
Regulation
  legal rights for robots, 173, 174
  needed for Internet of Things, 193

needed for smart wife industry, 198, 203,
    224
  right to repair laws, 106
  and sexbots, 141
Relational artifacts, 71
Reliability of smart wives, 31
Replika, 171
Representations of smart wives, 214–215
Resistance toward technology use, 45
Resource man, 18, 87–91
Rhee, Jennifer, 67, 191
Richards, Ellen, 33
Richardson, Kathleen, 55, 67, 70, 71, 137
Right to repair laws, 106
Robertson, Jennifer, 13, 62, 64, 65, 71, 74, 75
Robida, Albert, 150
"Robot," origins of word, 164
Robotics field, 9, 54
Robotic vacuum cleaners (robovacs)
  gender and use of, 40, 42
  iRobot Roomba, 27, 28, 34, 40, 195
  issues with, 33–34, 43, 46
  uptake of, 30, 52
Robots. *See also* Chatbots; Domestic
    (housekeeping) robots; Sex dolls and
    sexbots; Social robots
  abuse of, 160
  avoiding bias in speech, 171
  destructive image in sci-fi, 67
  Disney-inspired, 71, 73
  emotional intelligence, 52, 191, 192
  and ethics, 158, 172–173
  female voices in, 166
  honorary citizenship for, 146, 174
  legal rights for, 173, 174
  linguistic traits, 68
  male-identified, 16, 21, 71, 113–114,
    161–162, 165
  market for, 1, 27–28
  pet-inspired, 21, 51, 71, 77, 219–220
  plant-inspired, 21, 77
  public attitudes toward, 40
  as smart wives, 2